Political Traditions in Foreign Policy Series
KENNETH W. THOMPSON, EDITOR

The values, traditions, and assumptions undergirding approaches to foreign policy are often crucial in determining the course of a nation's history. Yet, the interconnections between ideas and policy for landmark periods in our foreign relations remain largely unexamined. The intent of this series is to encourage a marriage between political theory and foreign policy. A secondary objective is to identify theorists with a continuing interest in political thought and international relations, both younger scholars and the small group of established thinkers. Only occasionally have scholarly centers and university presses sought to nurture studies in this area. In the 1950s and 1960s the University of Chicago Center for the Study of American Foreign Policy gave emphasis to such inquiries. Since then the subject has not been the focus of any major intellectual center. The Louisiana State University Press and the series editor, from a base at the Miller Center of Public Affairs at the University of Virginia, have organized this series to meet a need that has remained largely unfulfilled since the mid-1960s.

HANS J. MORGENTHAU
AND THE ETHICS OF
AMERICAN STATECRAFT

Hans J. Morgenthau

AND THE ETHICS OF
AMERICAN STATECRAFT

GREG RUSSELL

LOUISIANA STATE UNIVERSITY PRESS

BATON ROUGE AND LONDON

Copyright © 1990 by Louisiana State University Press
All rights reserved
Manufactured in the United States of America
First printing
99 98 97 96 95 94 93 92 91 90   5 4 3 2 1
Designer: Barbara Werden
Typeface: Linotron Sabon
Typesetter: G & S Typesetters, Inc.
Printer and binder: Thomson-Shore, Inc.

Library of Congress Cataloging-in-Publication Data
Russell, Greg, 1955–
    Hans J. Morgenthau and the ethics of American statecraft / Greg
Russell.
        p.   cm.—(Political traditions in foreign policy series)
    Includes bibliographical references (p.   ).
    ISBN 0-8071-1618-1 (alk. paper)
    1. International relations—Philosophy.   2. United States—Foreign
relations—1945–   3. Morgenthau, Hans Joachim, 1904–   . I. Title.
II. Series.
JX1391.R85   1990
327'.01—dc20   90-5675
                                                                   CIP

Quotations from *Politics Among Nations: The Struggle for Power and Peace,*
5th edition, by Hans J. Morgenthau, copyright 1948, 1954, © 1960, 1967, 1972 by
Alfred A. Knopf, Inc., are reprinted by permission of the publisher.

The paper in this book meets the guidelines for permanence and durability of the
Committee on Production Guidelines for Book Longevity of the Council on Library
Resources.♾

To

KENNETH W. THOMPSON

CONTENTS

ACKNOWLEDGMENTS

I owe a profound debt of gratitude to a number of individuals and institutions that supported this undertaking in a variety of ways. The White Burkett Miller Center of Public Affairs was helpful in providing access to the Morgenthau Papers in the Alderman Library at the University of Virginia. Generous support was also extended by the Eric Voegelin Institute and the Department of Political Science at Louisiana State University. Among those whose own work and observations have been instructive, I must mention Kenneth W. Thompson, Cecil V. Crabb, Jr., Norman A. Graebner, Ellis Sandoz, Cecil Eubanks, Daniel G. Lang, W. David Clinton, and David A. Mayers. Invaluable editorial assistance was provided by Beverly Jarrett, Catherine Barton, and John Easterly of Louisiana State University Press, and Lois Geehr. Shirley and Annelise Russell weathered this undertaking with virtual equanimity and deserve a special tribute for their domestic forbearance.

HANS J. MORGENTHAU
AND THE ETHICS OF
AMERICAN STATECRAFT

PREFACE

The prominence of entrenched behavioral orthodoxy and pseudo-science in the study of politics and foreign policy now commands the reasoned dissent of an ever-widening circle of serious political thinkers. Political science has not only lost its relation to a transcendent value from which it could receive its meaning but, of more importance, it has also lost the awareness of the need for such a transcendent orientation. It is no longer aware of the need for moral distinctions to be made within the sphere accessible to human knowledge. As a subfield within the discipline of political science—uncertain of its professional inclinations and academic responsibilities—international relations is marked by the vast proliferation of research agendas unable to conceal the poverty of theoretical expression with rigorous methodological devices. The accumulation of factual detail leaves unimpaired the work of thoughtful minds in confronting the perennial questions regarding the nature of man's political existence in a world armed with weapons of mass destruction. Professor Hans J. Morgenthau was without equal in his profession in calling for the restoration of the intellectual and moral commitment to the truth about matters political for its own sake. His enduring contribution points to the primacy of political philosophy and ethics for calculating the moral resources of American power in world affairs.

The objective of this study is to differentiate Morgenthau's theory and philosophy of American realism from the normative roots and political concepts associated with the European heritage of *raison d'état*. In

1

addition to evaluating Morgenthau's provocative commentary on the nature of moral choice in man's political existence, arguments are presented to substantiate the process by which he reconciled the reformist values of the American diplomatic tradition (a strong commitment that many of his critics neglected) with the continuing relevance of the national interest and balance-of-power techniques in today's changing world. The ethical obligations of the prudent statesman have a direct bearing upon Morgenthau's understanding of the purposes and limitations of power and military force in the foreign policy of the United States.

Analysis throughout the several chapters will be guided by the hypothesis that Morgenthau's commentary on the many challenging issues raised by an increasingly interdependent multistate system differs from the classic rationale of "reason of state" intended for a Eurocentric international society characterized by common diplomatic objectives and values. This hypothesis is not intended to suggest the absence of any relationship of continuity between the continental tradition and the fundamental tenets of recent American realism. At issue, however, is the method or justification by which the inherited European tradition has been modified and subsequently adapted by realist interpreters to the exigencies of post–World War II United States foreign policy. An equally important consideration shaping Morgenthau's international thought is the recognition of persistent, and often contradictory, themes and principles that have influenced American foreign policy since the founding of the Republic—isolationism, legalism, idealism, and pragmatism—and that have received vivid expression in numerous doctrines, unilateral declarations, and diplomatic commitments of the United States.

Realist political philosophy is based upon the recognition of the sources of power and conflict at all levels of human existence and the methods by which expression of individual and national self-interest might be kept consistent with the requirements of order. For the realist, the realm of politics is the twilight zone where ethics and power meet. The recognition of this perennial political dilemma is virtually impossible without some consideration of the antecedent philosophical assumptions related to the problems of human nature and politics, order and disorder in society, the state of nature, and the quest for community. Moreover, the formulation of these core assumptions bears directly upon the possibility of compromise and reconciliation of divergent national interests backed by rival moral claims. From this vantage point, my objective will be to identify clearly any possible nexus between the precepts of *raison d'état* and the norms of Morgenthau's political realism in order to grasp the moral problem among nations, as well as the difficulty in defining viable and coherent guides to national action.

If a case can be made that Morgenthau's interpretation of the aims of American power in world affairs differs from the continental thinkers' vindication of "state necessity" in the conduct of diplomacy, knowledge of his views should serve two important purposes. First, insight into the normative roots of Morgenthau's world view should help explain some of the peculiarities, novel features, and recurrent traits of the contemporary American approach to world affairs that often puzzle foreign observers and lead them either to praise the special virtues of American policy or condemn what they consider its hypocritical pretense. Second, the ideals influencing the realist estimation of the appropriate methods and national aims of American foreign policy should help to promote critical self-understanding of America's moral presuppositions and of the deeply ingrained habits of thought affecting its foreign policy conduct in a sphere where emotion and value judgment play an important role. By identifying and paying tribute to an impressive intellectual ancestry for Morgenthau's conception of American realism, our understanding of international politics should gain in philosophical depth, historical perspective, and academic respectability.

The divergence between the classical formulation of *raison d'état* and the operative principles of American realism was noted by Arnold Wolfers' earlier and broad distinction between the Anglo-American approach to foreign policy and the contribution of such continental precursors as Machiavelli, Grotius, Spinoza, Rousseau, and Kant.[1] It would be misleading to suggest that all expressions of continental international thought have been Machiavellian; opposition to the views expressed in Machiavelli's *Prince* was voiced repeatedly throughout the centuries that followed its publication. In particular, Friedrich Meinecke provided an illuminating exposé of the debate between the Machiavellians and anti-Machiavellians.[2] However, Meinecke's analysis justifies the contention that continental theory centered around the idea of "necessity of state,"

---

1. Arnold Wolfers, *Discord and Collaboration* (Baltimore, 1962), 233–51.
2. Friedrich Meinecke, *Machiavellianism: The Doctrine of "Raison d'État" and Its Place in Modern History*, trans. D. Scott (London, 1957).

which was the focal point of Machiavelli's position. From the venue of continental *raison d'état*, the structure and practice of diplomacy was based upon the existence of independent territorial states, free from external control and able to pursue their interests by bargaining and fighting with one another. Diplomacy, balance of power, spheres of influence, and war were the means to power. The central question for continental theorists, therefore, was whether the statesman was under any moral obligation to resist these "compelling" demands of state necessity. From this horizon, a statesman found little leeway, if any, to reconcile the need for security with universal norms or laws applicable to an anarchic environment of sovereign states.[3]

On the other hand, English and American thinkers were less inclined to accept a rigid distinction between the requirements of the national interest and moral principles in foreign policy behavior. The Anglo-American approach took the form of a debate about the most appropriate way of applying accepted principles of morality to the conduct of foreign policy. The rationale for such efforts was the belief that statesmen enjoyed a degree of freedom in choosing the "right" path in their external policies (much as they did in their internal conduct). There was surely room, it was often held, to decide for the good ends and to preserve them with the least evil of available means. As Wolfers pointed out, this was a philosophy of choice, "which was bound to be ethical, over against a philosophy in which forces beyond moral control were believed to prevail."[4] Choice, in contrast to the political rationale of necessity, implies the freedom to decide what goals to pursue and what means to use in accordance with one's desires and convictions.

Wolfers' historical survey of competing theoretical traditions provides a useful typology for assessing the intellectual roots of Morgenthau's realism as a contemporary manifestation of Anglo-American thinking on international politics. This study demonstrates that the empirical and normative facets of Morgenthau's political philosophy drew upon a profound regard for the underlying purposes and ideals of American society. A strong case can and should be made that his philosophical and ethical commitments affirm the mix of classical and Christian principles at the core of what Edward S. Corwin called the "Higher Law"

3. Wolfers, *Discord and Collaboration*, 244.
4. *Ibid.*, 244–46.

background of American constitutional law. The transcendent purpose, which Morgenthau deemed essential for the workings of democratic government, encompasses a common conception of law and order based upon the natural rights of man. Because imperfect man aspires to the good but is frequently betrayed by a propensity for sin, the best system of government is one that harnesses his virtues to serve good purposes and limits his vices through legal and institutional restraints. In fact, the point can be made that Morgenthau's realism gives renewed expression to the familiar Anglo-American stipulation that statesmen are compelled to integrate two basic goals: one, the primary though prudently conceived objective of national self-preservation; the other, implied in such prudence, a fulfillment of the moral law to the maximum compatible with the primary duty of defense. For example, there is freedom of choice between more or less moderation, more or less concern for the interests of others, more or less effort to preserve the peace.

Before I turn to the organization of the book, a qualifying statement about the role of theory in international relations is in order. International relations theory is not philosophy in the broadest sense. As one scholar has noted, this theorizing does not seek to define the nature of truth or locate man's place in the universe. It does not ask with theology, What is the ultimate truth? Nor does it ask with philosophy, What is man's highest end in life?[5] This discrepancy has led some thinkers, such as Leo Strauss, to question the validity of a philosophy of world politics. Unless it sought to answer other questions, Strauss inquired whether a philosophy of international politics was not as problematical as, for example, a philosophy for New York's sanitation workers! To a degree, Strauss was correct in arguing that theorizing about interstate relations usually takes place at a more immediate and less universal level of discourse than general philosophy, and as a result, it suffers from the fact that common moral principles are difficult to discover in such theories.

Yet it would, at the same time, be at the expense of considerable intellectual arrogance for one school or discipline to claim a monopoly over philosophy. By way of analogy, it is instructive to reflect upon the dilemma of Edmond Cahn, a distinguished scholar of jurisprudence, who asked, Where is one to find the ideas and principles that help to illuminate the broad dimensions of his field? Writing in *The Sense of Injustice*,

5. Kenneth W. Thompson, *Morality and Foreign Policy* (Baton Rouge, 1980), 130.

Cahn pointed out: "The choice would be rather difficult if we did not have the benefit of indications vividly and repeatedly inscribed in the history of philosophy. . . . That is why the ideal is habitually set off against the positive, identity against time, the free against the determined, reason against passion." [6]

For this study, philosophy provides a number of interpretive and normative constructs by which to relate and assign meaning to recurrent patterns of international political behavior. Most social scientists seeking to understand the causes of war and the conditions of conflict resolution assemble and explain their data on the basis of assumptions about the nature of man, the internal organization of societies and governments, or the decentralized character of the international political system.

As a basis for contrasting Morgenthau's philosophy of realism with continental international thought, the opening chapter examines some of the leading European theorists and diplomatic practitioners of *raison d'état* (Thucydides, Machiavelli, Hobbes, Richelieu, and Bismarck). Although others could easily be added to this sample, these exemplars figure prominently in Morgenthau's writing on the nature of political ethics in the history of European statecraft. A preliminary section reviews the principal attributes and problems of theorizing about state relations in the history of European political thought. Subsequent treatment of the various spokesmen for *raison d'état* builds on such considerations as the philosophical understanding of human nature and politics characterizing each thinker's definition of state interest in foreign policy; the combination of domestic and external factors influencing a state's diplomatic and military objectives across all or part of Europe; the manner in which state interest, or state necessity, is manifested in alliance systems and balance-of-power arrangements; and the relevance of ethical commands in the state's relentless quest for power and security.

The remaining chapters evaluate Morgenthau's many literary works, both published and unpublished, in the areas of international politics and American diplomatic history. Chapter 2 examines his political philosophy and method of analysis. Following a brief account of Morgenthau's early life and immigration to the United States, emphasis is devoted to his principal academic and intellectual commitments. Various theological and philosophical assumptions about history and politics influenced his

6. Edmond Cahn, *The Sense of Injustice* (Bloomington, 1949), 2.

inquiry into the perennial problems of man's existence in society. Continental thinkers, in the tradition of *raison d'état*, claimed to observe a strict separation between the norms of state behavior and the moral responsibility of the solitary individual (*i.e.*, ethical dualism). By contrast, Morgenthau's writing was inspired by Anglo-American legal principles emphasizing constitutional restraints on the legitimate functions of government power. In essence, the morality of state behavior is shaped by, and inseparable from, certain self-evident principles of liberty and equality that find expression in the Christian-liberal-humanitarian ethos of the American mission. For the purpose of this study, attention turns to the question of how Morgenthau reconciles his allegiance to those transcendent principles embodied in American history with man's incurable ego and the exigencies of power politics.

Chapter 3 analyzes Morgenthau's ideas concerning the problems of conceptual definition that extend to competing interpretations of power, national interest, balance of power, diplomacy, and statesmanship. Evaluating his thought on this level entails identifying both domestic and external developments that contribute to the selection of appropriate criteria for definition and evaluation. Inasmuch as many of these principles were affirmed by prophets and practitioners of *raison d'état*, how did Morgenthau accommodate such new issues as growing military and economic interdependence among an ever-increasing number of nations, as well as the reliance on new modalities of power and influence (*e.g.*, economic, psychological, and ideological)? Morgenthau's definition of these concepts has considerable importance for the limits and possibilities of a democratic foreign policy.

Chapter 4 considers Morgenthau's ideas about the significance of continental *raison d'état* for American diplomacy as it points to the statesman's dilemma of having to balance the requirements of moral principle and national security. Morgenthau's objective, far from being a cynical vindication of ruthless power politics, was to harmonize the successful defense of the national interest with the promotion of desirable values in foreign policy. At issue is the extent to which America's national purpose in world affairs can be interpreted as an objective, value-free category exempt from *any* normative restraint transcending parochial interest. Contrary to allegations of many of his detractors, Morgenthau acknowledged viable universal norms for Americans in a troubled world menaced by the nightmare of nuclear catastrophe and ecological disaster.

Chapter 5 deals with Morgenthau's analysis of contemporary foreign policy developments. In addition to a deep appreciation for the philosophical and ethical roots of his tradition, Morgenthau was a dedicated political activist, always outspoken on the domestic and international issues of the day. Often overlooked by those critics who equate his realism with the tenets of *raison d'état* is how often he pointed to the limits and obligations of American power, in addition to the increasing obsolescence of the nation-state. Although a complete inventory of the many national issues he addressed throughout the postwar years is beyond the scope of this study, selective consideration is devoted to such topics as international law and world government, nuclear strategy and disarmament, intervention and American foreign policy in the Third World, and human rights and the American moral purpose in world affairs.

Chapter 6 contains a final overview that evaluates the significance of Morgenthau's work as an integral expression of a distinctive international perspective that has united a number of prominent American thinkers and diplomats over the years. In particular, the publications of Walter Lippmann, Reinhold Niebuhr, and George F. Kennan exemplify the evolution and development of realist doctrine over a volatile forty-five-year postwar period of United States foreign policy. Although these individuals have sometimes differed on policy matters, they do embody certain common conceptions of human nature, politics, and foreign-policy ethics that represent a fundamental departure from the canons of *raison d'état*. Perhaps more than that of any other American realist, however, Hans J. Morgenthau's political philosophy is unsurpassed in recognizing the tension between the state-centered principles of the continental tradition and the necessity to recognize the increasing importance of new domestic and transnational variables for American diplomacy and world affairs.

CHAPTER ONE

The Continental Heritage
Raison d'État *and* Realpolitik

This chapter examines the broad philosophical heritage of *raison d'état* from its moorings in the classical city-state system of Thucydides to its culmination in the Bismarckian conceptualization of *realpolitik* in nineteenth-century Germany. A number of key considerations will structure the inquiry into the evolution and interpretation of this millennial concept in the work of continental theorists and statesmen. First, how and why was *raison d'état* an early manifestation of theorizing about interstate relations? Second, what continuities and inconsistencies in conceptual understanding can be derived from a review of some of the prominent exponents of *raison d'état* in different historical periods? Finally, as a theory of international politics, how does *raison d'état* supply meaningful presuppositions for the successful exercise of European diplomacy and balance of power?

Machiavelli's doctrine of *raison d'état* as the servant of political necessity represented both a thesis and a justification that numerous European statesmen felt obliged to affirm and practice in their diplomatic and foreign-policy conduct. The doctrine was repeated in the words of Frederick the Great: "Princes are slaves to their resources, the interest of the state is their law, and this law is inviolable." Its spirit was similarly expressed when Bismarck suggested: "It is better to seek salvation via the sewer than to allow oneself to be choked or beaten to death." A more comprehensive summation of Machiavelli's principle was offered by the German historian Friedrich Meinecke, who pointed out: "*Raison d'état* is the fundamental principle of international conduct, the State's First Law of Motion. It tells the statesman what he must do to preserve the health and strength of the state. The state is an organic structure whose full power can only be maintained by allowing it . . . to continue growing; and *raison d'état* indicates both the path and goal for such growth."[1]

Raison d'état as interpreted and elaborated by continental theorists signified a pattern or tradition of thought that encompasses a *description* of the nature of international politics and also a set of *prescriptions* as to how statesmen should conduct themselves. For what has been termed the Machiavellian tradition in international politics—including such figures as Thomas Hobbes, Cardinal Richelieu, Frederick the Great, Georges Clemenceau, the twentieth-century realists such as E. H. Carr and Hans Morgenthau—the true description of international politics was one of international anarchy, a war of all against all, or a relationship of unending conflict among sovereign states.[2]

The structure of diplomatic practices was based on the existence of a number of independent territorial states, free from external control and able to pursue their own interests by bargaining and fighting with each other. Each national unit pursued objectives that best served the interests of its ruling (and largely aristocratic) class. These objectives, outlined in *The Prince*, involved a maximum extension of the territory and power of the state at the expense of rivals. The question of morality in international politics, at least in the sense of moral rules that restrained states in their mutual relations, either did not arise or was effectively subordinated to the competitive struggle for power.[3]

Raison d'État in the Tradition of European Political Theory

By what standards or criteria can *raison d'état* be interpreted or justified as a theory of international politics? Is it possible to identify the

1. Meinecke, *Machiavellianism*, 1; Richard Sterling, *Ethics in a World of Power* (Princeton, 1958), 239.
2. Hedley Bull, "Martin Wight and the Theory of International Relations," *British Journal of International Studies*, II (Spring, 1976), 104.
3. For additional commentary on the Machiavellian tradition of diplomacy and statesmanship, see Arnold Wolfers, "Statesmanship and Moral Choice," *World Politics*, I (January, 1949), 175–95; and Kenneth W. Thompson, "The Limits of Principle in Inter-

intellectual origins of *raison d'état* in the long history of European state-craft? As a theory or explanation of relations among independent states, how can *raison d'état* be distinguished from the emphasis of traditional political philosophy on the primordial fact of man's membership and obligations *within* separate states? Finally, what are the implications deriving from *raison d'état* for such fundamental topics in international thought as the nature and structure of international society, the relationship between human nature and state conduct, the role of power and diplomacy, the nature and conduct of war, and viable ethical guidelines above the state itself?

At the outset, it is important to address briefly the development and possibility of theory in international relations. Perhaps the prevailing view concerning the scope of theory is that the field is beleaguered by a plethora of theoretical approaches, models, and rival conceptual frameworks—that it is "in as much a state of change, chaos, and confusion as the contemporary world scene which it strives to comprehend"—and that theorizing about international relations is of only "fairly recent origin." Martin Wight suggests that if international relations theory "means a tradition of systematic investigation about relations between states, a tradition imagined as the twin of speculation about the state to which the name political theory is appropriated, it can hardly be said to exist at all."[4]

Wight's observation, perhaps expressing a consensus among contemporary observers of international politics, provides an initial platform by which to assess the consequences of political theory above the nation-state. Prior to the twentieth century, for example, speculation focusing on the society of states was largely confined to international law and such other sources as: (1) theorists who foreshadowed the League of Nations, such as Erasmus, William Penn, and the Abbé de St. Pierre; (2) Machiavellians and defenders of *raison d'état*, such as Machiavelli,

---

national Politics: Necessity and the New Balance of Power," *Journal of Politics*, XX (August, 1958), 437–67.

4. Klaus Knorr and Sidney Verba (eds.), *The International System: Theoretical Essays* (Princeton, 1961), 1. See also H. V. Harrison, *The Role of Theory in International Relations* (Princeton, 1964), 3–14; and Martin Wight, "Why Is There No International Theory?" in Herbert Butterfield and Martin Wight (eds.), *Diplomatic Investigations: Essays in the Theory of International Politics* (London, 1966), 17.

Hobbes, Meinecke, and E. H. Carr; (3) philosophers and historians who examined basic problems of international politics, as in David Hume's "The Balance of Power," Jean-Jacques Rousseau's "Project of Perpetual Peace," Jeremy Bentham's "Plan for an Universal Peace," Edmund Burke's "Thoughts on French Affairs," Leopold von Ranke's essay on the great powers, and John Stuart Mill's essay on the law of nations; and (4) speeches, dispatches, memoirs, and essays of statesmen, such as George Canning's classic dispatch of 1823 on the doctrine of guarantees, Bismarck's *Gedanken und Erinnerungen*, and Lord Salisbury's early essays on foreign affairs in the *Quarterly Review.*[5]

The often diverse and ambiguous expression of political theory above the nation-state can be explained in some measure by a number of assumptions that reinforce the gulf between political theory and international politics. The starting point for serious political theorists and philosophers has been the question of man and human nature. Plato's often-quoted phrase that a *polis* is man written large provides a general principle for the interpretation of society. Eric Voegelin pointed out that "as a general principle it means that in its order every society reflects the type of men of whom it is composed." Whenever the theorist wants to understand a political society, it will be one of his first tasks, if not the very first, to ascertain the human type that expresses itself in the order of the concrete society.[6] Although the typical starting point for the theorist is man, the question of human nature leads directly to a concern about the conditions that bring individuals together in association with others under government. In short, the political theorist frequently is led to develop a theory of politics and the state, as well as to explain the terms of man's membership in the state.

Does man live in one state or many? Although philosophers have raised the question of a truly global community free of parochial and self-interested nation-states, few thinkers have wavered from the conclusion that man lives and will always live in differentiated political and social structures. Although political theorists are apt to begin their work with an inquiry into human nature, they do not begin with mankind as a basis for distinguishing between the reason and unreason of the separate states

---

5. Kenneth W. Thompson, *Masters of International Thought* (Baton Rouge, 1980), 55–56.

6. Eric Voegelin, *The New Science of Politics* (Chicago, 1952), 61–62; Allan Bloom, *"The Republic" of Plato* (New York, 1968), 337–44.

into which he is divided.[7] The assumption of man's membership in separate states poses the fundamental dilemma for any political theory of interstate relations. If human nature and potential are fully actualized in the polity or state, what can there be for the theorist to say about international relations? Gerhart Niemeyer identifies the source of the problem by suggesting: "Foreign policy lacks the direct reference to human nature, since it deals not with the relation between the particular man as citizen and the community of citizens as a whole, but rather relations between wholes who are not 'natural' substances in the way each individual person is, and who have no center of normative experiences resembling the human soul." Niemeyer's cogent observation indicates that the duties of the statesman cannot be reduced to the citizens' good life, but rather, they operate to ensure "the continued existence of an artifacted whole neither the size, nor the configuration, nor the duration of which are given, as it were, by nature."[8] With what justification did European political thinkers reflect on the normative criteria that govern diplomatic conduct in a world of co-sovereign nation-states?

Whereas the older theoretical treatments of international politics are often unsystematic and highly dispersed, it is possible to ascertain a reasonable degree of coherence in matters of antecedent philosophical assumptions and conceptual definition. Specifically, the growth of classical international theory may be explained in terms of the general developmental pattern of scientific disciplines as outlined by Thomas S. Kuhn in *The Structure of Scientific Revolutions*. Arend Lijphart argued that continental thinking about interstate relations was, in fact, governed by what Kuhn calls a "paradigm," and this paradigm remained the basis of a research tradition that dominated the field until the 1950s. Kuhn identified science as a communal activity carried on by a community of scholars who share a common set of assumptions about the nature of their subject matter.[9] These assumptions and beliefs constitute a paradigm

7. Michael Donelan (ed.), "The Political Theorists and International Theory," *The Reason of States* (London, 1978), 75–76.

8. Gerhart Niemeyer, "Foreign Policy and Morality: A Contemporary Perspective," *Intercollegiate Review*, XV (Spring, 1980), 77.

9. Arend Lijphart, "The Structure of Theoretical Revolutions in International Relations," *International Studies Quarterly*, XVIII (March, 1974), 42–59; Thomas S. Kuhn, *The Structure of Scientific Revolutions* (Chicago, 1970), 92. See also Kuhn's "Reflections on My Critics," in I. Lakatos and A. Musgrave (eds.), *Criticism and the Growth of Knowledge* (Cambridge, Mass., 1970), 231–78.

within which normal scientific activity is conducted. A paradigm represents an accepted approach, model, or theory that constitutes the foundation for the cumulative growth of scientific knowledge.

For the purposes of this study, it is in the more global and philosophical sense (*i.e.*, comprehensive ways of looking at the subject matter, or world views) that European theorizing about international relations meets the criteria of paradigmatic thinking, as identified by Kuhn. According to Kuhn, a philosophical paradigm is both wider than and prior to theory. This kind of intellectual construct is what Michael Polanyi calls a "heuristic vision" that leads to the formulation of theory.[10] Kuhn's contribution permits us to approach the question of "theory" in the classical mold by shifting the intellectual focus to account for the philosophical world view that influences not only the identification of a reality between separate states but the adumbration of key concepts that illumine the nature and type of relations between separate states. A number of paradigmatic attributes distinguish the international orientation of continental theory. Peter Savigear noted that the theory of the state in Europe from its beginnings in the High Renaissance spawned a theory of international relations. In particular, early continental theorizing focused upon two features of the political landscape: the constitution (or nature) of the state and the dilemma of ethical guideposts imposing some minimal level of order in relations among states.[11]

Arnold Wolfers pointed out that the main question for continental theorists was whether statesmen and nations were under any moral obligation to resist these compelling demands of state necessity defined in terms of the struggle for power. The underlying tension between the unavoidable demands of state interests and the role of normative restraints in foreign policy rests on a number of presuppositions associated with a Machiavellian world view of international politics. It should be acknowledged that many European theorists who were proponents of *raison d'état* often exhibited significant differences in the scope and method of their theoretical examination of phenomena within the nation-state; how-

10. Michael Polanyi, "Commentary on T. S. Kuhn's 'The Function of Dogma in Scientific Research,'" in A. C. Gombie (ed.), *Scientific Change* (London, 1963), 375; Kuhn, *The Structure of Scientific Revolutions*, 175–82.

11. Peter Savigear, "European Political Philosophy and the Theory of International Relations," in Trevor Taylor (ed.), *Approaches and Theory in International Relations* (London, 1978), 32.

ever, regarding the structure of international society and the justification of state conduct, they identified a number of core themes as important for the development of *raison d'état* as a theory of international politics.

First, advocates of *raison d'état* have emphasized the inevitable expression of individual self-interest and the lust for power at all levels of human existence. Violence, coercion, and countervailing power are the principal means by which the state must protect the integrity of its political life and defend its security against external threats and subversion. From Machiavelli to Bismarck, *raison d'état* has been characterized by the tendency to differentiate sharply between the moral inclinations of the solitary individual and the immoral nature of political society both within and above the state.

Second, the state itself represents a moral force. The state did not simply exist as a set of institutions, but made a claim on the loyalty and service of its citizens and, as such, took on a moral quality that demanded priority and obedience. Machiavelli was one of the strongest advocates of this position in urging that the statesman's duty was to the political entity and its security, and not to any other moral code. The assumption that the public realm acquired a rightful authority that superseded private conscience led many theorists to assign primacy to the external strength of the state and adopt a more expedient view by which political actions would be evaluated.[12]

Third, the international environment exists and has structure. In terms of the structure of the international arena, a number of thinkers argued that the state was not defined *exclusively* by its internal ordering or territorial domain, but also by an understanding of the interests of other states. The ruler was obliged by the external circumstances of the state to formulate policy objectives by reference to the interstate environment. However, the interrelatedness and reciprocity of states was largely restricted to the norms of military capability and the successful defense of state sovereignty. International thought based on *raison d'état* portrayed international society as merely the sum of its individual parts and bereft of moral certainties transcending conflicting and competitive national goals. The task for the theorist was to provide some justification for the possibility of orderly political relations among states in an anarchic global setting where "Kings and Persons of Soveraigne authority,

12. *Ibid.*, 35–36.

because of their Independency, are in continual jealousies, and in the state and posture of gladiators; having their weapons pointing, and their eyes fixed on one another; that is, their Forts, Garrisons and Guns, upon the Frontiers of their Kingdoms; and continual Spyes upon their neighbors; which is a posture of war." [13]

Fourth, among the ideas integral to *raison d'état*—by many criteria, perhaps its pivotal idea—is the concept of power. It is from an understanding of the nature and role of power in political life that collateral concepts like balance of power, national interest, and diplomacy are largely derived. From the standpoint of many continental theorists, power politics as applied to relations among sovereign states constitutes a theory of survival by which statesmen seek freedom, security, prosperity, or even power itself.

Fifth, an important corollary to the idea that international politics is best described as a struggle for power and security is the idea that statesmen may define diplomatic ends in terms of religious, philosophic, economic, or social objectives. Ideological criteria and other normative sources, however, tend to disguise and distort the universal urge to power. Moral and ethical pronouncements can play a positive role in foreign policy only insofar as they function to legitimize successful policy initiatives and keep aspirations for power within socially tolerable bounds.

Sixth, although proponents of *raison d'état* were less than sanguine about the prospects of an authentic international community based on a harmony of values and interests, several thinkers turned their attention to the formulation of rules consistent with the possibility of a minimum level of orderly relations among states. The recognition of any rudimentary form of order among constituent states was predicated upon the preservation of state sovereignty (in addition to facilitating a wide margin of maneuverability in diplomatic strategy). In brief, the problem of order in international politics presented continental theorists with the challenge of defending both the *source* and *nature* of viable standards of state con-

13. Thomas Hobbes, *Leviathan*, in Sir William Molesworth (ed.), *The English Works of Thomas Hobbes of Malmesbury* (London, 1836–45), III, 115. Machiavelli went further and argued that the constitution of the state was in some measure a response to its international environment. See Allan H. Gilbert (ed.), *Machiavelli: The Chief Works and Others* (Durham, N.C., 1965), I, 269.

duct in a world that exhibited the indivisibility of peace and war. Both structural and procedural attributes identified as contributing to the maintenance of orderly interaction among states were subsumed under such principles as diplomacy and balance of power. The methods of diplomacy, as well as the operation of the balance of power, offered a conceptual basis by which European statesmen and thinkers attempted to build a coherent world view of a European system of state relations that acknowledged the interrelatedness of states based on the pursuit of interest and the recognition of the interests of others.[14]

International theory grounded in *raison d'état* built upon philosophical assumptions about human nature and political reality. These assumptions provided the justification for principles and concepts that functioned as both a description of the international milieu as well as a prescription for foreign-policy conduct. At this juncture, it will be useful to introduce a central paradox in classical *raison d'état* that is exhibited by several thinkers evaluated in this study. On the one hand, continental theorists clearly relied on ethical and political norms for the investigation of international phenomena. For example, the preoccupation with national self-interest grew out of the value placed on the existence of sovereign states. Similarly, emphasis on diplomacy and the balance of power reflected a concern for the sources of order and stability in an anarchic world. On the other hand, proponents of *raison d'état* distinguished between the private realm of ethical discourse affecting the individual and the morally neutral obligations incumbent on the statesman in the defense of state interests.

The emergence of such a paradox in international theorizing raises a number of significant questions. Have expositors of *raison d'état* clearly and convincingly demonstrated the importance of political ethics for the theory and practice of international politics? If such a justification can be found, does it find consistent support and interpretation from theorists in different historical periods? In addition, what is the exact nature of the relationship between philosophical thinking about ethical criteria applying to man's membership in the state and the nature and functions of norms of interstate behavior?

14. Savigear, "European Political Philosophy and the Theory of International Relations," in Taylor (ed.), *Approaches and Theory in International Relations*, 37.

European Philosophers and Statesmen: An Inquiry into a Theory of International Politics

This section evaluates several of the more prominent political thinkers who have drawn upon the primary assumptions of *raison d'état* in order to theorize about relations among sovereign states. Attention is devoted to both the intellectual heritage of *raison d'état* in the history of Western political philosophy (*i.e.,* Thucydides, Machiavelli, and Hobbes) and its culmination in the statesmanship of *realpolitik* associated with the classical age of European diplomacy following the Peace of Westphalia (*i.e.,* Richelieu and Bismarck). At issue is the manner in which philosophers and practitioners point to a connection between state "necessity" and the particular values impacting upon the methods *and* purposes of foreign policy.

THUCYDIDES (471? – 400? B.C.)

Whereas *raison d'état* has typically been associated with a description of conditions of multiple sovereignty since the period of the European Renaissance, its central assumptions and concepts received thoughtful attention by Thucydides in the *History of the Peloponnesian War.* Few surveys of the development of international political theory fail to assign his contribution a prominent position among other intellectual precursors of more modern political realism. Thucydides' *History* aimed not only at making future readers understand a singular event but also at describing generally the necessary logic of a certain kind of human behavior. His basic ambition was to illustrate how the combination of human nature, a certain structure of power, and the specific properties of rival states create an inescapable logic characteristic of world politics.[15] A leading student of the period has written: "He was writing, he said, for the guidance of men of all times and in all places, on the assumption that recurrent elements were present in varying historical circumstances. This assumption was based on the conviction that man has a nature."[16]

The *History* illustrates a number of enduring principles that have continuing relevance for contemporary international political theory. A

15. Stanley Hoffmann, *Primacy or World Order: American Foreign Policy Since the Cold War* (New York, 1980), 106–108.

16. Peter J. Fleiss, *Thucydides and the Politics of Bipolarity* (Baton Rouge, 1966), vii.

cursory inventory of topics encompassed by Thucydides' analysis includes the relationship between force and consent, the distinction between coalition and dominion, the nature of leadership, the effect of means upon ends, and the contrasting implications of land and sea power.[17] Our interest will be confined to Thucydides' understanding of how such seminal themes for *raison d'état* as human nature, the interest of the political community, and power cohere to form a theoretical world view or explanation of international politics.

Although the work of Thucydides can be read profitably as a treatise on war (its causes and effects), it ultimately belongs to the category of tragic drama. Throughout, there is a sense of destiny and the helplessness of men to save themselves from disaster. The downfall of Athens was attributed, in no small part, to a deterioration in human character in the toils of war. Thucydides' observations on human nature are explicit in his chronicle on the moral demise of Athenian statesmanship after the death of Pericles. In one of his most famous and often-quoted passages, Thucydides spoke directly about the eclipse of political morality under the strain of war: "In peace and prosperity states and individuals are governed by higher ideals because they are not involved in necessities beyond their control, but war deprives them of their easy existence . . . and brings most men's dispositions down to the level of their circumstances. So civil war broke out in the cities, and the later revolutionaries . . . derived new ideas which went far beyond earlier ones, so elaborate were their enterprises, so novel their revenges. . . . The cause of all these evils was love of power due to ambition and greed, which led to the rivalries from which party spirit sprung."[18] The tragedy of Athens, as Thucydides saw it, lay in its inability to live up to the moral standards and responsibility that had resulted from her own commitment to civic virtue.

The demoralization of Athenian political life and the increasing demagogy called into question the role played by human nature in the course of historical events and suggests the importance of differentiating between the impact of human and environmental factors. In assessing the

17. Thucydides, *The Peloponnesian War*, trans. R. Crawley (New York, 1910). See also William T. Bluhm, *Theories of the Political System: Classics of Political Thought and Modern Political Analysis* (Englewood Cliffs, N.J., 1965); and John H. Finley, Jr., *Thucydides* (Cambridge, Mass., 1942).

18. Louis J. Halle, *Civilization and Foreign Policy* (New York, 1955), 265, 272.

force of human nature vis-à-vis external determinants of the origin and conduct of the war, Thucydides turned his attention to two sources: the political necessities inherent in the circumstances that man can neither harness nor evade, and man's ambitious and passionate nature, which prevents him from exercising rational choices. Of major importance in his examination of the inexorable force of environmental factors that shape state conduct was the distribution of power among Greek states and its impact on the interest of the nation. Thucydides' diagnosis of the causes of the war received striking formulation in Book I: "The real cause I consider to be the one which was formally most kept out of sight. The growth of power of Athens, and the alarm which this inspired in Lacedaemon, made war inevitable."[19]

It is possible, from Thucydides' account of the Hellenic world (the *Archaeology*) and the creation of the Athenian empire (the *Fifty Years*), to understand his conception of power, how it operates, and its relation to the outbreak of the Peloponnesian War.[20] Briefly, power encompasses a number of important variables, including cumulative material resources (*e.g.,* capital combined with military-naval strength, national character, and leadership potential). The process of civilization is also a process of the growth of power. Power operates in a world of states much like a physical law; it expands until checked or balanced by countervailing power. Once checked, as Athenian power was, it dissipates, and the entire historical process toward higher organization and effective use of technological resources begins anew. In Thucydides' words: "The object of *interest* for the nation in its historical development is *dynamis*, power, and this means dominion over others. Fear and greed are the dominating motives on the road to imperialism, and there is no turning back" (emphasis added). Power becomes an amoral force that will grow until resisted by opposing power, and its very growth promotes conflict and opposition. Thucydides' statement that "identity of interests is the surest of bonds whether between states or individuals" simply affirms a key assumption associated with a philosophy of *raison d'état:* the idea of interest (defined in terms of power) is an objective category and the very

19. Thucydides, *The Peloponnesian War,* 51–52; Fleiss, *Thucydides and the Politics of Bipolarity,* ix, 25–26.

20. For a comprehensive overview of Thucydides' work, see A. W. Gomme, *A Historical Commentary on Thucydides* (Oxford, 1945–56).

essence of politics.[21] Thucydides introduced a number of insights and principles that form the core of a philosophy of *raison d'état* and were subsequently applied to the European system of states by continental theorists.

First, he called attention to the fact that the structure of the international system and the power relations between states are primary factors in individual state behavior. Second, his identification of system structure and the relations of power was based on a vision of human nature that reminds the reader of the tragic ambiguity of life and the irrational inclination toward hubris, which tempts the powerful to grandiose or arrogant policies. Third, he pointed to the gulf that separates the possibility of *dike* (justice) and moral obligation in the polity from the type of political morality that guides the statesman in the quest for successful policy. To understand such an apparent inconsistency, Thucydides argued that the statesman must be prepared to act in accordance with certain necessities that are not of his making, even if such actions do not conform to generally accepted moral standards.

Thucydides bequeathed to Western civilization one of the earliest and most original efforts to theorize about relations between states in terms of both recurrent and universal categories. However, the scope of his theoretical inquiry was circumscribed by two elemental factors: the specific configuration of rival city-states on the Greek peninsula in the fifth century B.C. and the absence of any explicit formula or criteria by which to differentiate the *ad hoc* assemblage of ethical prescriptions from empirical generalizations. Although more modern European thinkers in the tradition of *raison d'état* (and American "realists") acknowledge a normative or philosophical component in their theorizing, the vital nexus remains obscure and ambiguous in Thucydides' treatise.

NICCOLO MACHIAVELLI (1469 – 1527)

The Renaissance marked the decline of a comprehensive theocracy that had governed the feudal structure of international society. The appearance of a system of independent states in Italy, as well as a diminution in the status of the pope to prince, contributed to Machiavelli's for-

21. Fleiss, *Thucydides and the Politics of Bipolarity*, 121–26; Kenneth Waltz, *Man, the State and War* (New York, 1959), 216; Thucydides, *The Peloponnesian War*, 3–7; Hans J. Morgenthau, *Politics Among Nations* (5th ed.; New York, 1973), 8.

mulation of a "new morality" prevailing in the relations among sovereign states. Although Machiavelli was still far from having succeeded in elaborating a comprehensive conception of the new type of international relations that would characterize Europe just two centuries after his death, he was among the first to treat the study of international politics as a purely technical affair.

The elaboration of *raison d'état* (or *ragion di stato*) as a unifying theme for Machiavelli's understanding of state relations was heavily influenced by several important biographical and historical developments. As a secretary and diplomat of the Florentine Republic until 1512, Machiavelli observed the French and Spanish invasions that overtook Italy after 1494 and led to the decline of Neopolitan and Milanese independence, the change of government in Florence, and the collective impact of foreign powers on the entire Apennine peninsula.[22] Although Machiavelli's diplomatic and foreign-policy background endowed him with a working knowledge of Italian statecraft, it was not until the restoration of the Medicis in Florence (1512) that he was prompted to develop and express his own thoughts concerning the origin and nature of state behavior.

As a member of the party that had been overthrown, Machiavelli sought to reestablish himself by seeking the favor of the Medici rulers. A conflict thus developed between Machiavelli's own political and egocentric objectives, and the ideas of republican freedom he had long acknowledged. It was against such a political background that Machiavelli reflected on the relations between republic and monarchy, as well as the new national mission of monarchy on the Italian peninsula. In the words of one historical scholar: "It was in a context of all this that the whole essence of *raison d'état*, compounded of mingled ingredients both pure and impure, both lofty and hateful, achieved a ruthless expression. He had reached his fortieth year—the age at which productive scientific minds often gave of their best—when after 1513 he wrote the little book on the prince and the *Discorsi sopra la prima deca di Tito Livio*."[23]

Machiavelli's work was brought into being by an extraordinary conjunction of events—the coinciding of a political collapse with a spirit-

22. Meinecke, *Machiavellianism*, 30. See also James Burnham, *The Machiavellians* (New York, 1943); Herbert Butterfield, *The Statecraft of Machiavelli* (New York, 1956); Roberto Ridolfi, *The Life of Niccolo Machiavelli* (Chicago, 1963); and Leo Strauss, *Thoughts on Machiavelli* (Glencoe, Ill., 1958).

23. Meinecke, *Machiavellianism*, 30.

ual and intellectual renaissance. He wrote at a time when the personal loyalties of the feudal age were disappearing, when the moral restraints of the Middle Ages were felt less keenly, and when Italy was ruled by a number of petty tyrants. In studying the formation and background of Machiavelli's *Prince*, a leading political philosopher has written: "The mediaeval *Christianitas* was falling apart into the Church and the national states. . . . The disintegration of the *Christianitas* affected both the spiritual and temporal orders insofar as in both spheres the common spirit, inducing effective cooperation between persons in spite of divergence of interests as well as the sense of an obligation to compromise in the spirit of the whole, was seeping out."[24] The focus of attention had shifted from God to man, with the consequence that increasing attention was given to temporal security over eternal salvation. Displacing God, man became the center of the universe; the values of this new solar system were inevitably different from those of the God-created universe.

Machiavelli's passionate interest was the state—the analysis and computation of its different forms, functions, and conditions for existence. Indeed, it was in Machiavelli's analysis of the new secular state (divorced from ecclesiastical considerations) that the specifically rational, empirical, and calculating element in Italian Renaissance culture reached its peak. He was interested in the state as a self-sufficient entity in continual contact with other states and, therefore, in need of power. His contribution to *raison d'état* can, in no small part, be understood as an urgent plea to the princes for a new conception of politics in general, both at home and abroad. An attempt to distill the core attributes of Machiavellian *raison d'état* must acknowledge a sense of limitation at the outset. Meinecke pointed out:

> Machiavelli had not yet compressed his thoughts on *raison d'état* into a single slogan. Fond as he was of forceful and meaningful catch-words, he did not always feel the need to express in words the supreme ideas which filled him. . . . Critics have noticed that he fails to express any opinion about the final real purpose of the State, and they have mistakenly deduced from this that he did not reflect on the subject. But . . . his whole life was bound up with a definite

24. Eric Voegelin, "Machiavelli's *Prince*: Background and Formation," *Review of Politics*, XIII (April, 1951), 145. See also John Hallowell, *Main Currents in Modern Political Thought* (New York, 1950), 52.

supreme purpose of the State. And in the same way his whole political way of thought is nothing but a continual process of thinking about *raison d'état*.[25]

For our purposes, three basic themes of *raison d'état* were especially important in Machiavellian thought. Machiavelli's preoccupation with such principles as *virtù, fortuna,* and *necessita* sum up the demands he made of the state in terms of power politics. Consideration of these recurrent themes and their interrelation will also highlight many of the fundamental problems and topics integral to the historical development of *raison d'état*.

Machiavelli's deliberations on the meaning of *virtù* (or manly strength) have their origin in the effort to restore the sources of order for both individual and social existence as a result of the political humiliation inflicted by foreign powers on the Italian peninsula. Foremost among Machiavelli's objectives was to see Italy united in a condition of peace and security. The *virtù* of the conquering prince became the source of order; the political instability represented a challenge to a ruler with semidivine, heroic qualities to eject the barbarians and to restore the order of Italy through his *virtù*, which would overcome the adverse *fortuna*.[26]

Although the concept of *virtù* was taken over from antiquity and classical humanism by Machiavelli's era, it represented something of a new naturalistic ethic that denoted qualities of heroic political and military achievements, as well as the strength for the founding and preservation of states. Machiavelli broke with the dualistic and spiritualizing ethic of Christianity, which depreciated the natural impulses of the senses. Although he retained some of its structural ideas about the difference between good and evil, he strove primarily for a new naturalistic ethic that would follow the dictates of nature impartially and resolutely.[27] Indeed, the development of *virtù* by the prince was proclaimed by Machiavelli as the ideal and self-evident purpose of the state. Equally important was the connection Machiavelli made between *virtù* and monarchy. Perceiving the incurable corruption of republican rule, Machiavelli argued that the

25. Meinecke, *Machiavellianism*, 29.
26. Voegelin, "Machiavelli's *Prince:* Background and Formation," 165.
27. Meinecke, *Machiavellianism*, 31.

creative *virtù* of one individual should take the state in hand and revive it. Devoted to securing the authority of the Medicis, *The Prince* featured advice on the prerequisites of diplomatic success within the set of novel circumstances that had arisen in Renaissance Italy.

Before turning to the principal manifestations of princely rule, brief attention must be given to a serious problematic element in the whole character of *raison d'état*. This dilemma concerns the conflict between the ethical sphere of *virtù* (and the state animated by *virtù*) and the old sphere of morality and religion, represented by the Christian transcendental order. From Machiavelli's perspective, religion and morality were seen as indispensable in the influence they exerted toward *maintaining* the state. However, by this formulation, Christian ethics and morality became nothing but means toward the goal of the state animated by *virtù*. Insofar as the higher realm of *virtù* constituted the vital source of the state (*vivere politico*), it could be permitted to encroach on the moral world to achieve its ends.[28]

Reference must also be made to the concepts of *fortuna* (fortune or fate) and *necessita* (necessity) and how they influenced Machiavelli's reflections on the requirements of state conduct. Although Machiavelli viewed the unification of Italy as a present possibility, he was quick to acknowledge the role of fortune (*fortuna*) in human affairs. The drama of human existence achieves meaning by the dialectical interplay between the creative genius of the individual and the unsuspected revolutions of fate. Furthermore, "because, where men have little ability, Fortune shows her power much, and because she is variable, republics and states often vary, and vary they always will until someone arrives who is so great a lover of antiquity that he will rule Fortune in such a way that she will not have cause to show in every revolution of the sun how much she can do."[29] Machiavelli concludes that fortune can be an ally or adversary, depending on the circumstances. The true task of *virtù* is, therefore, the ability to suppress *fortuna*. Because *fortuna* is often malicious, so *virtù* must also be malicious when there is no other available option. That a man of *virtù* can conquer the vicissitudes of fate expresses the inner spirit-

---

28. For an analysis of how Machiavelli supplements the morality of the gospel with the martial vigor of ancient Rome, see Dante Germino, *From Machiavelli to Marx: Modern Western Political Thought* (Chicago, 1972), 42–43.

29. Gilbert (ed.), *Machiavelli: The Chief Works*, I, 411–12.

ual core of Machiavellianism and supplies an essential presupposition of *raison d'état*—the doctrine that, in national behavior, even immoral methods are sanctioned in the heroic defense and preservation of the state.

The triumph of *virtù* over *fortuna* was largely contingent on the intervening force of *necessita* (necessity) in human conduct. It is important to note that Machiavelli traced the origin of morality back to the idea of "necessity." In the *Discourses*, he suggests that men will never do anything good unless they are driven to it by some necessity. In a famous passage, Machiavelli pointed out: "In the actions of men, and especially princes from which there is no appeal, the end justifies the means. Let the prince, therefore, aim at conquering and maintaining the state, and the means will always be judged honorable and praised by everyone."[30] Machiavelli's conception of *raison d'état* was both amoral in essence and originated in ineluctable necessity. The state was a necessity; power was necessary to the state; and in order to secure power it was sometimes necessary to violate the laws of decency and morality.

Although religion, law, and morality were considered indispensable for the state's existence, the requirements of *necessita* sometimes compelled the statesman to set these aside whenever the need for national self-preservation required it. Machiavelli pointed out that, for the purpose of maintaining the state, a prince "is often obliged (*necessitato*) to act without loyalty, without mercy, without humanity, and without religion."[31] However, he does not offer dispensations for all human sins. Only the stern necessities of the state—not personal caprice nor any other personal consideration—justified doing evil. In summation, the struggle between *virtù* and *fortuna*, and the theory of *necessita*, worked together to legitimize the prince in the discriminating use of immoral methods.

Machiavelli identified two key elements that would shape continental theory about state relations for the next four hundred years: the state is a moral force and the international world exists and has structure. The Italian state system created its own patterns and demands that transformed the interest of the state by reference to the interstate environment. To illustrate this contention, Machiavelli refers to the analogous experi-

30. *Ibid.*, 67.
31. *Ibid.*, 66.

ence of Rome: "It was Rome's neighbors who in their desire to crush her, caused her to set up institutions which not only enabled her to defend herself but also to attack them with greater force, counsel and authority."[32] In short, the state was not defined simply by internal factors but also by the interests and objectives of other states.

Concomitant with the idea of the interrelatedness of states was the elevation of the state to the level of a new moral force in world politics. The axioms and principles of statecraft presented in *The Prince* and the *Discourses* were intended to apply to the intercourse of states as much as to internal politics. Discussing the requirements of successful political actions, Machiavelli reaches the conclusion that a ruler is often obliged to ignore considerations of religion and ethics (perhaps applicable to private relationships) and employ force and fraud where needed. Though Machiavelli never praises immorality for its own sake or denies the existence of values in this world, his writing affirms that in the situation of the statesman the rules of power have priority over those of ethics and morality; in fact, power becomes an end in itself. He confines his inquiry to the means that are best suited for acquiring, retaining, and expanding power. Morals are not to enter political relationships at all: the only question that need trouble a prince is whether the means he employs—and if necessary they might include assassination—are best adapted to the great end, the preservation or advancement of the state.[33]

Of equal importance to the study of international politics are the implications deriving from Machiavelli's assessment of human nature. Though one can find some evidence of a fragile optimism in the ability of institutions to channel human ambitions for public good, in the main, he seems to subscribe to the notion that "men are ungrateful, inconstant, deceitful . . . greedy and avaricious." That the prince must be as ferocious as the lion and as cunning as the fox is a reflection of Machiavelli's belief that history proves the most successful rulers to be those who do not scruple to break their pledges. Because most men are wicked and faithless, Machiavelli sanctions the sovereign's breach of treaty where fidelity to such an agreement would turn to the disadvantage of one who signed

32. *Ibid.*, 269.
33. Savigear, "European Political Philosophy and the Theory of International Relations," in Taylor (ed.), *Approaches and Theory in International Relations*, 36; F. Parkinson, *The Philosophy of International Relations* (Beverly Hills, 1977), 30–31.

it. Pope Alexander VI's success in extending his power throughout Italy, Machiavelli explained, was due to the fact that he was a past master of this stratagem.[34]

Unlike many of the later proponents of *raison d'état* in European politics, Machiavelli was both ambivalent and critical about the balance-of-power system. The ineffectiveness of the balance of power in the Italy of his day for creating unity against foreign aggression from the outside discredited the concept in his eyes. Prior to the invasion of Charles VIII of France, power was distributed among the Holy See, the Venetian Republic, the Kingdom of Naples, the Duchy of Milan, and the Florentines. Whereas the greatest of the five powers was Venice, it took an alliance of the other four to preserve a stable equilibrium on the peninsula. Rome was held at bay by fomenting discord among the Orsini and Colonna factions. Machiavelli admitted that this sort of arrangement was sound policy in the days when the balance of power was fairly stable in Italy, but he thought it would be mistaken in his own day.[35]

In addition, Machiavelli was critical of alliances, the working combination of states within the balance-of-power system. The chaos into which Italy had fallen, he thought, was largely the result of the use of disloyal mercenary and allied troops. Instead, Machiavelli advocated a policy of military self-reliance. He cited the case of Caesar Borgia, who began with allied troops, turned to mercenaries, and ended with his own forces. At the same time, he argued that no ruler can afford to ignore the workings of the balance-of-power system. For example, Machiavelli thought that the ruler was ill-advised to remain neutral in a conflict between two nearby powers, for he would lose no matter which side won, whereas he could lose only one way if he were committed.[36] In short, the prudent prince was one who was able to develop his own military arsenal and rely on it alone and never, unless compelled by necessity, on the power of allies.

Machiavelli's desire that Italy attain unity and freedom from foreign interference did *not* entail a state organized for peace rather than conquest. The Greek ideal of the small state free from preoccupation with

34. Gilbert (ed.), *Machiavelli: The Chief Works*, I, 45–46, 62; Frank M. Russell, *Theories of International Relations* (New York, 1936), 122.

35. John C. Dunne, "*Realpolitik* in the Decline of the West," *Review of Politics*, XXI (January, 1959), 135–36; Gilbert (ed.), *Machiavelli: The Chief Works*, I, 78–80.

36. Dunne, "*Realpolitik* in the Decline of the West," 135–36.

external affairs, absorbing its energies within itself, was not practical. He learned from Polybius that nothing is permanent in human affairs and that the fortunes of every state are repeated in a cycle of rise and fall. If organized only to live, with no thought of foreign conquest, necessity may nevertheless drive states to pursue conquest. With regard to international politics, Machiavelli assumed that there is a necessary and natural hostility among states and that the advancement of the interests of one must necessarily be at the expense of the other. Abandoning good faith as an essential requirement for public intercourse and elevating *raison d'état* above all other considerations, Machiavelli rejected the possibility of any moral premises uniting the larger community of sovereign states.

THOMAS HOBBES (1588 – 1679)

Before turning to the impact of Machiavellianism and *raison d'état* on European politics and statesmanship following the Treaty of Westphalia (1648), our intellectual perspective can profit by noting how the work of the English philosopher Thomas Hobbes supplies a number of interesting variations on the theme of *raison d'état* in world politics. Several reasons can be offered to justify his inclusion within the scope of this study. The philosophy of Hobbes provides an early and interesting example of how specific attributes of *raison d'état* impact on the Anglo-American tradition of theorizing about international politics. Moreover, such an investigation reveals how certain principles associated with *raison d'état* from the horizon of continental theorists have been revised and further developed by a distinctive Hobbesian world view. Finally, the tendency to associate postwar American realists with either a Hobbesian or Machiavellian world view of global affairs can be understood better by placing Hobbes within the intellectual context of *raison d'état*.

That the name of Hobbes is frequently employed by contemporary observers to characterize a particular vision of international politics is subject, however, to some qualification. Hobbes, for example, constitutes no exception to the general truth that may be stated about many of the greatest thinkers of the past: few ever devoted themselves primarily to the study of the subject. The historical drama in relation to which Hobbes's ideas take much of their relevance was, after all, not an international but an internal civil conflict. Aside from the more general objective of providing a scientific basis for moral and political philosophy, his thought seeks to contribute to the establishment of civic peace and amity and to the disposing of mankind toward fulfilling its civic duties.[37] The priority that Hobbes assigns to the pursuit of domestic or internal peace over international concord appears to reflect his belief that internal strife is more terrible than strife among states.

At the same time, a variety of historical and intellectual factors led Hobbes to reflect on the conditions of international conflict. Born in 1588—the year of the Spanish Armada—Hobbes lived through the struggles of the Hapsburg ascendancy, the last phase of the European wars of religion, and the early phase of the wars for naval and mercantile predominance. As a youth he was introduced to the subject by his readings of Thucydides' *History of the Peloponnesian War*, Francis Bacon's essay *The True Greatness of Kingdoms*, and John Selden's *Mare Clausum*. Of more significance, in Hobbes's time civil and interstate conflicts were clearly bound together. Civil wars brought opportunities for foreign intervention, and religious loyalties linked parties across state boundaries. In his account of the history of the English Civil War (*Behemoth*), Hobbes attempted to show that conflicts within states are often determined by relations among them. In fact, the institution of Commonwealth can be justified by reference to its capacity to ensure internal security as well as its ability to resist foreign intrusions effectively.[38]

In terms of his contribution to world politics, Hobbes seeks to account for the logic of relations between independent powers that find themselves in a situation of anarchy. Both descriptive and prescriptive criteria structured the direction of his inquiry. On the one hand, Hobbes explains why and how these powers do and must confront one another under the imperatives of international anarchy; on the other hand, he suggests what they should and sometimes can do to ensure a modicum of security even while remaining in this condition. Hobbes's view of international anarchy is premised on the idea of a "state of nature" that functions both as a description for the life of individual men as well as the condition of states in relation to one another. In a state of nature, prior

37. James L. Wiser, *Political Philosophy: A History of the Search for Order* (Englewood Cliffs, N.J., 1983), 194–95.
38. John Aubrey, *Brief Lives*, ed. Oliver L. Dick (Ann Arbor, 1957), 147–59; Hedley Bull, "Hobbes and the International Anarchy," *Social Research*, XLVIII (Winter, 1981), 718–19. See also Thomas Hobbes, *Behemoth; or, The Long Parliament*, ed. F. Tonnies (New York, 1969), 144.

to the establishment of civil society, man is at war with man, seeking to justify his own desires, to keep what he has, or to preserve his reputation. In such a condition, men live in "continual fear" and in "danger of violent death," the "life of man being solitary, poor, nasty, brutish and short." In this war of every man against every man, it is not until men enter into civil society that justice is possible, for "where there is no common power, there is no law: where no law, no injustice."[39]

Hobbes's understanding of human nature laid the foundation for his contract theory and defense of absolutism, and it also contributed to his rather fatalistic view concerning world politics. The life of individual men in the state of nature may be interpreted as a description of the existence of states in relation to one another. Nations, like individuals, before the latter are coerced by a supreme authority, exist within a state of nature, which is a state of war. At the same time, however, Hobbes stops just short of suggesting that *all* international politics is characterized by recurrent and unending warfare. The situation is not one of war, but of a "posture of war." The very vigilance of the state is itself a modification of a world of total chaos and implies, in however rudimentary form, some degree of order in the world of states.[40]

It is a feature of a condition of war that "the notions of right and wrong, justice and injustice have there no place." Where there is no common power to enforce compliance with legal requirements, force and fraud become the virtues by which the statesman acts to preserve the security of the state. The conception of international law, which Hugo Grotius had established as offering a limitation to conflict among nations, was refuted by Hobbes: "Concerning the offices of one sovereign to another, which are comprehended in that law, which is commonly called the law of nations, I need not say anything in this place, because the law of nations, and the law of Nature, is the same thing. And every sovereign hath the same right, in procuring the safety of his peoples, that any particular man can have in procuring the safety of his own body."[41]

It is Hobbes's conception of the natural right of states to take all appropriate actions to ensure their own survival that links him to the continental tradition of *raison d'état*. In asserting the ultimate freedom

39. Thomas Hobbes, *Leviathan*, ed. Michael Oakeshott (Oxford, 1947), 82–83; Russell, *Theories of International Relations*, 159.
40. Bull, "Hobbes and the International Anarchy," 720–21.
41. Hobbes, *Leviathan*, ed. Oakeshott, 101, 260.

of states from moral fetters, at least where the objective of self-preservation is concerned, and in his willingness to allow whatever measures are rationally judged necessary to achieve this objective, Hobbes stands within the broad tradition of Machiavellianism. It is important to remember that only the *internal* affairs of states, according to Hobbes, are susceptible to rational pacification by means of setting up an all-powerful Leviathan capable of restoring order and tranquillity in the commonwealth. In the absence of a supranational Leviathan with the power to transform the international state of nature (*bellum omnium contra omnes*), Hobbes's doctrine of natural right performs the function of hallowing self-interest.[42]

Yet it is also possible to point to a number of important differences between Machiavelli and Hobbes concerning the core assumptions of *raison d'état*. At the very least, it is questionable to what extent Hobbes subscribed to Machiavelli's understanding of the state as a living personality, which had a value of its own and which possessed, in *raison d'état*, a law governing the ongoing process of its own perfection. For Hobbes, the personality of the state is reduced to an artificial authority created by individual acts of will and embodied in an Absolute Sovereign Will. In other words, the sovereign becomes an artificial person who represents "the words and actions of another."[43] In return for obedience and the surrender of their natural right to unlimited self-defense (a precondition for civil society), the subjects may expect a sovereign to establish a milieu in which they can pursue felicity in reasonable tranquillity. The sovereign's task is not to repress men, but to help create those conditions under which they can express their individuality.

Although Hobbes's *Leviathan* is often considered the climax of the absolutist conception of the state and *raison d'état*, it does not celebrate absolutism for the sake of the idea itself. A completely individualistic and utilitarian spirit pervades everything that he has to say about the final purposes of the state. For Hobbes, the state was certainly a personality; however, it was an artificial one, a *homo artificiales*, fundamentally a

42. For a discussion of how Hobbes's doctrine of natural right was used by writers on international law from the eighteenth century on as a means of demolishing the claims of international society on its member states, or at least as a means of showing that they had only a contingent or tentative validity, see Bull, "Hobbes and the International Anarchy," 725.

43. See Oakeshott's Introduction to Hobbes, *Leviathan*, ed. Oakeshott, lv–lvi; and Germino, *Machiavelli to Marx*, 107.

piece of clockwork machinery manufactured by human ingenuity in order to promote the objects of individual men. An important role is assigned to the *commoda vitae*, the *delectatio*, the *jucundissime et beate
vivere* of the individual citizen. It was Hobbes's opinion that only in the
proper functioning of the state as a whole could individuals be properly
cared for. There is already here a portent of that "greatest happiness
of the greatest number," which was later to be proclaimed by Jeremy
Bentham.

It is precisely this attribute of Hobbes's political philosophy that
sets him apart from Machiavellian *raison d'état*. Whereas Hobbes's me-
chanically contrived state may call for blind obedience from its citizens
for the sake of public order and individual well-being, it cannot require
from them that devotion founded on faith and attachment to the truly
and living personal state. Two examples may be cited to illustrate how
Hobbes's mechanistic conception of the state differs from the *virtù* republic of Machiavelli. First, unlike Machiavelli, Hobbes argued that a citizen
who has been taken captive by an enemy country is justified in saving his
life by becoming an enemy subject. Second, Hobbes suggested that a citizen can ask to be released from military service to the state as long as he
can find a substitute.[44]

At the same time, Hobbes supplied a new intellectual justification
by which to assess and affirm the role of *raison d'état* in relations among
sovereign states. Hobbes's fatalistic equation of the international state of
nature with a condition of anarchy contains an important qualification,
relating to what Hobbes perceived as a fundamental tension between morality and power in foreign policy. In foreign politics, all the power measures and underhanded tricks of Machiavellianism are possible, because
the participants are bound by no contract and cannot be sure that the
laws of nature will be observed. Yet Hobbes was not prepared to divorce
himself totally from the tradition of natural law as the necessary ethical
basis for interstate relations. It followed that "the same law, that dictateth
to men that have no civil government, what they ought to do, and what
to avoid in regard to one another, dictateth the same to commonwealths,
that is, to the consciences of sovereign princes and sovereign assemblies;
there being no court of natural justice, but in conscience only."[45] Yet even

44. Meinecke, *Machiavellianism*, 213–15.
45. See Hobbes, *Leviathan*, ed. Oakeshott, Chap. 31; Parkinson, *The Philosophy
of International Relations*, 39–40; Bull, "Hobbes and the International Anarchy," 724–29.

here sovereigns are morally obligated to observe these laws as far as possible without jeopardizing the safety of their dominions, because otherwise there would be no respite from war. Reason, Hobbes argued, was the principal element in the law of nature and implied a striving toward some sort of international society. Imperfect as they might be, these laws of nature, "the articles of peace" as Hobbes called them, are the lifeline to which sovereign states in the international anarchy must cling if they are to survive.

CARDINAL RICHELIEU (ARMAND-JEAN DU PLESSIS, 1585 – 1642)

Throughout the course of European history, the definition and justification of governmental policy has been the most consequential issue that has forced its attention upon rulers, statesmen, and political thinkers alike. The consolidation of power commensurate with the emergence of the modern nation-state must be viewed against a background characterized by the breakdown of the community of belief (Christendom) that took place in the Reformation and was made manifest during the religious wars of the sixteenth and seventeenth centuries. The unity and moral reciprocity of the medieval *Christianitas* were rendered obsolete by the Treaty of Westphalia, which made the territorial state the cornerstone of the modern state system.[46] The new justification associated with the development and use of power within the modern state and in the community of nations was, in no small part, the achievement of Cardinal Richelieu while he served as prime minister of Louis XIII's France.

The same generation that observed the inability of Wallenstein to convert the Holy Roman Empire of the German nation into a modern state saw the consolidation of such a state in France under Richelieu. As prime minister, Richelieu was charged with the responsibility of preserving and strengthening the French state in the face of formidable foreign obstacles. These included not only the massive Hapsburg challenge abroad but also endemic governmental weakness, social fragmentation, and factionalism at home. In his celebrated *Memoires*, Richelieu described his conception of policy as consisting of three interrelated parts: destroying the Huguenot opposition, humbling the great nobles and re-

46. Morgenthau, *Politics Among Nations*, 272; Dunne, "*Realpolitik* in the Decline of the West," 136–37.

ducing them to subjects, and raising the royal prestige and power abroad to its deserved "place in the sun."[47]

At the core of Richelieu's domestic and foreign policy designs was one central ambition—aggrandizement of the royal power at home and abroad to the point where true sovereignty and independence would be realized. The relationship between Louis XIII and Richelieu was intensely personal and mutually advantageous. Although a sovereign of limited ability, Louis XIII had the judgment to support Richelieu as the embodiment of royal power and prestige. In turn, by making the achievement of absolute power by the king his overriding goal, Richelieu enhanced his own position accordingly. The political objectives of Richelieu have been summarized by Carl Friedrich: "Through him, a prince of the church, the claims of absolute secular authority were made to prevail, and the body corporate of the modern state came into being. . . . The state which Machiavelli had visualized as the most admirable work of art man can make thus emerged in true baroque style: not clearly against the church, but partly by its connivance."[48]

Although examining the full range of Richelieu's literary and political achievements is beyond the purposes of this study, specific consideration is given to his conceptual formulation of the state as a necessary moral end. Attention is also devoted to the implications of his philosophy of the state for diplomatic and political relations within the volatile European state system. To what extent did Richelieu draw upon or modify Machiavellian *raison d'état* in his justification of French absolutism? Is the politician or diplomat obliged to evaluate his actions exclusively from the standpoint of expediency and success, or should he pursue the paths of personal honor and righteousness though the end may be failure? Finally, in what respects did Richelieu's defense of the state provide a foundation of principles and precepts for the practice of power politics in international relations?

A leading biographer of Richelieu points out that "the concept of reason of state was the most important contribution of Cardinal Richelieu's generation to the growth of political thought in France."[49] Along with the development of divine-right sovereignty, the formulation of a

47. Carl J. Friedrich, *The Age of Baroque, 1619–1660* (New York, 1952), 198.
48. *Ibid.*, 199.
49. William F. Church, *Richelieu and Reason of State* (Princeton, 1972), 11.

viable *raison d'état* supplied the essential foundations for seventeenth-century absolutism. The latter concept was not new in that it concerned very old and continuing political problems; moreover, many of the political writers of Richelieu's period who were preoccupied with a new justification for the state rarely transcended the intellectual categories that they had inherited from the past. By contrast, Richelieu stands out as one of the few great thinkers who was able to synthesize prevailing political concepts in order to justify the policies he believed necessary to the continued success and expansion of the French state system. Before elaborating on the attributes of Richelieu's conception of *raison d'état*, it is important to take brief note of how "reason of state" in the service of French absolutism may be distinguished from the earlier Machiavellian version.

A number of philosophical and historical considerations produced a significant evolution in the meaning of *raison d'état* from Machiavelli's Italy to Richelieu's modern European state system. It will be recalled that the political mechanism and agents that so intrigued Machiavelli were not yet state personalities; instead, they were personalities of heroic figures who held a *stato* in their hands. For all practical purposes, in Machiavelli's conception, the chief meaning of *stato* amounted to a power apparatus. Despite the insight Machiavelli provided into the inner structure of the state (as well as the link between national vitality and external political power), he still permitted the philosophical (or ethical) presuppositions that lay behind the operations of power policy to fade out of the picture. Rather than calculating these operations themselves, his task was limited to judging what was expedient in the actions of individual statesmen.[50]

In addition, it was not until the rise of the modern nation-state system in seventeenth-century Europe that *raison d'état* could provide a new foundation for a more systematic account of the interrelationship among state interests. The growing empirical spirit of the latter period moved political thinkers to refine their perception that the suprapersonal *interessi di stato* governed the conduct of individual states (uniting one and disuniting another). The new thinkers and political practitioners inherited Machiavelli's conviction that the movement of politics proceeded from the deep-rooted vital forces of states; at the same time, however,

50. Meinecke, *Machiavellianism*, 149.

they arrived at a much clearer understanding that these vital forces had begun to differentiate themselves more strongly from one another in European state relations.

Although *raison d'état* was believed to be a motivating force for all national units, attention now turned to how various states began to shape their own special existence and destiny according to particular interests and needs. This produced an impulse in both political thought and statesmanship to go beyond the purely subjective aspect of statecraft and raw state egoism and identify the "objective" interconnections of state activity beyond national borders.[51] For the first time, *raison d'état* was elevated to the level of *a composite picture or principle of European state relations*. The first attempt to put forth this principle was made in France during the era of Richelieu.

The precise nature of Richelieu's contribution to *raison d'état* continues to elicit debate and disagreement among leading scholars and biographers. A number of authors tend to regard him as little more than a man of power, a Machiavellian statesman in cardinal's clothing.[52] Such a view unduly distorts the tension in Richelieu's policies between politics and morals, power and principle, ethics and expediency. Although a master technician of power, his ideals and conception of the good state were such that he was also a man of high principle as well. The religious character of the French state for whose good he committed many high-handed acts serves to indicate the distinction between Richelieu's world view and the secularism of Machiavelli. It must be emphasized that the functions and objectives of the French state were shaped to a considerable extent by its Christian traditions, values, and purposes. As for Richelieu himself, "the sincerity of his religious beliefs is generally accepted, and he was thoroughly convinced that they were in no way compromised by his often ruthless policies for the good of the French state."[53]

Cardinal Richelieu's use of power presented the problem of just government in a Christian monarchy and inspired widespread debate over the legitimate exercise of royal power in both foreign and domestic affairs. His version of *raison d'état* was built on the concept of the unique rights, nature, and purposes of the Christian state. The first foundation

51. *Ibid.*, 151.
52. W. F. Reddaway, *A History of Europe, 1610–1715* (London, 1952), 140.
53. Church, *Richelieu and Reason of State*, 8–12.

of the happiness of the state, said Richelieu, was the establishment of the reign of God. The divinely established relationship between church and state decreed that, in their sphere, the king and his minister were more knowledgeable than all others concerning the proper measures by which to guide France to its higher objectives.[54] From Richelieu's perspective, *raison d'état* provided a kind of means-end rationality and succeeded in justifying political measures that were in themselves morally objectionable but that benefited the state as a whole.

The application of a means-end rationality to state conduct implied a sharp distinction between the public and private spheres of ethical behavior. The critical problem in Richelieu's life was the uneasy interaction between public activity and religious standards. In an age of little faith in human goodness, Richelieu was pessimistic about humanity. He was convinced that the evil in man derived from a fallen nature and a propensity to sin. Freedom in the early seventeenth century meant, in practice, license; therefore, freedom (in theory) had to give place to the concept of order, a notion that appears more often than any other in Richelieu's writing.

Richelieu's approach gave rise to a dual moral standard in national and international affairs. In his *Memoires*, Richelieu acknowledged that "there is a difference between civil and political prudence, and this is so great that the moral order really makes two separate virtues of them." He once wrote: "In the course of ordinary affairs justice requires clarity and evidence of proof. But it is not the same when one is concerned with affairs of state, when one is dealing with the *summum rerum*, for often conjectures must stand in place of proof, considering that great designs . . . can never be verified except by their success or outcome."[55] The new force of *raison d'état* in French foreign policy and diplomacy illustrated that peripheral or *ad hoc* methods and aims of statecraft were gradually replaced by intensive and centralized control. It was no longer sufficient for the statesman simply to possess a special knowledge of the state itself in the pursuit of territorial independence and sovereignty. Indeed, contemporary statesmanship rose to a more comprehensive political vision

54. Reddaway, *A History of Europe*, 140–141; Church, *Richelieu and Reason of State*, 503.

55. D. P. O'Connell, *Richelieu* (New York, 1968), 314.

that brought within its focus the state in its relations with other states, how it is governed, and the relationship between rulers and subjects.

The outbreak of the Thirty Years' War (1618–1648) and the stirrings of a new great ambition on the part of France heralded a tendency toward pure power politics that had already flourished at the time of Machiavelli. However, the power politics of Richelieu can be distinguished from the simple, egocentric prescriptions of Machiavelli by an insight into Europe as a collective whole, a clearer perception of the connection between unity within the state and the external manifestation of power, a strong sense of the great and dominating powers, and a conscious reaction against permitting ecclesiastical and denominational considerations to obscure the simple interests of power. The significance of *raison d'état* for French power and independence in Europe can be illustrated by France's entry into the Thirty Years' War in 1635 and the subsequent attempt to counter the imperial designs of the Spanish and Austrian Hapsburgs. The justification for Richelieu's policies centered around the tension between politics and morals in the cardinal's devotion to the national interests of France at a time when the ancient unity of Christendom was beyond repair. That French diplomatic objectives in opposition to the formidable Hapsburg league were based on the interests of power over religious criteria is, however, subject to an important qualification.

As previously mentioned, *raison d'état* in seventeenth-century France assumed the character of a special means-end rationality. Questionable methods were often justified if they served the state as a whole. At the same time, there is little doubt that Richelieu operated upon the assumption that the purpose of the French state *was essentially religious* and that the cause of religion might therefore be served by less than ethical acts in support of French interests. In short, in Richelieu's thought, the subordination of moral-ethical factors to power considerations applied specifically to the sphere of means, as opposed to ends.

It is possible to identify briefly a number of key diplomatic principles and objectives integral to Richelieu's successful defense of French interests in Europe. All political writers of the period believed that the problem of international peace was best resolved by a theory of equilibrium. France and the Hapsburgs were seen as two poles of power, evenly balanced. As Philippe de Béthune, the French ambassador in Rome, wrote: "The security of states consisting principally in an equal counter-poise of power, and the aggrandizement of one prince implying the ruina-tion of his neighbors, it is wise to prevent it."[56] The means for balancing Hapsburg aggression was Richelieu's alliance with the leading Protestant powers of Europe.

Moreover, Richelieu's support of the balance-of-power principle derived from his conviction that the arsenal of diplomacy served as a weapon for the advancement of state interests. It is important to view his belief in the efficacy of diplomacy within the larger historical context of the "community of reason" characteristic of seventeenth-century Europe. Richelieu was a man of the time of Descartes and Corneille. In his *Testament Politique* he wrote: "The light of natural reason enables everyone to know that, since man is endowed with reason, he must do nothing except by reason, for otherwise he would act contrary to his nature, and as a result, contrary against Him who is its author."[57] What is important, however, is that Richelieu's confidence in reason extended beyond the range of the national community to the community of nations. If man was essentially reasonable and would be guided by reason, then the way to obtain what one wanted for one's own country was to reason with the representatives of others.

The tension between ethics and power in foreign policy is typified by Richelieu's position on the question of fidelity to treaty obligations. As for the king's relations with fellow princes, Richelieu found it indis-pensable that he keep faith and observe sworn treaties, once his word was pledged: "Kings should be wary of making treaties, but when they are made, they should religiously observe them. . . . But without consid-ering . . . what Christian faith may teach against such maxims, I maintain that since the loss of honor is greater than that of life, a great prince should risk even his person and interests of the state rather than break his word which he cannot violate without losing his good reputation."[58] On the supposition that the "community of reason" applied to the com-munity of nations, the statesman could not afford to disregard it by fail-ure to negotiate or by failure to observe the commitments entered into by way of diplomatic negotiation.

56. *Ibid.*, 162.
57. Dunne, "*Realpolitik* in the Decline of the West," 139.
58. Church, *Richelieu and Reason of State*, 501.

Richelieu believed that he had forged a justification for extensive application of discretionary power to achieve the state's higher purposes. The idea of a pure state interest, of the subordination of any fortuitous and instinctive impulse to the inexorable rule of *raison d'état*, was tempered by a commitment to the fundamentally religious end of the French state. However, the subsequent evolution of the nature and practices of the state gave *raison d'état* a different meaning. With the further development of state power and the expanding secularization of European culture, the exigencies of politics eventually undermined the fusion of religion and politics. When applied to the manifold relationships of state power in the eighteenth and nineteenth centuries, the doctrine of *raison d'état* rapidly deteriorated into a materialistic ability for calculation, into a purely utilitarian technique and mechanism of political trade.[59]

OTTO EDUARD LEOPOLD VON BISMARCK (1815 – 1898)

Appearing before the Prussian Parliament in 1881 for the purpose of defending the growing military budget and power of the empire, Chancellor Bismarck answered his progressive and liberal opponents: "I have always had one compass only, one lodestar by which I have steered; *salus publica*, the welfare of the state. . . . I have always acted according to the question, 'What is useful, advantageous, and right for my Fatherland, and—for my dynasty, and today—for the German nation?' I have never been a theorist. The systems which bind separate parties are for me of secondary importance. The nation comes first, its position in the world and its independence."[60] Although the precise motives and historical consequences of Bismarck's domestic and diplomatic machinations have long been debated by scholars, few have denied his brazen affirmation of *raison d'état* in the service of the Prussian state and German unification.[61]

As with earlier champions of *raison d'état* in world politics, it is possible to formulate several preliminary questions in order to help identify the salient themes contributing to Bismarck's defense of state objec-

---

59. Meinecke, *Machiavellianism*, 184.
60. Louis L. Snyder, *The Blood and Iron Chancellor* (Princeton, 1967), 15.
61. See Andreas Dorpalen, "The German Historians and Bismarck," *Review of Politics*, XV (January, 1953), 53–67.

tives in international affairs. First, what historical developments and events in nineteenth-century Europe and Germany were instrumental in the energetic drive to create a new German nation-state? Second, in what ways did *raison d'état* function as the foundation for the diplomacy of *realpolitik*? In particular, how was Bismarck's cabinet diplomacy and war policy affected by new, unpredictable factors (*e.g.*, public opinion, popular pressures, or ideologies) that jeopardized the very stability of the Concert of Europe? Finally, how did the peculiar admixture of might and right in Bismarck's "blood and iron" version of *raison d'état* contribute to the ultimate collapse of the Hohenzollern Empire in 1918?

Bismarck's rise to power can be traced to the revolutionary fervor that swept over Europe in 1848. The new liberal and democratic movement had shown itself powerless to create a German national state. Bismarck's repudiation of democratic doctrines and his protests against the subordinate part played by Prussia in the thirty-eight-member German Confederation, which had succeeded the old empire in 1815 under Austria's continued hegemony, had already gained for him the goodwill of the sovereign.[62] Only under a particularly favorable constellation of European powers could German nationalism risk a new attempt in this direction. Indeed, the danger of intervention by the great neighboring powers was all the more serious, because the Hapsburg monarchy was determined to reassert its old hegemony over Germany and minimize Prussian aspirations for leadership.

Upon assuming the position of minister-president in 1862, Bismarck announced that he did not believe that the German problem could be solved in any way but through "blood and iron." Rejected were the visionary hopes of his liberal antagonists that Prussia could build a united Germany by "moral conquests" or by arousing the support of public opinion. Without an armed struggle against Austria, the Prussian monarchy had virtually no prospect of asserting its claim to German leadership. German nationalism provided the moral issue by which to justify a war with Austria, the moral *élan* by which to gain the victory, and, finally, the centripetal force with which to consolidate the new state that would then emerge. The creation of a German nation-state was for Bis-

62. T. Walter Wallbank, Alastair M. Taylor, George B. Carson, and Mark Mancall, *Civilization Past and Present* (Glenview, Ill., 1969), II, 413–16.

marck not an ultimate objective but an incidental result of his striving for a more powerful state.[63]

Convinced that three wars must be fought before Prussia would be powerful enough to assert primacy in Germany, Bismarck sought and found occasions for them. The war with Denmark in 1864 gained for Prussia the duchies of Schleswig and Holstein. By defeating Austria in the "Seven Weeks' War" of 1866, Bismarck was able to end Austrian control of the old German Confederation. In its place the North German Confederation was formed under Prussian domination, with Austria and four southern German states excluded. Finally, the Franco-Prussian War of 1870 preempted French intervention in German affairs and made possible the integration of all the German states into a revived empire enlarged by the recovery of the old imperial territories of Alsace and Lorraine. Treaties were negotiated during the war stipulating that all of Germany should be united into a Hohenzollern empire. These agreements were given formal effect in 1871 when King William I of Prussia was invested with the title of German emperor and Bismarck became the first imperial chancellor.

Machiavelli's doctrine of *raison d'état* as the servant of political necessity became the powerful weapon by which Bismarck justified the power needs of the Prussian state. He rejected the admonitions of his conservative colleagues that the guiding principle of state policy should be the ethical command to resist revolutionary forces, and he argued that the ultimate norm of state behavior was derived from the immediate interests of the state itself. Realistic and successful policy could be formulated only if the statesman first looked to the specific needs and circumstances of his own state and then reflected on how those needs could be realized within the arena of international politics. Bismarck could and did ignore ethical-political doctrines that transcended or were alien to his own Prussian state.

Bismarck claimed that the state derived its norms of action primarily from itself and viewed any doctrine forbidding the state to consult its

63. Franz Schnabel, "The Bismarck Problem," in Hans Kohn (ed.), *German History: Some New Views* (Boston, 1954), 82–89; Gerhart Ritter, "The Last Great Cabinet Statesman," in Theodore Hamerow (ed.), *Otto von Bismarck: A Historical Assessment* (Lexington, Mass., 1972), 149.

own interests as either self-deception or hypocrisy. State egoism was the fundamental presupposition of the *realpolitik* that Bismarck practiced in diplomatic affairs. In opposition to nineteenth-century political romanticism, he suggested: "The only healthy basis for a great state . . . is state egotism. . . . It is unworthy of a great state to contend for something which does not correspond to its own interests." It is interesting to note that the most eminent German historian of the nineteenth century, Leopold von Ranke, coupled the premise of state egotism with the idea of a moral purpose that the state must fulfill.[64] Bismarck was much less concerned with such philosophical questions and was inclined to leave moot the question of state morality. He contended that the possibility of more pragmatic political achievement obligated the prudent statesman to think exclusively in political categories.

In addition, the strict separation of politics from morality was no more vividly exemplified than by the diplomatic maneuvers and foreign-policy aims associated with Bismarckian *realpolitik*. Amid the great powers of the continent, there was no possibility of "splendid isolationism" or insular aloofness typical of England's liberal empire. Instead of calm repose and conciliation, the cardinal virtue of a statesman was strict vigilance and the exertion of all energies in behalf of the state. Bismarck justified the authoritarian nature of his state by the pressure of an international situation constantly threatened with struggles for power.[65] Moreover, he argued that the foreign policy of such a state could be successfully conducted only under the completely unrestrained sovereignty of a monarchical government independent of fleeting parliamentary majorities. It was from this point of view that Bismarck's attitude on diplomacy, power, and war must be understood.

Whereas William Gladstone was the extreme champion of English and insular statecraft, Bismarck was perhaps the most powerful representative of a continental, hierarchically organized, actively belligerent great power.[66] In fact, the chancellor was the last great representative of cabinet diplomacy that governed the fate of Europe from the seventeenth to the

64. Meinecke, *Machiavellianism*, 377–92; Sterling, *Ethics in a World of Power*, 74.

65. Friedrich Meinecke, *The German Catastrophe: Reflections and Recollections*, trans. Sidney B. Fay (Cambridge, Mass., 1960), 10–11.

66. Ritter, "The Last Great Cabinet Statesman," in Hamerow (ed.), *Otto von Bismarck*, 147–48.

nineteenth century. The resourcefulness and restraint of his diplomatic overtures reflected the traditions of Richelieu, Mazarin, Kaunitz, and Metternich. These past masters of diplomacy operated on the basis of known quantities—rulers, ministers, court favorites. They did not have to concern themselves with such new pressures as public opinion and militant ideology. Yet the time when these new elements could be ignored was drawing to an end; the age of mass communication and political movements was rapidly approaching. To Bismarck, diplomacy remained a technique whose prudent maneuvers ought not to be deflected by popular demands. In general, he felt strong and secure enough either to ignore or manipulate these forces, and diplomatically he was largely successful.[67]

At the same time, however, it is important to take brief note of how Bismarckian cabinet diplomacy can be distinguished from the statesmanship and political strategy associated with the "community of reason" that was to supply the foundation for the Concert of Europe. Following the dissolution of the community of reason at the time of the French Revolution and Napoleonic Wars, there was an attempt at the Congress of Vienna (1815) to revive it under the Concert of Europe. Concert members (France, England, Prussia, Austria, and Russia) were to act jointly to maintain national "stability" through monarchical rule and international "tranquillity" through the balance of power. On a number of occasions, however, concerted action was possible only when it happened to coincide with the several national interests of the powers. In a famous remark about Europe's representing little more than a geographic expression, Bismarck proclaimed: "That Europe cannot give way is a proposition that I cannot accept, for I do not admit the conception of Europe as a joint liability. The five powers have agreed on precise measures whose possible inadequacy was recognized from the very beginning."[68] In contrast to the cosmopolitanism of Metternich, Castlereagh, and Talleyrand, Bismarck lacked any sense of a transcendent European community united by the "traditions of civility." The only viable order left in the West, as far as he was concerned, was the community of mutual fear, the balance of power.

As noted by George F. Kennan, Bismarck's European policy was

67. Dorpalen, "The German Historians and Bismarck," 55–57.
68. W. N. Medlicott, *Bismarck, Gladstone, and the Concert of Europe* (London, 1956), 160.

based on the maintenance of a reasonable balance of power between Austria and Russia and the avoidance of any major conflict between those two powers.[69] The new German Reich was a political arrangement that Bismarck had found necessary to create in order to assure what he believed to be Prussia's proper place in the Central European scheme of things. After emerging victorious from the war of 1870–1871, Bismarck's diplomacy grew essentially defensive, with the purpose of protecting a unified Germany from the threat of hostile coalitions. Specifically, he was determined to preempt a French war of revenge by depriving France of possible allies. Similarly, his diplomacy toward both Austria and Russia sought to deprive each power of any incentive to ally with France or confront each other in the Balkans. The Three Emperors' Alliance (*Dreikaiserbund*) among Germany, Austria, and Russia that was engineered by Bismarck in 1881 had the dual effect of ending the chances for a revival of the European Concert and balancing the various national claims impinging on the destiny of Central Europe.[70]

Bismarck's outlook on war did not originate in the passions of a conqueror or unrestrained militarist, but in the sober *raison d'état* of a military state. As Gerhart Ritter points out, "he is a spiritual descendent of Frederick the Great in a completely altered world."[71] As one of the last great cabinet statesmen of European history, he represents a lonely figure, somewhat alien in his own time. The European cabinets of the seventeenth and eighteenth centuries waged war with a sober calculation of power interests of the state, in contrast to the moral and religious passions that had been aroused during the age of religious wars. For both Richelieu's "community of reason" and Metternich's Concert of Europe, *raison d'état* represented the harmonization of separate national interests with European-wide political and cultural objectives.

By contrast, Bismarck's political and military achievement consisted of harnessing *raison d'état* with specific national aims at a time when the vision of an organized international order based on the willing partnership of self-governing units was illusory. For Bismarck, war was not seen

69. George F. Kennan, *The Decline of Bismarck's European Order: Franco-Russian Relations, 1875–1890* (Princeton, 1979), 277–78.

70. Dunne, "*Realpolitik* in the Decline of the West," 143–44.

71. Ritter, "The Last Great Cabinet Statesman," in Hamerow (ed.), *Otto von Bismarck*, 148.

as a crusade for the cause of God or some abstract sense of the nation, but as a political struggle to determine superior power.[72] Even though Bismarck was somewhat harsh about human nature and progress, the causes of war were located within an international environment where conflicting power interests could be peacefully reconciled. In this sense, morality and politics were sharply differentiated in his thought. This provided a vivid contrast to the normal turn of military and diplomatic events since the French Revolution, when almost every political conflict tended toward the total antagonism and moral destruction of the opponent as an "enemy." What separated Bismarck from his German nationalist successors was thus a devotion to prudent *raison d'état*, unobscured by passion, imposing firm restraints on the deployment of power, and pursued with the skill of a born diplomat who knew the great courts of Europe as no other knew them.

Finally, in what ways did Bismarck's commitment to *raison d'état* in both domestic and foreign affairs contribute to, or fail to prevent, the collapse of the Hohenzollern Empire in 1918? Such important figures as Jakob Burckhardt and Constantin Franz argued that Bismarck's policy meant the victory of Machiavellianism over the principles of morality and justice in international relations. It let perish the higher and finer things in culture, owing to a relentless striving after power and pleasure. On the other hand, there were a number of voices to defend Bismarck. They called attention to all the similar experiences of Machiavellian practices in the rest of Europe of that day and especially to the fact that Bismarck himself acknowledged some limits to his policy of force (*e.g.*, the defensive character of German diplomacy after 1870). Moreover, Bismarck did not stand alone in the battle against Catholics and Progressives or in the bitter struggle with the Socialists. Yet he helped to determine the nature of these struggles. Irrespective of whether or not he considered himself a "maker of history," Bismarck did face alternatives and made conscious choices.

It is difficult to determine the extent to which Bismarck shared the conception of a synthesis of power and culture as it was understood by leaders of the movement for German unification. As Meinecke pointed

72. G. P. Gooch, "The Divorce of Politics from Morals," in Hamerow (ed.), *Otto von Bismarck*, 164. See also Gooch, "Bismarck's Legacy," *Foreign Affairs*, XXX (July, 1952), 527–30.

out, however, the inevitable result was that "in the synthesis of power and culture, of the things of the state and the things of the spirit, the preponderance steadily shifted further over to the side of power and its domain."[73] The center of gravity between might and right, which was at best in a precarious balance, kept shifting slowly towards the former. It was to become a serious omen for the future that ideas about the all-powerful state and Machiavellianism, at first expressed as mere theories, might become potent weapons in the hands of the ruling authorities. In the end, Bismarckian *realpolitik* knew no appeal to the imagination of the nation, no vision of a richer future; nor did it exhibit an abiding faith in humanity that gave true significance to the birth of the American and French republics.[74]

Raison d'État and World Politics

An attempt carefully to inventory the primary assumptions and concepts associated with continental *raison d'état* must acknowledge a number of significant caveats. At the outset, it is important to note that *raison d'état* defies the narrow limits of any one specific doctrine or conceptual definition. In one perspective, *raison d'état* is a mixture of moral and power considerations, "a bridge between *ethos* and *kratos*." In another light, it has been described as the valuing of power above law and morality. In still another and more comprehensive sense, *raison d'état* is "the law governing the movement of the state. . . . It tells the statesman what to do in order to maintain the state's health and vigor." The implication of determinism in this conception is unmistakable in that "to live in liberty and independence the state must . . . obey the laws dictated by *raison d'état*."[75]

Although subject to a number of interpretations, *raison d'état* has also functioned as a description and explanation of state behavior in a wide variety of historical and political circumstances. Although its earliest antecedents may be traced back to the civil strife among Greek city-states, the first attempt to provide any kind of detailed account of the underlying diplomatic norms and realities of interstate behavior was sup-

73. Meinecke, *The German Catastrophe*, 13–15.
74. Dorpalen, "The German Historians and Bismarck," 67.
75. Sterling, *Ethics in a World of Power*, 234–35; Meinecke, *Machiavellianism*, 3–5.

plied by Machiavelli during the wars of unification in fifteenth-century Italy. Machiavelli's vivid portrayal of the instrumentalities of power in the service of state necessity was later reinforced by Hobbes's elaboration of an anarchic international arena, bereft of effective legal and ethical restraints. Statesmen were seen to confront each other in the uneasy posture of combative gladiators.

Both *raison d'état* and divine-right sovereignty supplied the basis for seventeenth-century absolutism. In defense of French national interests and the so-called European community of reason, Cardinal Richelieu interpreted *raison d'état* as a special kind of means-end rationality that would fulfill the unique rights, nature, and purposes of the Christian state. Following the virtual collapse of the Concert of Europe in the midst of nineteenth-century revolutionary ferment, Bismarck's "blood and iron" method of unifying Germany satisfied the conventional definition of *raison d'état* as reliance on armed strength for national ends. By insisting that the state derives its norms of action primarily from itself, he established a pattern of thought that expressed itself in German diplomacy as a penchant for "calling a spade a spade" and that in popular vocabulary came to be known as *realpolitik*. In short, the meaning and utility of *raison d'état* for the statesman was largely determined by an evolving constellation of political and historical forces impinging on a state's diplomatic objectives at any particular time.

Moreover, it would be somewhat misleading to suggest that *raison d'état* has *always* functioned as an *a priori* set of immutable diplomatic guidelines. The determinism traditionally associated with the concept has gone little beyond the assumption that the imperative of state survival might require moral or immoral actions; once that state was accepted as supreme, the ruler had no choice but to obey. However, the requirements of state survival and the necessity for either moral or immoral measures were meaningful only in relation to specific and concrete challenges and opportunities that confronted the statesman. Indeed, the assumption of state survival reveals little about the significance of important domestic factors or the distribution of power in the international political system that inevitably influences the formulation and implementation of foreign-policy goals. It was not until the rise of the modern European state system after Westphalia that the chief spokesmen for *raison d'état* began to turn their attention to a more systematic assessment of state activity across national borders. It was only with Richelieu and Bismarck that one finds *raison d'état* elevated to the level of a composite world view of European state relations.

While being mindful of the often disparate historical forces that help mold both personalities and national policies over time, it is possible to isolate several key tenets or elements that distinguished *raison d'état* as an approach to world politics. Although by no means an exhaustive list, the following concepts and themes received repeated attention and varying degrees of affirmation by the major figures discussed thus far in this study. Moreover, it must be admitted that theorists and practitioners of *raison d'état* almost never sought to relate and develop *all* of these tenets into an integrated theory of international politics.

NATION-STATES AS PRIMARY ACTORS

The nation-state represents both a moral agent and the most significant actor in international politics. As far back as the Greek city-state system of Thucydides, the organized political community was viewed, not merely as a collection of institutions, but as an enduring moral entity that could compel the loyalty and service of its citizens. Writing about the political world at the birth of modern European theory, Machiavelli established the proposition that every other value must bow to the survival of the state: "Where the very safety of the country depends upon the resolution to be taken, no consideration of justice or injustice, humanity or cruelty, nor of glory or shame, should be allowed to prevail." [76] After the emergence of the modern European nation-state, both Richelieu and Bismarck echoed Machiavelli's judgment that the statesman must take only the course of action that will secure the state's life and liberty.

INTERNATIONAL STATE OF NATURE

The necessities of a *raison d'état* policy arise from the unregulated competition of states. Sovereign states, recognizing no higher authority, are in a Hobbesian state of nature; the resulting security dilemma forces them to live in a condition of mutual competition and conflict. *Raison d'état* in international politics represents a "natural tendency" of the state to restrict its foreign policy behavior, therefore, to the realm of self-interest. Possibilities for orderly and peaceful exchange between nation-

---

76. Hallowell, *Main Currents in Modern Political Thought*, 58.

states are subordinate to the statesman's calculation of selfish and tangible advantages for the state. In addition, for the figures included in this study, the perception of an anarchic international system is reinforced by a pervasive pessimism about man and human nature in general.

UBIQUITY OF POWER

The Machiavellian or Hobbesian view of the international political system is geared to the assumption that the broader aspects of interstate politics can be characterized by a relentless struggle for and extension of state power. Each state seeks safety by relying on its own power and viewing with alarm the power of its neighbors. Accordingly, the *ulta ratio regum* of sovereigns in dealing with other sovereigns is force. Proponents of *raison d'état* have generally emphasized that the power of prime concern to the statesman is, in the final analogy, military power or fighting capacity. Concern with military capability derives from the observation that each state can best preserve its power by expanding it and can most surely guarantee its own security by depriving others of theirs. For the purposes of *raison d'état*, the pursuit of power tends to become an end in itself rather than a means to other ends. No other end matters if the state lacks power to serve its ultimate end—self-preservation.

ETHICS AND FOREIGN POLICY

Nowhere does the contradiction between professed ethical principles and actual behavior appear so patent and universal as in the conduct of foreign relations. Down through the centuries, Machiavellianism has stood for a doctrine that places princes and sovereigns under the rule not of ordinary morality, but of "reason of state." Unlike the solitary individual who may claim the right to judge political action by universal ethical guidelines, the statesman will always make his decision on the basis of the state's interest and survival. Perhaps the ultimate irony of the ethical dualism associated with *raison d'état* is the idea that political ambition could, in a limited sense, contribute to the strengthening of particular moral values. Despite the fact that few could assert the ego of the state in the ruthless tone of Machiavelli, the Florentine's idealism expressed itself in the thought that *necessita*—understood as the imperative of survival—could conceivably provide the means to salvage the decline of moral energies in the Italian state system. That political ambition and the struggle for power could *augment* moral values was echoed by Hobbes's assertion that one need not fear "that the Leviathan would misuse its power . . . because the power wielder would be compelled by his own interests to rule with reason and advance the public welfare."[77] In seventeenth-century France, Richelieu suggested that the true interests of the state required concessions of tolerance to the Huguenots in order to safeguard the freedom of the state from foreign influence and to develop its internal strength.

At the same time, however, the precarious balance between considerations of national interest and moral conduct in state relations gradually shifted to accentuate the role of the former. The thesis that state egotism is justified by the values it serves was brought into question by recurrent power struggles of the state, which tended to destroy the ethical and cultural values that might function as the state's ultimate justification. Indeed, Bismarckian *realpolitik* represented the eclipse of state necessity or interest from higher ethical or moral considerations.

BALANCE OF POWER

Perhaps no other concept or principle has been so frequently associated with *raison d'état* as has the illusive balance of power. Whereas *raison d'état* may be taken as an indication of the methods by which foreign policy is conducted and rationalized, balance of power purports to explain the international result that such methods produce. For many observers, it has become an "avowed principle of foreign policy, accepted and acted on so consistently by all the great states that it may well be viewed as the central theme about which the web of diplomacy is woven."[78] It should be recognized that the precise origins and operations of the balance of power have been subject to widespread debate. David Hume traced the origins of the idea to the shifting coalitions of Greek city-states (*poleis*) at the time of the Peloponnesian War. J. M. Robertson,

77. Sterling, *Ethics in a World of Power*, 221.
78. Frederick L. Schuman, *International Politics* (6th ed.; New York, 1958), 66. See also Kenneth Waltz, *Theory of International Politics* (Menlo Park, Calif., 1979), 177; Ernst B. Haas, "The Balance of Power: Prescription, Concept, or Propaganda," *World Politics*, V (July, 1953), 361–80; Martin Wight, "The Balance of Power and International Order," in Alan James (ed.), *The Bases of International Order* (London, 1973), 85–115; Morgenthau, *Politics Among Nations*, 167–221; Greg Russell, "Balance of Power in Perspective," *International Review of History and Political Science*, XXI (November, 1984), 1–16.

writing his biography of Emperor Charles V, made the case for the balance as the creation of the fifteenth-century Italian state system.[79]

Although Machiavelli emphasized military self-reliance and was skeptical about the balance of power as an effective technique to bring about Italian unity, he also suggested that no prince can afford to disregard its workings. Indeed, he thought that the ruler was ill-advised to remain neutral in a conflict between two nearby powers. However, as Frederick Schuman pointed out, during the fifteenth and sixteenth centuries the states of Europe pursued balance-of-power policies without the principle itself receiving any clear and universal formulation. Contrary to Hume's contention that the balance doctrine originated in antiquity, Sir Herbert Butterfield argued that the idea of a balance operating throughout the international system as a whole became implanted in European thought only in the seventeenth century, along with the notion that European politics formed a single system.[80] The key question affecting both theorists and statesmen was the nature and degree of interrelatedness and reciprocity of the new European order of states.

Richelieu's affirmation of a community of reason (*une negociation continuelle*) operating on diplomats and statesmen merged with the idea of "equilibrium" among major European powers. Whereas state interest remains the essential guide for foreign policy, its realization is made possible by the community of reason among nations that is operative in the negotiations of diplomats. With France and the Hapsburgs seen as two poles of countervailing power, Richelieu sought to balance the Hapsburg threat by an alliance system with the leading Protestant powers of Europe. The negotiations required by the community of reason (and the obligations emanating therefrom) were simply conditions for the maintenance of a desired balance of power. For both seventeenth- and eighteenth-century theorists, balance-of-power policies reflected the belief in a rationally induced world, a diplomacy conforming to clear and often mechanistic rules productive of order among states.

Similarly, Bismarck was the managing director of a state that played

79. David Hume, "Of the Balance of Power," in *Essays Moral, Political, and Literary* (London, 1875), I, 348–57; Savigear, "European Political Philosophy and the Theory of International Relations," in Taylor (ed.), *Approaches and Theory in International Relations*, 41.

80. Butterfield and Wight (eds.), *Diplomatic Investigations*, 133; Schuman, *International Politics*, 70.

the role of a great power in the European system of five major powers and many smaller powers. Bismarck's European policy aimed at the preservation of a reasonable balance of power between Austria and Russia and the avoidance of any major conflict between these two powers. It will be useful to recall that an effort was made to revive the community of reason at the Congress of Vienna after the violence of the Napoleonic Wars. The five predominant powers, acting as the "Concert of Europe," frequently resorted to balance-of-power tactics based on the conception of Europe as a joint liability, an interdependent world of great powers united by "traditions of civility." By contrast, Bismarck found the concert formula inimical to the purpose of building a unified German state in central Europe. Much like Machiavelli, who worked to upset the balance of power in Italy to create a unified Italian state, Bismarck's wars were designed to set up a *new* balance of power in Europe with a unified Germany as one of its principal weights.

RAISON D'ÉTAT AS THE SPORT OF KINGS

The continental tradition of *raison d'état* in international politics remained the sport of kings or the preserve of cabinets—the last refuge of secrecy, the last domain of largely hereditary castes of diplomats.[81] The democratization of foreign policy was effectively preempted on two counts. First, proponents of *raison d'état* consistently emphasized that the foreign policy of a state constantly threatened with struggles for power could only be conducted with the unrestrained sovereignty of a monarchical government independent of parliamentary majorities. Second, only a well-trained core of aristocratic elites could engage in the kind of diplomacy required by the balance-of-power principle without undue concern about the reactions of public opinion, the need to consider ideological values, or attention to the nation's image in the minds of foreigners.

Finally, in what ways is it possible to speak of continental *raison d'état* as a distinctive theoretical or philosophical approach to the study of international politics? Although theorists and statesmen of *raison d'état* attempted to describe a permanent logic of state behavior, most were careful to avoid explicit generalizations, "if . . . then" propositions,

81. Stanley Hoffmann, "An American Social Science: International Relations," *Daedalus*, CVI (Summer, 1977), 42.

and analytic categories relevant to the sphere of international political behavior. Even though Machiavelli stands out in his belief that politics has its own laws, discernible by reason and rooted in political interest, he failed to develop any theory that would explain the operation of such laws beyond the level of the state itself.[82] What often passes for theory in the continental tradition is usually a mixture of statements in which concepts are ill-defined, the connections of the theory's components are loosely specified, and possible conclusions wear the guise of assumptions. Such problems reinforce the strength of Wight's observation that, in the classical (European) tradition, "international theory, or what there is of it, is scattered, unsystematic, and mostly inaccessible to the layman," as well as "largely repellant and intractable in form."[83]

A less stringent but perhaps more revealing inquiry into the patterns of coherence of *raison d'état* in international politics can be developed by interpreting the continental tradition as governed by what Kuhn has termed a "metaphysical" or "philosophical" paradigm. From this vantage point, *raison d'état* would constitute the wide-ranging assumptions and beliefs about the international milieu (as well as its key components) shared by a community of scholars and statesmen. Reduced to its essentials, the principal assumptions and beliefs of *raison d'état* may be summarized as follows: the ruler's, and later the state's, interest provides the spring of action; the necessities of policy arise from the unregulated competition of states; calculation based on these necessities can discover the policies that best serve a state's interest; success is the ultimate test of policy; and success is defined as preserving and strengthening the power of the state. *Raison d'état* identifies the methods by which foreign policy is conducted and provides a rationale for them; the balance-of-power concept provides a rough explanation of the result that such methods produce.[84]

82. Waltz, *Theory of International Politics*, 117.
83. Wight and Butterfield (eds.), *Diplomatic Investigations*, 17–18.
84. *Ibid.*

CHAPTER TWO

Roots of an American Thinker

In the decades before and after World War II, the leading spokesmen of the American realist tradition exhibited a persistent philosophical
and historical interest in the relation between power and moral purpose
in American statecraft. Scholars such as Walter Lippmann, Reinhold Niebuhr, and George F. Kennan clearly rejected classical *raison d'état* as an
appropriate standard for United States foreign policy; at the same time,
however, they deplored the tendency of idealists and naïve moralists to
sacrifice the prudent calculation of American national interest for the
promotion of moral absolutes in international politics. Although strongly
committed to American liberal-democratic values, realist thinkers recognized that a nation's achievement of either universal ideals or national
goals depends on its making an accurate assessment of the configuration
of world power and an objective calculation of the most effective means
to an end. In summarizing the rise of political realism as it applied to
American foreign policy in the postwar era, one scholar has written:
"Ideal goals are not obtained in the real world of conflicting national
purposes by moral fervor alone but only by a pragmatic calculation of
the means to an end, by a rational anticipation of the actual consequences
of a given action."[1]

The career of Hans J. Morgenthau, who fled Nazi Germany, stands

1. Robert Osgood, *Ideals and Self-Interest in America's Foreign Relations* (Chicago,
1953), 437.

56

as a vivid testament to realism's moral sensibility to American self-interest in world affairs. Unlike Lippmann and Niebuhr, Morgenthau was a professor of political science whose voluminous writings in the field of international politics have been at the forefront of the discipline for over forty years. As subsequent pages suggest, the accomplishments and frustrations Morgenthau experienced in public life lend credence to his conviction that the intellectual lives in a world that is both separate from and potentially intertwined with that of the politician. The difference lies in the particular values relevant for each sphere of activity. On the one hand, the intellectual is oblivious to power and is committed exclusively to the disinterested pursuit of the truth. The politician, on the other hand, relegates the pursuit of truth to an instrumentality, or means, to serve his own self-centered ends. As much as the very existence of power has a bearing on the expression of truth, Morgenthau's writing recapitulated the essence of classical *episteme politike* and applied it to the struggle for democracy and civic virtue in America. In calling for fundamental changes in the curriculum of political science, Morgenthau's primary concern was with "the restoration of the intellectual and moral commitment to the truth about matters political for its own sake." Against social and political pressures protecting the institutions and values of an established order, Morgenthau warned his colleagues: "If the political scientist cannot resist these pushes and pulls by repairing to the vision of the searcher for the political truth, which Plato brought to the world, and of the professor of political truth, which the prophets exemplified, what will become of him as a scholar, and what will become of a society which has deprived itself of the ability to measure the conflicting claims of interested parties against the truth, however dimly seen?"[2]

One measure of Morgenthau's success can be obtained by consulting the judgments of leading scholars and public officials. Robert Osgood declared that Morgenthau was without equal in exhorting Americans to come to terms with the realistic management of power on the international stage. He "expounded the gospel of *Realpolitik* and exorcised the moralistic illusions nurtured during the nation's long isolation from the mainstream of international politics." Furthermore, those who charged that Morgenthau's message excluded morality from foreign policy ne-

2. Statement by Hans J. Morgenthau on Political Science, n.d. (TS in Hans J. Morgenthau Papers, Box 4, Alderman Library, University of Virginia, Charlottesville).

glected the extent to which he wrote about the ideals embedded in the founding of the United States. As Osgood suggested, the moral dignity of the national interest lies in the responsible use of power in full recognition that moral satisfaction seldom coincides with the imperatives of national security.[3]

For former Secretary of State Henry Kissinger, Hans Morgenthau was both teacher and friend through all of the intellectual upheavals and disputes over two and a half decades. He "made the study of international relations a major discipline" and "sought to transcend" the disparate tendencies shaping the American world view—legalism, pragmatism, and a sense of moral mission. The perception among many that Morgenthau exemplified a doctrinaire conservatism in politics and diplomacy could not be more erroneous. His liberal political credentials were matched by a willingness to confront the statesman's fundamental dilemma—"that moral aims can be reached only in stages, each of which is imperfect. . . . Morality provides the compass course, the inner strength to face the ambiguities of choice."[4]

Speaking as one of America's leading diplomatic historians, Norman Graebner pointed out that Morgenthau judged history as an essential, if not exclusive, foundation for the study of international relations. Morgenthau saw clearly that "the primary dilemma that confronts students of human society is that of distinguishing the specific from the general and dealing meaningfully with both." Even in attempting to construct a theory of international politics, Morgenthau understood that the best the theorist can do is to trace the tendencies that, as potentialities, are inherent in international developments. "He can point out the different conditions which make it more likely for one tendency to prevail than another, and, finally, assess the probabilities for the different conditions and tendencies to prevail in actuality."[5]

Kenneth W. Thompson, director of the White Burkett Miller Center of Public Affairs, has written: "Because Morgenthau had a clear concep-

3. Chicago *Tribune*, July 27, 1980, Sec. 3, p. 5.
4. Henry A. Kissinger, "Hans Morgenthau," *New Republic*, August 2–9, 1980, pp. 12–14.
5. Norman Graebner, "Morgenthau as Historian," in Kenneth W. Thompson and Robert J. Myers (eds.), *Truth and Tragedy: A Tribute to Hans J. Morgenthau* (New Brunswick, 1984), 66–68. See also Morgenthau, *Politics Among Nations*, 21.

tion of man and the historian's sense of what is unique and recurrent, he approached Soviet-American relations from a perspective which continues to have enduring value." From the formulation of the Truman Doctrine to the Vietnam War, he warned American policy-makers of the "confusion which does not see that the real issue is Russian imperialism and Communist revolution only insofar as it is an instrument of that imperialism." In an essay written before the Cold War, Morgenthau explained: "Practical political action is not often a subject for authoritative moral judgments of universal scope. Those who act in the political field must deal with the possible, not with the ideal; they must try to get the relatively good, the lesser evil; they cannot without frustration reject whatever is not wholly good; they cannot be satisfied with proclaimed ends but must deal with actual means."[6]

To a greater extent, perhaps, than any of his intellectual predecessors, Morgenthau's analysis of the behavior and diplomacy of nations reflected, as it broadened, periodic debates within his profession regarding the theoretical and methodological commitments of the practicing political scientist. Throughout his long career, Morgenthau reminded his colleagues of the normative element in all political analysis and illustrated how the commitment of a "value-free" political science is itself a philosophical predisposition rooted in beliefs about man's nature and the meaning of his political existence. For Morgenthau, political science is based upon a total world view—religious, poetic, as well as philosophic in nature—the validity of which it must take for granted.[7]

Morgenthau drew upon the resources of both classical and modern political philosophy in developing a theory of politics. His vigorous critique of modern social science in *Scientific Man vs. Power Politics* (1946), as well as the "six principles of political realism" outlined in *Politics Among Nations* (1948), specify the content and boundaries of an American philosophy of power politics. The point of departure for Morgenthau's realist philosophy of politics is the proposition that "power politics, rooted in the lust for power, which is common to all

6. Kenneth W. Thompson, *Moralism and Morality in Politics and Diplomacy* (Lanham, Md., 1985), 101–106. See also Townsend Hoopes, *The Devil and John Foster Dulles* (Boston, 1973), 118.

7. Hans J. Morgenthau, *Dilemmas of Politics* (Chicago, 1958), 32.

men, is . . . inseparable from social life itself."[8] The truth of political science, he claimed, is the truth about power, its configurations, and its laws.

Morgenthau applied to practical affairs a philosophy of international politics that recognized the many forms, and stressed the limits, of power. Diplomacy, peace, and war—the conditions of their existence and the reasons for their success or failure—were for him the fundamental ingredients of international life.[9] His many books and essays probed the limits and possibilities of statesmanship for a postwar world in which American policy-makers face the increasingly difficult task of reconciling security interests with transcendent principles that have sustained the country's previous projections of power abroad. Morgenthau's thinking on international politics throughout the 1960s and 1970s provides ample evidence from which to judge the strength and limits of the realist approach in accounting for such new developments as the "obsolescence" of the sovereign nation-state in world politics, the emergence of new and influential nonstate actors, the rise of new centers of economic and military power, the redistribution of economic and political strength among industrialized and poor countries, and the dilemma of democratic states in projecting civilizing values abroad while preserving them at home.

In addition, Morgenthau was perhaps the first American realist to develop a systematic and broad-gauge theory of international politics. Any international political theory, he argued, is a reflection of certain philosophic propositions. The intellectual horizon of the political theorist extends to the identification and analysis of objective, general truths that exist regardless of time and place. Morgenthau drew actively upon the tradition of the great political philosophers who "were also the great political scientists deriving concrete, empirically verifiable propositions from abstract philosophic ones." In discussing the normative element of political theory and the moral commitment of the political scientist, he suggested: "Without . . . the assumption that objective, general truths in matters political exist and can be known, order and justice and truth itself . . . become the mere by-products of ever-changing power relations.

8. Hans J. Morgenthau, *Scientific Man vs. Power Politics* (Chicago, 1946), 9.

9. Graebner, "Morgenthau as Historian," in Thompson and Myers (eds.), *Truth and Tragedy*, 70.

In such a society the political scientist still has an important part to play: he becomes the idealogue who gives the appearance of truth and justice to power and the claim for it."[10]

The Education of an American Realist

Although he was often vilified by his critics as an expositor of "Old World" values and power politics, Morgenthau's career can be considered something of an American success story. Much of his reputation was earned by pointing to basic problems with the principles and problems of American foreign policy. Against a crusading, ideologically oriented foreign policy, he called for a more realistic world view emphasizing national interest in terms of a nation's power vis-à-vis other nations. Yet Morgenthau's analysis of the instruments and consequences of diplomacy cannot be understood in isolation from his unequivocal commitment to the values of America's liberal and democratic heritage. One of his least read but most important volumes, *The Purpose of American Politics* (1960), affirmed his strong commitment to America's unifying national purpose, which he defined as "achieving equality in freedom." In his revealing interview with Bernard Johnson, Morgenthau concluded with the rather sentimental conviction: "There is no doubt . . . that I would never have been able to establish myself as a scholar were it not for the opportunity offered me by the United States. . . . I did have the opportunity to show what I could do and by showing it, was able to advance. It is this uniqueness which from the very beginning has been the most distinctive characteristic of American society."[11]

Morgenthau was born in 1904 in Coburg, a small town in central Germany and now part of northern Bavaria. His first political reflection extended back to the Tripolitanian War of 1911 between Italy and Turkey and the First Balkan War of 1912 between Bulgaria, Greece, and Serbia on the one hand, and Turkey on the other. Morgenthau "sympathized with the enemies of Turkey and was particularly fascinated by the

10. Morgenthau, *Dilemmas of Politics*, 35.
11. Hans J. Morgenthau, *The Purpose of American Politics* (New York, 1960), 8; "Bernard Johnson's Interview with Hans J. Morgenthau," in Thompson and Myers (eds.), *Truth and Tragedy*, 385. Hereinafter cited as "Interview."

Bulgarian siege of the Turkish fortress of Adrianople."[12] As a schoolboy, he read extensively about the events leading up to World War I and witnessed the betrayal of enlightened liberal convictions that the progressive march of civilization transformed warfare into a social anachronism. Morgenthau's autobiographical recollections are especially vivid about the revolution that swept over Germany in 1918, the swift disintegration of the Imperial government, and the inability of the Weimar regime to stem the rising tide of political fanaticism prompted by the enormous economic and moral devastation following the war.

Morgenthau's own reflections of his early life and formative experiences as a youth were clouded with painful disappointment and frustration.[13] He recalled the personal trauma of being an only child and the anxiety of being emotionally victimized by a neurotic and oppressive father. Although exhibiting a promising young mind in the classroom, he suffered from frequent illness and inveterate shyness. Morgenthau admitted, many years later, that he still experienced considerable difficulty with initiating casual and impromptu conversation in chance encounters with other people. Raised a Jew in an authoritarian family committed to uneasy coexistence in German society, he was often the target of gross anti-Semitic provocations and institutionalized discrimination. In September, 1922, as an eighteen-year-old, Morgenthau had the opportunity to come to terms with his aspirations and expectations as a senior in the Gymnasium. Assigned a composition with the title "What I Hope for My Future and the Foundations for That Hope," he wrote: "My hopes for the future move in two directions. I hope for the lifting of the pressure to which I am exposed by the social environment, and I hope to find a direction and a purpose for my future activities. The latter cannot be realized before the former is fulfilled."[14] With obvious bitterness, Morgenthau found in the German character a cruel and sadistic streak that was reinforced by the intrinsic authoritarian elements in both family and government. Unlike Lippmann, for example, who retreated from his Jewish roots, Morgenthau's sense of deep injustice over religious persecution remained a prominent concern throughout his life. The support he would later offer

12. Hans J. Morgenthau, "An Intellectual Autobiography," *Society*, XV (January–February, 1978), 63.

13. "Interview," 338–40.

14. Morgenthau, "An Intellectual Autobiography," 63.

to Jewish emigrés throughout Eastern Europe and the Soviet Union, as well as to an Israeli state with secure borders, was strengthened by many of these early memories.

Morgenthau's formal academic training began in 1923 when he enrolled at the University of Frankfurt. Much to his father's chagrin, he displayed a keen interest in the disciplines of philosophy, literature, and art. His sanguine belief that philosophy would provide an answer to the riddles of the universe was sorely tested by an introductory course in which the instructor, a disciple of Bishop Berkeley and David Hume, treated the study of man and nature as a problem in epistemology. Believing philosophy to be a purely rational and scientific enterprise, the professor dismissed as irrelevant Morgenthau's reference to Aristotle and the "wonderment" or "shock" that accompanies the philosopher's first encounter with the mystery of existence. Outside the classroom, the family emphasis on assimilation into the German environment led to his participation in a dueling fraternity from which he incurred a number of permanent facial scars.

Discouraged by the prevailing positivist credentials of his professors, he transferred in 1924 to the University of Munich in order to concentrate more specifically in the fields of public law and European diplomatic history. To a considerable extent, Morgenthau decided to study law "not because I was interested in it, but because my father would not allow me to study literature." He compensated for this unattractive choice by limiting his attendance at law lectures to the bare minimum and "taking courses whose subject matter and, more particularly, whose professors interested me."[15]

One such scholar was Heinrich Wölfflin, an art historian who founded the school of aesthetics that revolutionized the criticism and understanding of art. Wölfflin treated each work of art as the concretization of "intuitive forms" common to a particular epoch in art history. Building on the theory of "prefiguration," Wölfflin's approach accounted for changes in style, especially from Romanesque to Gothic, in terms of the transformation of fundamental forms rather than of mere chronological sequence. Another important influence was Herman Oncken, a diplomatic historian who lectured on nineteenth-century European diplomatic

15. Hans J. Morgenthau, "Fragment of an Intellectual Biography," in Thompson and Myers (eds.), *Truth and Tragedy*, 6.

history. As a scholar of unusual sensitivity, Oncken impressed Morgenthau by the way "he entered into an historic period or personality and reconstructed it, laying bare the hidden connections of motivations, actions, and consequences." In particular, the heritage of Bismarck's diplomacy was especially significant for the young Morgenthau's thinking on the principles of foreign and military policy. "For the first time, I felt the impact of a coherent system of thought . . . a distillation of Bismarck's *Realpolitik*, that appeared to support my . . . impressionistic judgments on contemporary issues of foreign policy." [16]

In addition, a seminar by Professor Rothenbücher on Max Weber's social and political philosophy provided Morgenthau with a model for the practicing political scientist. "Weber's political thought possessed all the intellectual and moral qualities I had looked for in vain in the contemporary literature and outside the universities." Against the general moral and intellectual degradation of German public life, he summarized Weber's importance by writing: "While as a citizen he was a passionate observer of the political scene and a frustrated participant in it, as a scholar . . . [he viewed] politics without passion . . . or political purpose beyond the intellectual one of understanding." [17]

Morgenthau also profited, intellectually and personally, from a course in international law with Professor Karl Neumeyer. The entire semester was devoted to a philosophical and conceptual content analysis of the first twenty-five pages of a standard international law text. Finding "hardly a sentence in those pages that was philosophically sound or empirically provable," Morgenthau learned "to take nothing for granted in the so-called scholarly literature." [18] In addition, Neumeyer was one of the few German professors who made no effort to conceal his Jewish faith and who took a personal interest in Morgenthau and his work. One of the first articles Morgenthau wrote after arriving in the United States was an obituary for Neumeyer in the October 1941 issue of the *American Journal of International Law*.

Two prominent intellectual and social movements within the German universities had a largely negative impact on Morgenthau's world view. The influence of Marxism on German society in the decade fol-

16. Morganthau, "An Intellectual Autobiography," 63.

17. Morgenthau, "Fragment of an Intellectual Biography," in Thompson and Myers (eds.), *Truth and Tragedy*, 7.

18. Morgenthau, "An Intellectual Autobiography," 65.

lowing World War I was heralded by a younger generation of scholars affiliated with the *Institut für Sozialforschung* at the University of Frankfurt. Marxist concepts and tools of analysis provided a disintegrating society with a method of accelerating the pace of disintegration under morally respectable auspices and, then, reconstituting the social structure on a more firm and just foundation. Occasionally taking part in the work of the *Institut* as an outsider, Morgenthau objected to "that particular type of Marxist who considers Marxism to be a closed intellectual system, containing ready-made answers to all possible questions, to be elicited by correct answers." Morgenthau's disaffection was reinforced further by *Institut* members who, with the Nazi enemy at the gate, engaged in "futile hair-splitting" and debated the true meaning of one statement by Marx against another. More and more, Morgenthau appreciated Marx's admonition to his son-in-law: "*Moi, je ne suis pas Marxiste!*"[19]

Morgenthau's dissertation research led him to recognize the need for a broad theoretical approach that would substantiate the relationships between politics and law that he found in international relations. Intrigued by new work in the field of psychoanalysis, he experimented briefly with Freudian concepts and principles in hopes that they would yield a systematic view of political life. The unhappy result was an unpublishable manuscript along with the solemn realization that both Marxist and psychoanalytical theories of politics suffer a common dilemma—the impossibility of explaining systematically the complexities and contingencies of man's political existence by the static categories of a reductionist theory, whether economic or psychological.

After passing his law exam in Munich, Morgenthau returned to the University of Frankfurt in 1929 to complete his doctorate. More interested in political and philosophical questions than legal and administrative case studies, the title of his dissertation read: "The International Judicial Function: Its Nature and Its Limits." Against those who sought to outlaw war by noble covenants, Morgenthau argued that the weakness of international law stems from the intrusion of international politics. What really mattered in the relations of nations, he thought, was not international law but international politics and the pursuit of power.

Until 1931, Morgenthau remained in Frankfurt as a legal assistant to Professor Hugo Sinzheimer, who was a leading specialist in the areas

19. Morgenthau, "Fragment of an Intellectual Biography," in Thompson and Myers (eds.), *Truth and Tragedy*, 66–67.

of criminal and labor law. Sinzheimer was a prominent Social Democratic intellectual who had been elected in 1919 to the National Assembly that drafted the Weimar Constitution. Although Morgenthau helped to draft briefs for the Supreme Court, he thought these activities were marginal to the crucial issue of the distribution of political power within the Republic. Following brief service as acting president of the Labor Law Court in Frankfurt, Morgenthau took a leave of absence and would never again render a judicial decision. From this brief period, he would establish lifelong friendships with such notable figures as Franz Neumann, Ernest Frankel, and Karl Freund.

From 1932 to 1935, he taught public law at the University of Geneva. With Hitler's rise to power in 1933, Morgenthau left Germany to teach at an institute for economic and international studies in Madrid from 1935 to 1936. His immigration to the United States the following year led to teaching appointments at Brooklyn College (1937–1939); the University of Kansas City (1939–1943); the University of Chicago (1943–1971); the City College of New York (1968–1975); and the New School for Social Research in New York (1975–1981). Morgenthau taught classes in American politics, law, political philosophy, and international relations. His lectures on American foreign policy were always popular if not contentious forums of debate concerning America's military and diplomatic responsibilities in the postwar world. In addition, his commitment to a philosophy of politics and his distrust of a quantified political science represented a sharp departure from the discipline's prevailing orthodoxy of behavioral science and data-based empirical theory.

Whereas the philosopher's political involvement may be corrupted by the temptation of power and its rewards, Morgenthau exemplified the political scientist who stood both within and outside the political arena. Encouraged by George Kennan, he joined Niebuhr and others as a consultant to the State Department's Policy Planning Staff. Following an official trip to Austria in which he was assigned to report on the transition from military to civilian rule, his association with the State Department came to an abrupt halt in 1951. Morgenthau was particularly frustrated when, in 1954, Washington neglected to draw upon his expertise and personal connections in negotiating a bases agreement with Spain. He also served as a consultant to the Pentagon from 1962 to 1965, only to be fired because of his opposition to the Vietnam War. His stand against the commitment of American troops to Southeast Asia was based on a time-honored principle of classical diplomacy: The statesman should never commit his nation's security and prestige to a position from which he cannot retreat without loss of face or from which he cannot advance without undue risk.

In fact, his criticism of American intervention prompted the Johnson Administration to establish a desk known as "Project Morgenthau," an in-house operation to discredit him for which, he claimed, McGeorge Bundy and Zbigniew Brzezinski became the official spokesmen. One of the more conspicuous and offensive attempts to impugn Morgenthau's integrity was made by Freedom House, which published an article in 1967 that associated his position with that of pacifists, communists, and traitors. In his final years, Morgenthau grew increasingly skeptical about the power of truth to move men. Speaking for a generation of political thinkers, he concluded: "We came to realize . . . through political experience, what some of us had concluded before by way of philosophic reflection, that power positions do not yield to arguments, however rationally and morally valid, but only to superior power. We came to realize that the distribution of power in America favors the continuation of policies that we regard to be indefensible on rational and moral grounds." [20]

The many texts he published throughout the decades of Cold War and détente reflected an increasing recognition in the United States that "power" in myriad forms holds a central place in the study of international relations. His commentary on American foreign policy (*e.g.*, *In Defense of the National Interest* and *A New Foreign Policy for the United States* [21]) exposed the intellectual confusions about the realities of the international environment in which the United States would have to pursue its security after World War II. The crucial choice for American decision makers was between a crusading foreign policy motivated by universal ideological appeals and a realistic foreign policy that emphasizes the nation's interests in terms of its power vis-à-vis other nations. He revealed how the optimism and pragmatism characteristic of American intellectual life was blinded by the tragic character of political and social problems, how these issues are incapable of any clear-cut solutions and cannot be remedied by some kind of technological or political con-

20. Hans J. Morgenthau, *Truth and Power: Essays of a Decade, 1960–1970* (New York, 1970), 5; "Interview," 381–83.

21. Hans J. Morgenthau, *In Defense of the National Interest* (New York, 1951); *A New Foreign Policy for the United States* (New York, 1969).

trivance. According to Morgenthau, those who seek to remake the world in the image of America's own commitment to liberty and equality misunderstand the relation of universal principles to self-interest in a nation's foreign-policy conduct. Certainly, Morgenthau acknowledged that the statesman's moral obligation both within and above the nation-state is essential to the formulation of particular interests and objectives; at the same time, however, he cautioned that the ethical criteria by which political actions are judged must be applied with a prudent regard for expected and unanticipated consequences in an anarchic world arena.

Shortly before his death in 1980, Morgenthau had grown quite frail in stature yet remained consumed with his obligations as a scholar and critical observer of world affairs. He never wavered from his commitment to the classroom and spoke frequently of how much teaching meant to him. The ambiguity and tragic choices he had experienced in his personal life nurtured a healthy skepticism about the necessity of "redefining American identity and mission" in the wake of the Indochina War and Watergate. With George Kennan, Morgenthau warned that the militarization of the Cold War delivered successive American leaders down the treacherous path of failing to relate vital national interests to the internal purposes of a democratic nation.

Morgenthau's American Philosophy of Power Politics

Morgenthau's primary intellectual interest from the beginning of his academic career was not foreign policy or even politics in general, but philosophy. Following World War II, his decision to focus on American foreign policy was based on the practical conviction that "the existence of the United States and . . . mankind depended on a sound foreign policy." [22] He saw little point in abstract philosophy for a troubled world that could be reduced to radioactive rubble in a matter of years or decades. Morgenthau may have sacrificed a life devoted to philosophical reflection for self-imposed public service; however, his analysis of domestic and foreign policy revealed a consistent awareness of both the limits and possibilities of the philosopher in politics. He was seldom hesitant to cite the great philosophical systems in Western thought and evaluate their

22. "Interview," 381.

relevance for such perennial topics as power, legitimacy, freedom, natural law, revolution, and majority rule.

Commenting on the inclinations of those political scientists who seek to emancipate the scientific study of politics from "value-laden" political philosophy, Morgenthau warned: "Contemporary political science, predominately identified with a positivistic philosophy which is itself a denial of virtually all of the philosophic traditions of the West, has . . . mutilated itself by refusing itself access to the sources of insight available in the great philosophic systems of the past. Yet without that access it cannot recognize . . . some of the perennial problems of politics which contemporary experience poses with . . . unprecedented urgency."[23] As subsequent pages illustrate, the interrelation of science and humanism in Morgenthau's philosophy had considerable significance for the practical imperatives of statesmanship. His philosophy of power politics pointed to both the prospects and limitations of a just world community committed to supranational political values. Finally, his vigorous commentary on the struggle for liberty and equality in the United States had a direct bearing on his estimate of America's moral mission in world affairs.

Whether discussing the nature of American democracy or foreign policy, Morgenthau's principal contribution was to illumine the intellectual and moral dilemma of understanding politics and acting within the political sphere. His realism gained in depth by drawing on a general political philosophy, a set of general principles that shaped his analysis of concrete problems and have universal applicability. The task of the great political philosophers, from Plato onward, has always been to identify the defects of the existing political order and to reverse the political decline by thinking about the nature of politics and the right political order. Few political thinkers, however, ever succeeded in stemming the political decline of their respective societies; rather, their work tends to demonstrate in retrospect the inevitability of that decline. Their continuing ability to teach posterity the truth about politics testifies to their success. Political science, Morgenthau believed, was inherently a philosophical discipline in that "man . . . cannot live without a philosophy which gives meaning to his existence, by explaining it in terms of causal-

23. Morgenthau, *Dilemmas of Politics*, 33.

ity, rationalizing it in terms of philosophy proper, and justifying it in terms of ethics."[24]

Morgenthau noted that any political philosophy with enduring value is shaped by three different but closely related influences. The first, what Alfred North Whitehead termed the "climate of opinion," encompasses those unconsciously accepted presuppositions that help determine what men think about the nature of the universe, what can and cannot happen in it, and the nature of man and his potential to lead the good life. The second, and more concrete, evolves out of the political conflicts of the time and embraces those theories and concepts by which groups and classes of men interpret specific political measures. The third derives from the mind and temperament of the individual who gives to the philosophy its ordered literary form. Whether philosophic expression is able to transcend time and place will depend upon the extent to which its fundamental prerequisites have a universal validity—the extent to which they express some essential and perennial truth about nature and the life of man.[25]

Unfortunately, far too few of the existing commentaries on Morgenthau's realism and political thought elucidate the depth of his philosophic convictions or illustrate how his international perspective grew out of a profound regard for the intellectual and moral foundation of Western civilization. The principles of foreign policy and diplomacy outlined in *Politics Among Nations* have an organic connection to substantive theoretical and ethical topics Morgenthau addressed in numerous essays, both published and unpublished, as well as in such books as *Science: Servant or Master?* and *Truth and Power*. For example, his writing on the distinctive characteristics of the nuclear age and its probable human and material consequences pointed to the need for "a new way of thinking," and, beyond this, a "transformation of man himself in his moral, rational, and political qualities." Along other lines, Morgenthau's judgment on the role of power and force in modern diplomacy reflected a consistent regard for the manner in which self-interest and its hypocritical concealment in human nature give rise to the new moral force of

24. Morgenthau, *Scientific Man*, 2–6. See also Hans J. Morgenthau, *The Decline of Democratic Politics* (Chicago, 1962), 1–3, 10–13, 41–42, 227, 332–34. Vol I of Morgenthau, *Politics in the Twentieth Century*.

25. Hans J. Morgenthau, "Modern Political Theory Research File," n.d. (TS in Morgenthau Papers, Box 80), 1.

nationalistic universalism in world politics. The international morality that in past centuries kept a nation's aspiration for power within certain bounds has, except for certain fragmentary restraints, given way to the morality of individual nations.

A number of interrelated themes in the philosophic and scientific study of man's political existence led Morgenthau to reflect upon what he regarded as the "philosophy of scholarship." These may be classified in the following order: (1) theoretical thinking and action as typical modes of human behavior; (2) human consciousness and the experience of tragedy and guilt in the existential drama of man's quest for self-identification; (3) the nature of objective and relative criteria in the expression of truth in matters political; (4) the values that give meaning to the struggle for liberty and equality in American democracy; (5) the scientific study of politics; and (6) realism as a political philosophy.

THE REQUIREMENTS OF THEORY AND ACTION IN POLITICS

Morgenthau cited the experience of the classical political thinkers who vividly portrayed the necessity of that unbridgeable chasm, or eternal tension, between politics and a theoretical science of politics. In Plato's *Theatetus*, Socrates profiles the intellectual disposition of the philosopher, the man of knowledge, in contrast to the atheoretical practical man. The philosopher's "outer form . . . only is in the city. His mind, disdaining the littleness and nothingness of human things, is 'flying all abroad' as Pindar says, measuring earth and heaven . . . interrogating the whole nature of each and all in their entirety, but not condescending to anything which is within reach. . . . He is searching into the essence of man, and busy in enquiring what belongs to such a nature to do or suffer different from any other." [26] The philosopher's commitment to truth for its own sake and his divorcement—morally and intellectually, in judgment and action—from the political sphere makes him a scandal in the eyes of the multitude. By contrast, the man of moral virtue and practical wisdom (*phronesis*) seeks to transcend the empirical limits of his existence through action and to overcome that finiteness through the objective permanence of a great deed. Such a man, as Goethe remarked, "hates all that only instructs him without increasing or directly stimulating his

26. Morgenthau, *The Decline of Democratic Politics*, 17.

activity." However deeply theoretical reflection may penetrate the mysteries of the universe, it cannot accomplish what even defective action achieves: change the world.[27]

The conceptual antithesis between the *vita contemplativa* and the *vita activa* is not merely a false dichotomy that brings together exclusive categories of theoretical abstraction and subjective feeling; the tension that exists between theoretical thought and politics in the sphere of concepts and values reappears in the real world. As Morgenthau observed, the inspiration for theoretical thought is impeded when the consequences of political action correspond with the mental image that the practitioner has formed of the political world. Alternatively, when man's political power declines and reality threatens to pass from his grasp, he seeks to assure himself of his intellectual mastery by providing a theoretical account of the reasons for decline and disorder in political life. The increasing visibility of the philosopher, then, is symptomatic of man's inability to create a purposeful political world. Morgenthau alluded to Hegel's observation: "When philosophy paints its grey in grey, then has a shape of life grown old. By philosophy's grey in grey it cannot be rejuvenated but only understood. The owl of Minerva spreads its wings only with the falling of the dusk."[28]

Morgenthau argued that politics, specifically the *animus dominandi*, or lust for power, poses the primary threat to human existence in the modern age. In particular, the phenomenon of totalitarianism "puts in doubt certain assumptions about the nature of man and of society which we took for granted" and "overwhelms legal processes on which we had come to look as self-sufficient instruments of control." Man thus becomes both an exponent and victim of the force that shakes society to its foundation and administers to human consciousness the shock of wonderment that is the beginning of a meaningful science of politics. According to Morgenthau, the vital task of our age is to "transform the shock of wonderment that has its source in politics to the theoretical, systematic understanding of that source. That understanding . . . has two purposes: to create a philosophical order in our minds through the transformation of an unintelligible and discordant reality into a theoretical

27. Hans J. Morgenthau, "Thought and Action in Politics," *Social Research,* XXXVIII (Winter, 1971), 612.

28. Georg Wilhelm Friedrich Hegel, Preface to the *Philosophy of Right,* trans. T. M. Knox (New York, 1976), 13.

system for its own intellectual sake and to serve as a preliminary to the elimination of threats to human existence by transforming reality."[29]

Yet the theoretical understanding of politics and its pragmatic value as a guide to action pose a dual paradox. Morgenthau relied on both historic and personal experience to show how vulnerable the functional relationship between theoretical knowledge and political action is to being severed by the intrusion of factors the control of which is beyond the competence of the theorist. The potential value in any political theory derives from the postulation of a rational order within which the relationship between ends and means can be clarified; however, and as Morgenthau suggests, what successful political action more often requires, especially in a democracy, is not just theoretical knowledge about the hierarchy of conceivable ends but "moral support for making the intellectually obvious choice of means and ends."[30] At this juncture, the political actor is in the realm of the contingent, the accidental, the indeterminate will. Between reason—assimilating theory and fact—and action, the human will intervenes, and that will may or may not translate into action what reason suggests. The first paradox, then, appertains to the inescapable normative element that shapes the tasks of political theory. Theoretical thinking about politics is by necessity thinking for politics.

In addition, Morgenthau maintained that the reactions of the will are less predictable in terms of conformity to theoretical propositions under the conditions of modern democracy and totalitarianism. During the centuries of aristocratic rule in Europe, the predictability of policy was a function of the extent to which sovereigns shared common moral convictions regarding both the normative order of society and the rules of diplomatic intercourse. The statesmen who became masters of events and thus conscious creators of history—the Richelieus, Napoleons, and Bismarcks—had one quality in common: they combined a general conception of foreign policy, of its direction and aim, with the ability to manipulate concrete events in light of that conception. Referring to the rise of mass political movements, as well as the emergence of new technologies of power, Morgenthau suggested that modern governments

29. Hans J. Morgenthau, "Notes on Political Theory," Summer, 1964 (TS in Morgenthau Papers, Box 80), 1–3; *Science: Servant or Master?* (New York, 1972), 33; *Truth and Power,* 219; "Hannah Arendt on Totalitarianism and Democracy," *Social Research,* XLIV (Spring, 1977), 127–28.

30. Morgenthau, *Science: Servant or Master?* 41.

hardly ever try to master reality; rather, they only react when it appears to threaten what they regard as the national interest and, more particularly, the status quo. The statesman, lacking a vision that would bring a measure of rational order in that chaos, is left with little more than his fear of change and the primitive urge to prevent that change from being consummated.[31]

The separation of thought and action by a recalcitrant will points to still another paradox. Morgenthau documented how much of social science research operates upon the fallacy that the problems of social life are comparable to the problems of physical nature. In the same way that the natural scientist can, through experimentation and hypothesis testing, understand the laws of nature, the social thinker can create a gigantic social mechanism that is at the command of the scientific master. The models of scientific reason offer the "value-free" theoretician a corrective to the uncertainty of choice in politics by, in effect, replacing the will of the statesman with the technical application of scientific solutions. In an opposing vein, Morgenthau stressed that the object of the social sciences is man, not as a product of nature, but as both the creature and creator of history in and through which his individuality and freedom of choice manifest themselves. A viable theory of politics is one that builds upon the assumption that the human will is not primarily informed by scientific theory but by wisdom. "Wisdom is the gift of intuition, and political wisdom is the gift to grasp intuitively the quality of diverse interests and of power in the present and future and the impact of different actions upon them."[32]

CONSCIOUSNESS OF BEING AND TRANSCENDENCE

Another seminal theme distinguishing Morgenthau's philosophical orientation is the existential drama within which the uncertainty and doubt in human nature is reflected in the struggle for power and justice in society. In an unpublished essay entitled "The Significance of Being Alone," Morgenthau traced the biblical antecedents of man's self-doubt and subsequent efforts to overcome the mystery of existence. According to the Book of Genesis, man as created by God exhibits five attributes: he is created in the image of God; he has dominion over the animal king-

31. Morgenthau, "Thought and Action in Politics," 618.
32. *Ibid.*, 620.

dom and inanimate nature; he is to fill the earth with his descendants and subdue it; the good man cannot be defined apart from others; and the day he eats from the tree of knowledge of good and evil he will perish. Of these prophecies, Morgenthau elaborated on man's separation from God as the starting point for theoretical reflection on the desires and aspirations of man as a political animal.

For God, the question of whether or not it is good for Him to be alone cannot arise. The essential quality of His being apart, of being in, yet ultimately distinct from that which is created, is a necessary corollary of His perfection. "God is perfection and goodness, wisdom and power; He is complete and suffices unto Himself; for Him to have a companion in perfection is not only unnecessary but unthinkable." Man is imperfect by nature, yet he carries within himself the vision of perfection. This vision encompasses both the contemplation of eternal verities as well as the desire for perfection and a meaning to his life that transcends the mere prerequisites of corporeal existence. The Fall, the eating from the tree of knowledge, symbolizes man's restless search for a perfection from which he is precluded by his own nature. Subsequently, the inborn loneliness of man takes on new significance. Able to know good from evil, man acquires a sense of tragedy and guilt by recognizing the chasm that divides what he is in contrast to what he should but can never fully become. Man's guilt, like that of Prometheus, emanates from the hubris that leads him to overstep the bounds of his nature. Like Sisyphus, his tragedy is that he must labor in vain until the end of time, trying and failing.[33]

Nowhere is this theme more evident than in Morgenthau's writing on the roots of narcissism in modern political culture. Although the fascination with individuality is often regarded as an immutable feature of psychological life, the rediscovery of the self was the achievement of the Renaissance. Throughout the Middle Ages, man's self-identification was inseparable from such general categories as race, people, family, and corporation. The dissolution of the Medieval *Christianitas*, in tandem with outbursts of individual creativity in art, literature, and politics, appeared to supply empirical proof of man's ability to overcome alienation through his own unaided efforts. In varying degrees, the systems of Hegel, Marx, and Freud seek to emancipate the individual from the shackles of dog-

33. Hans J. Morgenthau, "The Significance of Being Alone," n.d. (TS in Morgenthau Papers, Box 110), 1–5.

matic theology and metaphysics. For Hegel and Marx, individual freedom was embodied in the progress of objective reason, which would culminate in either an identity of the real and rational or in the substitution of the administration of things for the domination of man by man. The individualism of Freud finds its objective point in reference to the norms of a particular society, which are hypothesized, at least for the purpose of therapy, as absolute.[34]

The self-confidence of the modern mind is confronted by two manifestations of alienation: one existential, in which all human beings share; the other historic, for which contemporary narcissism is a response. Man's existential dilemma is the need to find meaning in a life that is finite, whereas human imagination and aspiration are limitless. Morgenthau examined the process of human consciousness within which the experience of alienation or anxiety gives rise to efforts, either religious or secular, to reintegrate man with himself and with the cosmos of which he forms a part. In addition, he shared the concern of classical political thinkers in restating the experiential challenge to the philosopher: The depths of the human soul, driven on by the shock of wonderment, strive to reconstruct the unity between the world and reflective consciousness. The shocking paradox of man's ability to master nature and his helplessness to control the results of that mastery, his supremacy over what is inanimate and alien and his impotence in the face of man, is at the root of the contemporary revolt against science, society, and politics-as-usual.[35]

Before turning to that illusive point of balance or harmony shaping the philosopher's consciousness of the ground of being, Morgenthau identifies two deceptive, and ultimately false, solutions to the mystery of existence. First, man can seek salvation from empirical misery and metaphysical doubt by an unconditional activism; he seeks to transform reality by the vital force of his own individuality. Against the empirical threat—the desire to maintain the range of one's own person with regard to others—man may devise structures of countervailing power directed against any challenge to his freedom. This impulse is strictly relative and may be available only under particular fortuitous circumstances; more-

34. Hans J. Morgenthau, "The Roots of Narcissism," 1978 (TS in Morgenthau Papers, Box 109), 1–11.

35. Morgenthau, *Science: Servant or Master?* 47.

over, the mere presence of action for its own sake cannot convey a normative standard, or end-in-view, that imparts substance or direction to man's proper task of becoming conscious of himself and the world.

Once man's activist confidence has been shattered by the ineluctable limits of human action, subsequent efforts to relieve the metaphysical shock may involve the political actor in a second deception of an intellectual nature. Unable to recognize his real strength (*i.e.*, to become conscious of experience through thought), man tries to overcome uncertain political knowledge by drawing on the illusory security of ideological pseudoknowledge. Modern man, threatened with atomization by unintelligible and unmanageable social forces, embraces the collective ideology of a nation, race, or class. Morgenthau summarized the essential dilemma of all political ideologies: "By seeking security in collective myths rather than in his own soul, man abandons his creative solitude for a collectivization in which he loses the fearful disquiet in the face of the incomprehensible and, with it, the ability to comprehend." In the political arena, the purpose of ideology is not to understand reality as it actually is, but to justify and rationalize the position and interest of a particular individual or group in regard to that reality. "It is not for want of admirable doctrine," wrote Shelley in the *Defence of Poetry*, "that men hate and despise and censor and deceive, and subjugate one another."[36]

The restoration of human consciousness, the quest for transcendence and salvation in the midst of the constant flux of life, begins with man's experience of existential disorder only superficially stilled by action. In the words of Georges Sorel: "Philosophy is perhaps after all only the recognition of the abysses which lie on each side of the footpath that the vulgar follow with the serenity of somnambulists."[37] Morgenthau considered it to be a distortion of the hierarchy of human values to assign to political action, especially in its collective form, the highest rank. To be conscious of himself through thought, of his fate in the world, is man's proper task. Hamlet's tragedy, for example, exemplifies the experience of a man whose awareness of the absurdity of action cannot maintain itself

36. Morgenthau, *Scientific Man*, 155–56; "Thought and Action in Politics," 625–26.

37. Georges Sorel, *Reflections on Violence*, trans. T. E. Hulme and N. Rolfe (New York, 1950), 30.

against his moral conscience through which society commands him to act. It is not conscience but action that "does make cowards of us all." Thinking man is by nature suffering man whose reflective consciousness transforms the tranquilizing feeling of not being alone into the experience of man living dangerously among men. "To become fully conscious of that fate does not mean to escape it; but by thus becoming conscious of it man transcends his fate."[38] Consciousness, therefore, does not save man from perdition so much as it instructs him on the origin and end of his fate.

To a considerable extent, Morgenthau's comments on the fundamental motivating structure of philosophical consciousness affirms a seminal proposition shaping the epistemological orientation of the classical political philosophers. The philosopher stands as the self-reflective man open to the horizon of wonder and mystery that intimates the existence of man and all that is out of nonexistence. The process of reality becomes intelligible in human consciousness through participation in all levels of reality, from the corporeal to the divine ground of being. The insight is gained that consciousness is formed and exists in the "In-Between" (*metaxy*) of the tension bounded by the polarities of immanent and transcendent being. Both Plato and Aristotle struggled to clarify the formative center of experience, the *metaxy*, and to defend the noetic core (*i.e.*, reason as the source of order in the soul of man) against the deformative forces prevalent at the time.

The *metaxy* is a symbol of rich complexity and depth, drawing on the language of divinity and of spirits as well as of man and *psyche*. Clarifying Plato's symbolization of the tension of man's existence as revealed in the *Symposium*, Eric Voegelin wrote:

> Man experiences himself as tending beyond human imperfection toward the perfection of the divine ground that moves him. The spiritual man, the *daimonios aner*, as he is moved in his quest of the ground, moves somewhere between knowledge and ignorance (*metaxy sophias kai amathias*). "The whole realm of the spiritual (*daimonion*) is halfway . . . between (*metaxy*) god and man" (Symp. 202a). Thus, the in-between . . . is not an empty space between the poles of the tension but the "realm of the spiritual"; it is

38. Morgenthau, *Science: Servant or Master?* 53–55.

the reality of "man's convergence with the gods" (202–203), of the mutual participation (*methexis, metalepsis*) of human in divine, and divine in human, reality.[39]

The order of the individual soul is dependent upon its orientation towards the ground of being, and the order of society depends on its analogy to the structure of the order of the soul in the well-developed man. The In-Between of existence, as Voegelin suggested, represents the meeting ground of the human and divine in a consciousness of their distinction and interpenetration. The philosopher is not allowed to settle down on the positive pole of existential tension; only the tension in its polarity of real and nonreal is the full truth of reality.

Morgenthau's discussion of reflective consciousness exhibits a similar concern with the tension and limits of man's participation in a multidimensional reality. Between the cognitive impulse and the reality to be understood, thinking "exists in tension between the darkness of not knowing and extinction from an excess of knowledge." On the one hand, Morgenthau acknowledged that consciousness of the human fate is to live within the presence of death; consciousness, aware of its own transitoriness and deprived of an ultimate meaning, may find through the deliberate act of dying a way of changing the world through its own inner force. In the language of Socrates in the *Phaedo*, right philosophizing is the practice of death. As Aristotle observed in the *Nicomachean Ethics*: "Such a life . . . is more than merely human; it cannot be lived as man *qua* man but only by virtue of the divine that is in him."[40]

On the other hand, Morgenthau emphasized that man is incapable of being conscious simultaneously of the fullness of his vital forces and reflective thoughts. In the struggle between life that wants to maintain itself and reflection that wants to fulfill itself through its own sacrifice, consciousness reaches its limit in the heroic renunciation of this inner contradiction. Certainly, Morgenthau appreciated what the classical thinkers found to be the tension, that dynamic movement, that designates

39. Eric Voegelin, *Anamnesis*, trans. Gerhart Niemeyer (Notre Dame, 1978), 103. See also Ellis Sandoz, *The Voegelinian Revolution* (Baton Rouge, 1981), 161, 192, 199, 209, 211, 218n, 249.

40. Morgenthau, *Science: Servant or Master?* 57; Aristotle *Nicomachean Ethics* (trans. M. Ostwald) 290.

the poles of human consciousness—the immanent-transcendent. In one of Morgenthau's most important passages, yet neglected by his critics, he pointed to the fundamental experience engendering the philosopher's symbolization of the "In-Between" in human existence.

> In the middle, thinking comes to rest: the rest of creation when in this middle the tension is kept in equilibrium, the rest of lassitude and of the attrition of what is specifically human in man's existence when consciousness dissolves the tension by dropping out of it. That rest is the end of all movement . . . in the consciousness toward the unknown. . . . In this tension, thinking bears witness to the perils to which man is exposed as a seeker after all knowledge and as a creature endowed with the will to live.[41]

Man's spirituality is a product of his psychic nature when, shaken in his soul by the rift between his consciousness and the world, he seeks union with the world by becoming conscious of its mysteries. Ultimate knowledge is beyond any human possibility: "Man cannot become God, for the separation of his consciousness from the world is of his essence and thus he cannot cease to suffer." To suggest, however, that Morgenthau dismissed any divine presence in human reality misrepresents his position. Although the divine and human poles of consciousness are not coterminous (*i.e.*, in the completeness of consciousness), the suffering of man is inexplicable without reference to a transcendent standard within, and yet beyond, ephemeral human experience. By raising his suffering into reflective consciousness, man contemplates suffering as God contemplates the world. As Morgenthau described the experience: "In the fullness of the consciousness of his suffering, he becomes like God and is assured of his divine kinship."[42]

THE NATURE AND REQUIREMENTS OF POLITICAL JUSTICE

The boundaries of human consciousness led Morgenthau to consider the meaning of truth in man's political existence. In fact, Morgenthau characterized the history of political thought as a dialogue between

41. Morgenthau, *Science: Servant or Master?* 58.
42. *Ibid.*, 68–69.

the teachings of tradition and the needs of the contemporary world. The philosopher's task is anchored to an inescapable dilemma: What of the tradition is perennially true, and what is simply a manifestation of specific interests and circumstances? Goethe remarked to Eckermann that the one who acts is always unjust and that nobody has justice but the one who observes. That epigram calls into question the nature of both objective and relative judgments about political truth.[43] Morgenthau referred to the ambivalent moral position of the historian and political scientist in society.

There will, in varying degrees, be a certain relativism implicit in the social vision of the thinker who is a product of the society which it is his mission to understand. No social institution can completely transcend the limitations of its origins. Morgenthau contrasted the detachment and objectivity of mind that characterized the great historians of ancient Greece, Herodotus and Thucydides, with the modern historians who have become partisans of nation or class. Leopold von Ranke's work is "a panegyric to the virtues and greatness of Prussia, a testimony to the author's nationalism." Similarly, Theodor Mommsen judged Rome—praising the Republic and Caesar, condemning Caesar's enemies and Caesarism—by the standards of nineteenth-century liberalism. The core of Woodrow Wilson's international message—that democracy is the best form of government toward which all nations aspire—is but another example of this tendency.[44]

Although never doubting the "personal equation" of the political scientist, Morgenthau noted that the very possibility of political theory is based upon the existence and accessibility of objective, general truth. Specifically, it is man's ability to rethink and to put himself in contact with the political thought of his predecessors that is the basis for assuming the existence of objective general theory. As a result of common experiences, political philosophy draws upon a common fund of rational ability as a basis for meaningful communication across the ages. Morgenthau pointed to the Kantian categories of reason as applicable to all men in their experiences. "It is in the same reason meeting the same experi-

43. Morgenthau, *Truth and Power*, 68.
44. *Ibid.*, 70. See also Morgenthau, "Notes on Political Theory" (TS in Morgenthau Papers, Box 80), 1.

ences that there is an empirical foundation for a political philosophy that is able to claim objectivity and political truth."[45]

Although men may share in a broad community of political experience and common categories of reason, Morgenthau was quick to stipulate that the *particular* expressions of a political philosophy are tied to time and place. Plato and Aristotle reflected on the nature of man in order to preserve the declining Athenian *polis*. Machiavelli raised into consciousness the tension between right political action and right moral action with the aim of instructing the House of Medici on the causes of political decay in Italy. The thought of Hobbes and Locke tried to come to terms with the legacy of the English revolution, as Montesquieu and Rousseau anticipated the French one in the decline of monarchical rule. In the history of political theory, there is a dialectical movement consisting in a particular truth's becoming established within a particular period.

The process by which Morgenthau adapted the principles of ethics and philosophy to the constant flux and ambiguity of human existence is evident in his writing on the limits of historical justice in all political action. His tragic conception of the human condition acknowledged that norms of social justice must be seen within the context of man's capacity for both self-transcendence and self-deception. "Man," to quote Pascal, "is neither angel nor beast and his misery is that he who would act the angel acts the brute."[46] Historical judgments on either the reality or the illusion of justice derive from a particular view of the world, of its constitution and purpose, and of man's place within it. For Morgenthau, the proper role of the political philosopher is to seek that fragile point of congruence between universal norms that apply to all men and striking a meaningful balance between freedom and power in a particular society.

Is it possible to assert that the concept of justice has any objective content, or is it reducible to the dogmas of partisan ideology? Morgenthau argued for the reality of justice while stipulating that its realization in political life will forever be incomplete. The invocation of justice is built into the very structure of politics and points to the objective universality of justice. "Man alone is . . . suspended between heaven and earth:

45. Morgenthau, "Notes on Political Theory" (TS in Morgenthau Papers, Box 80), 2.

46. Morgenthau, *Scientific Man*, 200.

an ambitious beast and frustrated god. For he alone is endowed with the faculty of rational imagination that outpaces his ability to achieve." The aspiration for justice, however feeble and ephemeral it may be, derives from man's capacity for transcending himself, for trying to see himself as he might look to others. At the same time, Morgenthau conceded that "it is not given to man to comprehend the *substance* of objective justice" and described the dilemma in the following terms: "Yet where rational, objective knowledge is precluded from the outset, as it is with justice, the propensity for self-deception has free rein. . . . Since man cannot help but judge and act in terms of justice and since he cannot know what justice requires, but since he knows for sure what he wants, he equates with a vengeance his vantage point and justice. Empirically we find . . . the absolute majesty of justice dissolves into the relativity of so many interests and points of view."[47]

From Morgenthau's standpoint, the principle that justice requires that men give to others, and receive from others, what is their due lacks any real content. Criteria interpreting the adequacy of what men give and receive have meaning only in prudential situations and become substantive only in a particular context. For Callicles and Thrasymachus in *The Republic:* "In all states there is the same principle of justice which is the interest of the government; and as a government must be supposed to have power, the only responsible conclusion is that . . . there is one principle of justice which is the interest of the stronger." Morgenthau categorically rejected the equation of might with right but averred that this conception of justice "has been echoed in modern times from Machiavelli, Hobbes, and Spinoza to Marx and Kelsen, and history seems to bear it out." All such formulations have one common characteristic: The powerful defend the status quo as just and condemn those who oppose it as unjust. Morgenthau referred to Justice Holmes who, in a letter to Sir Frederick Pollock, embodied the ultimate tribute that justice pays to power: "I have no practical criticism except what the crowd wants."[48]

Modern ideological currents testify to the absence of consensual standards by which to balance the machinations of power with a vision of the common good. Order and stability within liberal-democratic soci-

47. Morgenthau, *Truth and Power*, 61, 65.
48. Plato *Republic* (trans. Benjamin Jowett) 328E; Morgenthau, *Truth and Power*, 62.

ety grow out of an equalitarian conception of public welfare, which assumes that justice requires keeping disparities in wealth and power to a
minimum. Libertarian and modern conservative movements will identify
justice and freedom, and will be relatively unconcerned with the issue of
inequality, at least in its economic manifestation. Revolutionary political
agendas inspired by the writings of Marx and Lenin seek justice in the
violent liberation of an oppressed class, which, in turn, moves history
along a progressive path to its predetermined consummation. Aristocratic philosophies tend to acknowledge a natural order of inequality
among men and view justice as a function of the asymmetrical distribution of power and valued goods. Even theology, which Morgenthau
deemed essential for any understanding of the hierarchy of values reflecting the objective order of the world, is as much at a loss as secular norms
when it involves applying abstract principles to concrete cases.

The relativity of justice, the manner by which particular interests
are justified in terms of universal principles, is rooted in man's struggle
for survival and well-being within the dialectic bounded by the polarities
of power and justice. In *Scientific Man*, Morgenthau warned that this
antinomy is insoluble because the poles creating it are immutable. The
end of Machiavellianism "is not of this world" and "neither science nor
ethics can resolve the conflict between politics and morality into harmony." In another essay, he wrote: "In that dialectic between justice and
power, power gets the better of justice. For the work of justice is never
done and always dubious; the work of power . . . is clearly seen and
simply enjoyed."[49]

Yet Morgenthau was equally cognizant of several limitations, or
qualifications, affecting the philosopher's contribution to political life.
First, the requirements of formal political philosophy are different from
those that inform political reality, always in a "period of transition," re-
plete with empirical contingencies and systemic irrationalities. Second,
political philosophy is exposed to two kinds of corruption: either of becoming subservient to the existing political reality by rationalizing it, or
of becoming subservient to an anticipated and desired future reality by
justifying it.[50] From this standpoint, political philosophy fails when it is
reduced to either ideology or utopia. Morgenthau stressed that each ep-

49. Morgenthau, *Scientific Man*, 176–78; *Truth and Power*, 67.
50. Morgenthau, *The Decline of Democratic Politics*, 2–4.

och of history has the responsibility to abstract from the tradition of Western philosophy those truths that fit its own experience and, in turn, to separate out of its own manifold experience the perennial configurations of political life.

In view of the contrast between the systematic rationality of philosophy and the contingencies that determine the reality of politics, Morgenthau argued for an approach that is systematic in substance but takes its form from political life itself. Specifically, he pointed to the writings of Edmund Burke, who spoke of the need for an "issues-oriented" philosophy that applies the theoretical principles of politics to a wide variety of political issues. The thought processes of the philosopher seek to elucidate a particular issue both for the sake of theoretical knowledge as well as for the benefit of the political actor. Two examples from Morgenthau's work illustrate the philosopher's role in the political arena. The concrete issue of nuclear war moves the philosopher to reflect on the meaning of death in which human survival is predicated on the maintenance of an uncertain balance of terror. That philosophic reflection, carried on for its own sake, can help to illuminate the actor's mind, and through it, to fashion political action designed to minimize risks and multiply the sources of international stability. In addition, the concrete economic issues of the day lead the philosophic observer to theorize about the relationship between the concentrations of private power, on the one hand, and the government and the individual, on the other. This analysis leads to a reexamination of the nature of freedom and its prerequisites in the modern world.

Morgenthau's political thought, by synthesizing both the normative and empirical halves of theory, serves two important purposes. First, philosophic reflection carried on for its own sake helps to illuminate the actor's mind and, through it, to encourage or limit political action. Second, political philosophy helps make explicit for statesmen the relation between their knowledge of political things and their action, the dilemma confronting them, and the ethical problem involved in the political act. Seeking to reconcile the dispassionate contemplation of the philosopher and the practical art of the statesman, Morgenthau wrote: "The sum total of such reflections constitutes a political philosophy in substance; for these relations seek in an issues-oriented form the same kind of coherent theoretical understanding which is the obvious aim of systematic philosophies. They try to compensate for the lack of . . . systematization with their avoidance of . . . the more obvious ideological and utopian temptations and with their direct relevance for the political concerns of the times."[51] In an attempt to speak the truth to power, he assessed political action not by the levels of expediency but according to certain higher standards and principles that are true but can never be fully realized in practice.

DEMOCRATIC VALUES AND THE AMERICAN NATIONAL PURPOSE

At a time when philosophers and pundits decry the poverty of American higher learning and the pervasive moral indifference eroding a public commitment to the commonweal, partisans to this national debate in the 1990s might profit from Morgenthau's writing on the American national purpose and the contemporary crisis of democratic government. That his published and unpublished works in this realm have been largely neglected by other commentators does him injustice on several counts. First, these sources vindicate Morgenthau from the egregious allegation that his political thought is archetypical of the traditional conservative regard for power in the service of individual conformity and societal order. Second, the oversight has led to the erroneous belief that Morgenthau calculated the national interest in foreign-policy conduct on the exclusive basis of how power is distributed among states in the international arena. Finally, Morgenthau's statement of America's purpose, if not conclusive, does illustrate that he did not summarily cast aside the natural-law tradition in American constitutional thought.

The contemporary crisis of American government, Morgenthau asserted, is a crisis of the national purpose. In *The Purpose of American Politics*, he substantiates the thesis that "the immediate objectives of our policies . . . have lost the organic connection with the innermost purposes of the nation." Morgenthau took exception to those cynics who view the idea of the national purpose as a political ideology to which nothing corresponds in verifiable experience. To reason in such a fashion risks confounding the abuse of reality with reality itself. Philosophy and religion, both integral for a statement of America's distinctive purpose, "are

51. Tang Tsou, "Scientific Man vs. Power Politics Revisited," in Thompson and Myers (eds.), *Truth and Tragedy*, 46; Hans J. Morgenthau, *The Restoration of American Politics* (Chicago, 1962), 2. Vol. III of Morgenthau, *Politics in the Twentieth Century*.

not figments of the imagination or artifacts of deception, but express in rational or symbolic terms the reality of an inner experience, which is not less real for not being of the senses." In order to comprehend the reality of the national purpose, "it is necessary to consult the evidence of history as our minds reflect upon it." Moreover, Morgenthau realized that the great nations and civilizations worthy of our remembrance have contributed to the affairs of men more than the successful defense and promotion of their national interests. The reality of the American purpose, then, can be found in the political and social history of the nation, in a continuum of actions and policies that reveal a common and unique pattern pointing to a common and unique purpose.[52]

Morgenthau's appraisal of the American purpose takes the form of a historical inquiry into divergent national ideals that nevertheless testify or point to a distinctive experience. Two contradictory conceptions of the national purpose were operative at the very threshold of American history. Speaking for the Anti-Federalists at the Federal Convention, Charles Pinckney limited the task of American government to the development of democratic institutions in order to ensure the happiness of all citizens. "Our true situation appears to me to be this.—a new extensive Country containing within itself the materials for forming a Government capable to extending to its citizens all the blessings of civil & religious liberty—capable to making them happy at home. This is the great end of Republican Establishments. We mistake the object of our government, if we hope or wish that it is to make us respectable abroad." Arguing for the Federalists, Alexander Hamilton maintained that the very purpose of assuring happiness required strength abroad. "It has been said that respectability in the eyes of foreign Nations was not the object at which we aimed; that the proper object of republican Government was domestic tranquility & happiness. This was an ideal distinction. No Governmt. could give us tranquility & happiness at home, which did not possess sufficient stability and strength to make us respectable abroad."[53]

Neither of these conceptions, however, was distinctive with American statesmen. For example, Morgenthau noted that the components of Pinckney's world view stem from classical Greek philosophy with its em-

52. Morgenthau, *The Purpose of American Politics*, 3, 8.
53. Max Farrand (ed.), *The Records of the Federal Convention of 1787* (New Haven, 1911), I, 402, 466–67.

phasis on the good life, from the apolitical individualism of the Roman Stoics, and from the modern liberal spirit proclaiming the primacy of domestic over foreign policy. Similarly, Hamilton's view of the national purpose "simply applies the European tradition of reason of state to the American scene." Moreover, the exalted vision of America as the "chosen people" can "be traced to Puritan England, to which an identical mission was attributed in identical terms." The new, or distinctive, aspect shaping the American purpose was "not the idea but the environment, and from the impact of a new environment upon old ideas grew the originality and uniqueness of American political philosophy." This philosophy looked to America as the expression of certain objective truths to which both the cosmic order and human society were thought to owe their existence. That order, as Morgenthau noted, was conceived in both religious and secular terms. "The religious order ran the gamut from English High Church through puritanism to the Quakers, and the rational order was received through the teachings of the Romans, Locke, and the French Encyclopedists." These established beliefs "were not so much transformed in substance as infused by a new spirit and endowed with a new quality by two peculiarly American experiences: the equalitarian conditions of society and the absence of serious competition from abroad."[54]

To maintain that achievement in "equality of freedom" within the United States has been the fundamental and minimal purpose of America. To have substantive meaning, however, equality (*i.e.*, equal access to political rule) and freedom (*i.e.*, freedom from permanent political rule) must be related to some transcendent purpose derived from some conception of an objective order. For example, how is the commitment to equality qualified by the principle of merit and the commitment to freedom by the requirements of societal order? To these questions, Morgenthau concluded that no single answer can be given. The American purpose "consists not in a specific substantive ideal and achievement but in a peculiar mode of procedure, a peculiar way of thinking and acting in the social sphere, in a peculiar conception of the relations between the individual and society." On the procedural aspect of the American purpose and how it has been related historically to a variety of substantive norms, Morgenthau wrote: "The persistence of that variety is accounted

54. Morgenthau, *The Purpose of American Politics*, 17–18.

for by the natural environment and the principle of equality of freedom. The natural environment made for a diffusion of power which precluded the victory of one conception of order over all others, and the very principle of equality in freedom, applied to the realms of religious faith and philosophic conviction, encouraged and sanctioned their variety. . . . The assumption of such a substantive, transcendent, and objective order, however conceived, gives meaning to the American experience of equality in freedom."[55]

The problematic, if not unresolved, element in Morgenthau's judgment is whether he can draw a clear and meaningful distinction between changing substantive formulations of the national purpose and the enduring, or transcendent, principles from which such substantive expressions arise. In what sense do the transcendent principles impact upon the process by which the political actor is forced to make proximate and discriminate political judgments? For example, the formal principles of equality and freedom have received meaning through the invocation and application of substantive principles of justice to the issues of the day, such as slavery, state sovereignty, or social reform. The general principle of social justice is immutable, but particular circumstances give it content. Yet, in equating consent with the fundamentals of political society without which government could not function, he acknowledged that "it is only the rules of the game that are not subject to change." In this category Morgenthau included such principles as succession to power, rule of law, fair play, checks and balances, and judicial review.[56] From where do these norms, even if only as regulative principles, receive their content? Morgenthau assumed that America's pluralism goes hand in hand with the relativist attitude toward political truth; however, his argument is less illuminating on how transcendent principles, or self-evident truths, can contribute to a view of the public interest and harmonize competing interests and representations of the national purpose.

This last issue is particularly important in light of Morgenthau's observations on the contemporary crisis and challenges to the American

55. *Ibid.*, 20–22.
56. Morgenthau, "Notes on Political Theory" (TS in Morgenthau Papers, Box 80), 5.

national purpose. The dynamic process by which America's aspiration for equality in freedom was tested and renewed over time by a number of social and economic crises has been replaced by conformity as the integrating principle of American society. By ultimately identifying the status quo with material well-being, the hedonism of production and the disappearance of great issues from the political scene lead to the decline of objective standards of excellence. In the popular mind, nothing precedes and transcends society; whatever exists in the social sphere has been created by society itself. From these preferences, Morgenthau noted, "there is no appeal to a higher law, rational or moral, aesthetic or economic, political or religious. Man-in-the-mass, the majority of men in a given society at a given time, become the measure of all things." On the loss of those objective criteria from which civilized man has learned to distinguish a work of art from trash, a good man from a scoundrel, Morgenthau wrote: "What the crowd desires and tolerates becomes the ultimate standard of what is good, true, beautiful, useful and wise. What you can get away with . . . is morally permitted; what you can get accepted in the market place, to paraphrase the . . . saying of Holmes, becomes the test of truth; art is what people like; what can be sold is useful." [57]

Concomitant with the eclipse of a public realm based upon objective standards of universal validity has been the degeneration of representative democracy into a majoritarian tyranny. In consequence, the pluralistic variety of objective standards by which each political action can be judged according to its merits is replaced with the monistic and formal standard of the individual will. The supreme dual paradox of contemporary democracy, Morgenthau argued, is that the expansion of democratic methods goes hand in hand with the recession of actual popular control of government and that this decline in the power of the people is not compensated for by a corresponding increase in the power of government. Suggesting that we are in the presence of a new feudalism, Morgenthau described how governmental power "is being arrogated by numerous semi-autonomous public and private agencies, business enterprises, and labor unions." Morgenthau judged as obsolete the reassuring simplicity of the formula for preserving freedom at the core of the Manchester *laissez-faire* liberalism: diminish the power of the state by law or

57. Morgenthau, *The Purpose of American Politics*, 59–64, 225–28.

social arrangements and thereby increase the sphere of individual liberty. Individual liberties of today, however, are threatened not only by a strong government, but also by concentrations of private power, by private governments that the public government has great difficulty in controlling and regulating. Morgenthau stated the central dilemma of modern government in the following terms: "A government too weak to threaten the freedom of the individual is also too weak to hold its own against the new feudalism; and a government strong enough to keep the new feudalism in check in order to protect the freedom of the many is also strong enough to destroy the freedom of all."[58]

In discussing the restoration of the national purpose, Morgenthau points to a solution that embraces both the traditions of realism and natural law. In one respect, he suggests that these tasks can best be met by relying upon "what Machiavelli called *virtù* and *fortuna*. The one, the quality of our wills and minds, is in our hands; the other, the benevolence of fate, is beyond our reach." Specifically, Morgenthau looked to the decisive leadership of a strong president who could have an impact upon the consciousness of the nation by restoring the government's ability to act, and of the people's ability to control in a polity committed to the rule of law. Once again returning to the indispensability of some operative conception of an objective order in which all rational humans participate, Morgenthau agreed that "private happiness is a function of public happiness—that is, of the public welfare—and that in terms of both the allocation of resources and resolution of conflicts the public power must take precedence." Consider also the following statement on the meaning of morality offered in reference to the Van Doren scandal at Columbia in 1959: "The moral law is not made for the convenience of man, rather it is an indispensable precondition for his civilized existence. It is one of the great paradoxes of civilized existence that, in contrast to the existence of animals and barbarians—it is not self-contained but requires for its fulfillment transcendent orientations."[59] One would expect a Machiavelli to deny this point and argue that politics can be most successful when it ignores transcendent reality and the demands made by it

58. Hans J. Morgenthau, "The Future of Freedom," n.d. (TS in Morgenthau Papers, Box 110), 1–7; "Our Thwarted Republic," *Commentary,* XXX (June, 1960), 473–82.

59. Morgenthau, *The Purpose of American Politics,* 311–23, 358.

upon men. Precisely how Morgenthau would combine the two traditions, at least in a way that would be different from what Walter Lippmann had to say in *The Public Philosophy*, is a debatable proposition.

THE DILEMMA OF SCIENTIFIC MAN

Noteworthy also was Morgenthau's powerful dissent from almost all of the prevailing beliefs shaping the theory and practice of contemporary social science. His *Scientific Man* was much more than a narrow treatise on methodology; rather, it sought to evaluate the many philosophic currents that brought the scientific study of social phenomena into being. Perhaps more than any subsequent publication, this brief and contentious work constitutes the core of Morgenthau's contribution to political philosophy and statecraft in the United States.

Referring to the rise and fall of the Roman Empire, Morgenthau found that the political crisis confronting the West in the first half of the twentieth century resided in "the general decay in the political thinking of the Western world." Specifically, Morgenthau took exception to "the belief in the power of science to solve all problems and, more particularly, all political problems which confront man in the modern age."[60] The underlying philosophy of modern Western civilization (whether in the guise of rationalism, scientism, liberalism, or pacifism) sought answers for the great human problems with abstract mechanical formulas, blind to the fact of evil still at work in the world and, therefore, disarmed by it. Morgenthau's critique built on three interrelated components: (1) to indicate how this belief in the redeeming powers of science is misplaced; (2) to point to the elements in philosophic and political thought from which this belief has arisen; and (3) to identify those intellectual and moral faculties of man to which alone the problems of the social world will yield.

Morgenthau's sweeping and often loosely worded indictment of the social and political philosophy of modern Western thought was based on a number of derivative and corollary ideas, which may be summarized briefly.

First, the modern philosophy of rationalism is rooted in two erroneous assumptions: the conception of the social and physical world as being intelligible through the same rational processes, and the conviction

60. Morgenthau, *Scientific Man*, vi.

that understanding in terms of these processes is all that is needed for the rational control of the social and physical world. The practical cognition of physical nature consists of a multitude of isolated facts over which human action has complete control. That the same kind of knowledge and control holds true for the social world has often found expression in the "method of the single cause"—the tendency of the social sciences and contemporary political thought to reduce the contingencies of human existence to simple chains of cause and effect, after the model of the natural sciences. Morgenthau cited William Graham Sumner, who stipulated that "social science is still in the stage that chemistry was in when people believed in a philosopher's stone, or medicine, when they believed in a panacea, or physiology, when they believed in a fountain of youth, or an elixir of life." [61]

Second, the rationalist mode of thought supports a philosophical structure that gives the appearance of yielding eternal verities to certain anthropological, social, and political assumptions that are true, if at all, under the conditions of a particular historic experience. The principles of scientific reason are always simple, consistent, and abstract; by contrast, man's political and social existence is always complicated, incongruous, and concrete. Whereas the natural sciences concentrate on isolated causes operating upon motionless objects, the social observer must come to terms with interminable chains of causes and effects, each of which is the cause of another reacting effect. Morgenthau never denied the legitimate tasks of empirical social or political theory so much as he emphasized the limits of scientific investigation of social causation among the vast number of tangible and intangible variables shaping the manifold relations of groups and nations. Under such circumstances, "the social sciences can, at best, do what is their regular task, that is, present a series of hypothetical possibilities, each of which may occur under certain conditions—and which of them will actually occur is anybody's guess." Morgenthau viewed politics as an art and not a science; the wisdom and moral strength of the statesman takes precedence over the calculating rationality of the engineer. The social world yields only to that fragile combination of moral and material pressures that the art of the statesman creates and maintains. Morgenthau quoted Burke who, in his "Speech on

61. William Graham Sumner, "Liberty and Responsibility," in *Earth Hunger and Other Essays* (New Haven, 1913), 218.

the Petition of the Unitarians," remarked: "A statesman differs from a professor in a university; the latter has only the general view of society; the former . . . has a number of circumstances to combine with those general ideas, and to take into consideration. Circumstances are . . . variable and transient; he who does not take them into consideration is not erroneous, but stark mad,—*dat operam ut cum ratione insaniat,*—he is metaphysically mad. A statesman, never losing sight of principles, is to be guided by circumstances; and, judging contrary to the exigencies of the moment, he may ruin his country forever."[62]

Third, modern liberal reason misunderstands both the nature of man and his political existence. It does not see that man's nature has three dimensions: biological, spiritual, and rational. By neglecting the biological and spiritual facets, it misconstrues the function reason fulfills within the whole of human existence, distorts the problem of ethics, and perverts the natural sciences into an instrument of social salvation. The failure of dogmatic scientism results from an inability to recognize that the irrational pursuit of self-interest and power is inseparable from social life itself. The key to the laws of man is not in the facts from whose uniformity the sciences derive their laws; rather, "it is in the insight and the wisdom by which the more-than-scientific man elevates his experiences into the universal laws of human nature."[63] In order to eliminate from the political sphere not power politics—which is beyond the ability of any political philosophy—but the destructiveness of power politics, rational faculties are needed that are different from, yet superior to, the reason of the scientific age.

Fourth, the epistemological orientation of modern rationalism treats the social scientist as a detached, passive observer of social events, but this obscures the impact of "purposive action" and "the creative influence of the human mind" on the initial stages of knowing the social world. Morgenthau noted that the relationship between the mind and the physical world is not exclusively cognitive even when the mind confronts nature for the limited purpose of perception. Testifying to how the qualities of the mind must be reflected in the picture we have of nature, Sir James Jeans wrote: "We saw nineteenth century science trying to explore nature

---

62. Hans J. Morgenthau, "The Limitations of Science and the Problem of Social Planning," *Ethics*, LIV (October, 1943), 175–76; Morgenthau, *Scientific Man*, 220–21.
63. *Ibid.*

as the explorer explores the desert from an aeroplane. The uncertainty principle makes it clear that nature cannot be explored in this detached way; we can only explore it by tramping over it and disturbing it."[64] Nature is subject to human action; it is the human mind that actually creates it, and the creation must bear witness to the quality of the creator. The human mind fulfills the same function for the social world insofar as the social scientist stands in the streams of social causation as an acting and reacting agent. Describing the essential unity of the natural and social sciences, Max Planck wrote:

> The most impressive proof that the individual will is independent of the law of causality will be found if the attempt is made to determine in advance the subject's own motives and actions on the sole basis of the law of causality—by a method of intense introspection. Such an attempt is condemned to failure in advance because every application of the law of causality to the will of the individual and every information gained in this way is itself a motive of acting upon the will, so that the result which is being looked for is continually being changed. . . . This impossibility of foretelling the subject's actions on purely causal lines is not based on any lack of knowledge, but on the simple fact that no method by whose application the object is essentially altered can be suitable for the study of this object.[65]

Fifth, the modern science of peace operates on the assumption of a world that is rational throughout and that contains all the elements necessary for the harmonious cooperation of mankind. For rationalism, international relations reveal their true nature in the harmony of interests, which is still temporarily deprived of its beneficial effects by the atavism of power politics. Conflicts among nations are the result of maladjustments arising from lack of understanding and the influence of ideological passions. Recounting the blessings of scientific reason in the international arena, Proudhon observed: "Truth is everywhere identical with itself: science represents the unity of mankind. If therefore science, instead of religion or authority, is taken in each country . . . as the sovereign arbiter of interests . . . all the laws of the universe will be in harmony. Nationality

64. Sir James Jeans, *The New Background of Science* (New York, 1933), 235.
65. Max Planck, *The Philosophy of Physics* (New York, 1936), 79–80.

or fatherland will no longer exist in the political meaning of the term; there will only be birthplaces. . . . Harmony will reign among the nations, without diplomacy nor council; nothing from now on shall disturb it." According to C. E. M. Joad, "The duty of the pacifist today is above all things to be reasonable. He should . . . rely on the use of his own reason in making his appeal and he should assume that other men may be brought to theirs. . . . Truth . . . will win out, if people are only given a sufficient chance to find it."[66] Territorial claims, sovereignty over national minorities, the distribution of raw materials, the struggle for markets, disarmament, the relation between "haves" and "have nots," peaceful change, and the peaceful organization of the world in general—these are not political problems to be solved temporarily and always precariously on the basis of the distribution of power among competing nations. They are "technical" problems for which reason will find one—the correct— solution, to the exclusion of all others—the incorrect ones.

Sixth, truly successful and rational social action is impossible without a knowledge "of the eternal laws by which man moves in the social world." The Aristotelian truth "that man is a political animal is true forever; the truths of the natural sciences are true only until other truths have supplanted them."[67] Political wisdom, therefore, builds on two experiences—one intellectual, the other moral. The intellectual experience is doubt about the meaning of history in terms of its recurrent and unique elements. The moral dilemma results from the tendency of man to claim for his position in history more in terms of his moral dignity than he is entitled to. The position of the political actor is morally ambivalent, and that ambivalence, in conjunction with the logic inherent in the political act, corrupts his moral judgment.

A REALIST POLITICAL PHILOSOPHY

Morgenthau's intellectual perspective, by contrast, attempted to provide a foundation for systematic political inquiry as well as a normative guide for the practicing statesman. A realist political philosophy, he believed, is distinguished by several important principles. First, the realist

---

66. Pierre Joseph Proudhon, "Idée générale de la révolution au dix-neuvième siecle," in *Oeuvres Completes* (Paris, 1868), X, 300; C. E. M. Joad, "Pacifism: Its Personal and Social Implications," in G. P. Gooch (ed.), *In Pursuit of Peace* (London, 1933), 61, 63.
67. Morganthau, *Scientific Man vs. Power Politics*, 220.

believes that politics forms an "autonomous" field of behavior and inquiry. Against those who would apply natural-science methods to the
study of political behavior, the realist holds that the historic arena—the
human universe—is essentially different from the natural universe. The
political theorist is one who thinks in terms of interest defined as power,
as the economist thinks in terms of interest defined as wealth; the law-
yer, of the conformity of action with legal rules; the moralist, of the conformity of action with ethical principles. The concept of power allows
the observer "to distinguish politics from other social spheres, to orient
himself in the maze of empirical phenomena which make up the field,
and to establish a measure of rational order within it." [68]

Second, a realist theory of politics evolves from certain philosophical conceptions about the human condition and political society. Perhaps
with some oversimplification, Morgenthau reduces the history of Western
political thought to the story of a contest between two schools that differ
in their conception of man, society, and politics. One—the horizon of
political idealism—assumes the essential goodness and infinite malleability of human nature; it blames the failure of the social order to measure up to the rational standards of a progressive society on lack of
knowledge and antiquated institutions. The idealist in politics is inclined
to place his optimistic faith in education, reform, and a minimum reliance on the instrumentalities of power and coercion. By contrast, the
tradition of political realism acknowledges that forces inherent in human
nature prevent man from achieving a thoroughly rational or moral political order. [69] The realist views man as a self-interested creature whose
ego is inevitably contaminated by the propensity for sin and evil. In seeking fundamental political changes, the statesman must work with those
forces, not against them. Integral to the realist world view is the primary
assumption that power conflicts are an ineradicable feature of all political
relationships—more so perhaps among nation-states than any other level
of political intercourse.

Morgenthau's pessimism was a function of his beliefs concerning
the omnipresence of the lust for power or the universal desire of the self
to dominate others. To the extent that politics can be defined as the exercise of power over man, politics is rooted in evil in that it degrades and

68. Morgenthau, *Dilemmas of Politics*, 39.
69. Morgenthau, *Politics Among Nations*, 3–4.

relegates man to a means for other men. Yet Morgenthau did distinguish between human selfishness and the ubiquitous impulse to power. The typical goals of human selfishness (*e.g.*, food, shelter, and existence) have an objective relation to the survival needs of the individual; their acquisition represents the prerequisites for survival under the particular natural and social conditions in which man lives. On the other hand, the desire for power concerns itself mainly with man's position among his fellows once survival has been achieved. Whereas the selfishness of man has objective limits, his will to power has none. "For here," as Morgenthau insisted, "the *animus dominandi* is not merely blended with dominant aims of a different kind but is the . . . essence of the intention . . . the constitutive principle of politics as a distinct sphere of activity."[70]

Third, the realist believes that politics is governed by objective laws that have their roots in human nature. For realists the possibility exists, therefore, of developing a rational theory of politics that reflects, however imperfectly, these objective laws. Moreover, any theory of politics must be submitted to the dual tests of reason and experience. For Morgenthau, the concept of power "provides a kind of rational outline of politics, a map of the political scene." In commenting on the rational requirements of any political theory, he observed: "Such a map does not provide a complete description of the political landscape as it is in any particular period of history. It . . . provides the timeless features of its geography distinct from their ever-changing historic setting. . . . A theory of politics, by the . . . fact of painting a rational picture of the political scene, points to the contrast between what the political scene actually is and what it tends to be, but can never completely become."[71]

The struggle for power by both men and nations in a wide variety of historic settings supplies the nexus between reason trying to understand politics and the facts to be understood. In expounding his theory of international politics, Morgenthau exhorted the student to assume the position of the statesman who is called upon to meet a certain problem of foreign policy under specific circumstances. In so doing, "we ask our-

70. Morgenthau, *Dilemmas of Politics*, 247; *Scientific Man*, 192–93.

71. Morgenthau, *Dilemmas of Politics*, 39; *The Decline of Democratic Politics*, 48; "International Relations: Common Sense and Theories," *Journal of International Affairs*, XXI (1967), 207–14.

selves what the rational alternatives are from which a statesman may choose who must meet this problem under these circumstances . . . and which of these rational alternatives this particular statesman . . . is likely to choose." [72] It is the testing of this rational hypothesis against the actual facts and their consequences that imparts meaning to the patterns of international political behavior. The validity of a realist theory, Morgenthau believed, does not hinge on its strict conformity to preestablished methodological criteria; rather, it is subject only to the "pragmatic" requirement that it broaden our knowledge and deepen our understanding of what is worth knowing.

Fourth, Morgenthau's theory of international politics also contains a normative element. The political realist values the rational elements of political action for practical reasons: Political realism assumes that a rational foreign policy is, of necessity, *good* foreign policy. It minimizes risks and maximizes benefits and, hence, complies with the moral precept of prudence and the political requirement of success. [73] In short, a realist theory of international politics offers not only a guide to understanding but an ideal for action.

Fifth, realism treats the concept of interest defined as power as an objective category that is universally valid, but it does not endow the concept with a meaning that is fixed once and for all. Morgenthau observed that the significance of interest in state relations is surpassed by the variety of configurations through which man transforms the abstract concept of the national interest into foreign policy. Taken in isolation, the determination of a nation's interest in a concrete situation is relatively simple: it encompasses the integrity of a nation's territory and political institutions, and of its culture. However, an objective determination of a foreign policy designed to ensure national survival in a particular period depends on the specific mix of political and cultural factors impacting on the decision-making process. Morgenthau repeatedly warned: "While the realist . . . believes that interest is the perennial standard by which political action must be directed, the contemporary connection between interest and the nation state is a product of history, and is . . . bound to disappear. Nothing in the realist position militates against the assumption

72. Morgenthau, *Politics Among Nations,* 5.
73. *Ibid.,* 8.

that the present division of the . . . world into nation states will be replaced by larger units . . . more in keeping with the . . . potentialities and
the moral prerequisites of the contemporary world."[74]

Sixth, political realism holds that multiple factors affect moral reasoning and that "universal principles cannot be applied to the actions of
states in their abstract . . . formulation, but . . . must be filtered through
the concrete circumstances of time and place." Therefore, in a hostile
world arena, moral principles can never be fully realized, but can only be
approximated through the temporary balancing of interests and the precarious settlement of conflicts.[75] As will be discussed at some length in
the pages that follow, Morgenthau avoided a conception of ethical dualism segregating the morality of man from that of the state. Yet, and in
giving expression to perhaps the high paradox in the history of political
ethics, he acknowledged that the standard (or criterion) of judgment for
moral man is different from the requirements of political morality governing state behavior. Whereas the individual may justly claim the right
to self-sacrifice in defense of moral law, the state has no right to let its
moral disapprobation get in the way of successful political action. The
operative moral strategy for politics, then, is to choose the lesser evil and
minimize the intrinsic immorality of the political act.

Finally, political realism does not identify "the moral aspirations
of a particular nation with the moral laws that govern the universe."
Morgenthau held that crusading and pretentious idealism contains two
principal defects. On the one hand, the idealist falls victim to world-
embracing ideals which, because of their vagueness and generality, can
provide no national guidance for resolving concrete political problems.
On the other, the idealist dresses parochial interests in the garb of universal moral principles and then presumes that the rest of the world, in
refusing to grant his policy cosmic righteousness, is *ipso facto* less moral
(or rational) than he.[76] Alternatively, Morgenthau stipulated that the national interest itself commands a certain moral dignity, because it func-

74. Kenneth W. Thompson, "Moral Reasoning in American Thought on War and
Peace," *Review of Politics*, XLIX (July, 1977), 392. See also Morgenthau, *Dilemmas of
Politics*, 68–69; *Politics Among Nations*, 10.

75. See also Hans J. Morgenthau, "National Interest and Moral Principles in Foreign Policy," *American Scholar*, XVIII (Spring, 1949), 210–12.

76. Morgenthau, *Politics Among Nations*, 10–11; "National Interest and Moral
Principles in Foreign Policy," 207, 211; *In Defense of the National Interest*, 35.

tions as the protector of minimal world values in a world lacking order and moral consensus beyond the bounds of the national state.

Morgenthau's observations on a just world community and operative supranational values in relations between states raise a number of problematic questions, not the least of which was his judgment of *raison d'état* as a basis for American diplomacy both past and present. Although this theme will be explored at greater length in Chapter 4, it will be useful to introduce his approach to the moral dilemma of international politics. At a minimum, Morgenthau's thought exhibited a curious ambivalence regarding the gap between national interest and viable norms transcending state interest.

In a more pessimistic assessment, Morgenthau once wrote: "There is a profound and neglected truth hidden in Hobbes' extreme dictum that the state creates morality as well as law and that there is neither morality nor law outside the state." Universal moral principles, such as justice and equality, apply to concrete situations only in the measure in which they are given content by a particular society. Specifically, Morgenthau doubted the existence of acceptable standards of justice and human rights in the absence of a politically and morally integrated international society. Reflecting on what has euphemistically been termed the "society of nations," Morgenthau remarked: "Not only are there no supranational moral principles concrete enough to give guidance to the political actions of . . . nations; there is also no agency on the international scene to promote the interests of the individual nations themselves. . . . If a nation is . . . to escape the Scylla of national suicide, the threat of which is ever present in the emphasis on moral principles to the neglect of national interest, it is likely to fall into the Charybdis of the crusading spirit which is the great destroyer of morality among nations."[77]

Yet, in opposition to those critics who have portrayed his international thought as Machiavellian or Hobbesian, Morgenthau retorted: "I have always maintained that the actions of states are subject to universal moral principles and I have been careful to differentiate my position . . .

---

77. Morgenthau, *Dilemmas of Politics*, 80–81; "National Interest and Moral Principles in Foreign Policy," 211. For an early refutation of Morgenthau's position, see A. H. Feller, "In Defense of International Law and Morality," *Annals of the American Academy of Political and Social Science*, No. 282 (July, 1952), 80.

from that of Hobbes." He consistently stressed that moral reasoning in the political sphere does not imply a simple choice between a moral principle and a standard of action that is morally irrelevant or even immoral. He wrote: "Moral rules do not permit certain policies to be considered at all from the point of view of expediency. Such ethical inhibitions operate in our time on different levels and with different effectiveness. Their restraining function is most obvious . . . in affirming the sacredness of human life in times of peace."[78] Although Morgenthau hoped to distance American political realism from European *raison d'état*, the question remains as to the exact relation of interest to norms transcending interest.

78. See J. E. Hare and Carey B. Joynt, *Ethics and International Affairs* (New York, 1982), 34–42. See also Morgenthau, *Dilemmas of Politics*, 81; *Politics Among Nations*, 231; "The Machiavellian Utopia," *Ethics*, LV (January, 1945), 145–47; *Scientific Man*, Chaps. 7, 8; "Views of Nuremberg: Further Analysis of the Trial and Its Importance," *America*, December 7, 1946, pp. 266–67; and "The Twilight of International Morality," *Ethics*, LVIII (January, 1948), 79–99.

CHAPTER THREE

A Realist Theory of International Politics

The rise to prominence of American political realism following two world wars generated a distinctive intellectual orientation and approach to the study of international relations. As the previous chapters emphasized, the realist world view was informed by philosophical convictions regarding the nature of man, his existence in political society, and the moral problem in a decentralized world of sovereign nation-states. More so than his predecessors, however, Morgenthau used the philosophical and moral resources of realism in order to specify the limitations and prospects of a theory of international politics. His attention focused on such objectives as identifying key concepts and categories of analysis; weighing the impact of science, philosophy, and ethics on generalization about international political behavior; and stipulating the intellectual and political functions a theory of international relations ought to perform.

For Morgenthau, the calculus of the national interest functions as the central concept for a theory of international politics. "All successful statesmen of modern times from Richelieu to Churchill," he wrote, "have made the national interest the ultimate standard of their policies, and none of the great moralists in international affairs has attained his goals." In international politics, the national interest is shaped by the "struggle for power . . . for national advantage."[1] Idealistic detractors of the na-

---

1. Morgenthau, *In Defense of the National Interest*, 34.

tional interest jeopardize the welfare and security of the nation by failing to act on the fundamental lesson of all diplomatic history: a foreign policy based upon moral abstractions without consideration of the national interest is bound to fail, for it accepts a standard of conduct alien to the nature of the action. Self-preservation for individuals and societies is both a biological and psychological necessity; in the international realm, the attainment of a modicum of order and the realization of a minimum of moral principles are contingent upon the existence of national communities capable of preserving order and realizing moral values within the limits of their power. For general purposes, Morgenthau's observations on the importance of national interest in world politics can be evaluated according to problems of definition and classification, American diplomatic history and competing versions of American national interest, and the norms and purpose of American national interest in a changing postwar global setting.

American Diplomatic History and the National Interest in World Affairs

Morgenthau refused to consider the national interest as a static, self-evident principle of statecraft whose formulation is immune from the complex interaction of domestic and external influences on the decision-making process in foreign policy. Like the "great generalities" in the United States Constitution (*e.g.*, due process and general welfare), the concept of the national interest "contains residual meaning . . . inherent in the concept itself, but beyond these minimum requirements its content can run the whole gamut of meanings that are logically compatible with it."[2] Therefore, the meaning of the national interest is affected by the political traditions and the overall cultural context within which a nation formulates its foreign policy.

Morgenthau clearly emphasized that the concept of national interest contains two elements: one that is logically necessary and relatively permanent, and one that is variable according to changing circumstances.[3] The permanent "hard core" of the national interest stems from three criteria: (1) the nature of the interests to be defended; (2) the inter-

2. Morgenthau, *Dilemmas of Politics*, 65.
3. *Ibid.*, 66.

national milieu within which the interests operate; and (3) the rational necessities limiting the choice of means and ends by all foreign-policy actors. The survival of the political identity of the nation is the irreducible minimum, the necessary element of its interests vis-à-vis other nations. In a global setting where a number of sovereign nations compete for power, the foreign policies of all nations strive to protect their physical, political, and cultural identity against the aggressive designs of rival forces. Moreover, Morgenthau stipulated that the nature of the threat to which the hard core is exposed remains relatively constant over long periods of time. For example, the chief threat to Great Britain has resided in hegemonic aspirations of one or more European nations. Russian security has been threatened by a great power having uncontested access to the plains of eastern Europe. The successful defense of American national interest has encompassed such goals as unrivaled American superiority in the Western Hemisphere and preserving a balance of power in both Europe and Asia.[4] Bipartisanship in foreign policy, especially in times of war, has been most easily achieved in the promotion of these minimum requirements of the national interest.

The rational character of the national interest derives from the reasoning by which the statesman translates abstract goals into concrete foreign-policy options. Governments throughout history attempted to uphold a nation's core interests by pursuing such policies as competitive armaments, balance-of-power tactics, defensive alliances, and subversion. In commenting on the relation between rational necessities of foreign policy (*i.e.*, selecting one of a limited number of alternatives through which to bring the nation's power to bear upon the power of other nations) and the universal character of the national interest, Morgenthau remarked: "It is this assumption of universality of the national interest in time and space which enables us to understand the foreign policies of Demosthenes and Caesar, Kautilya and Henry VIII, of the contemporary statesmen of Russia and China. Regardless of all the differences in personality . . . and environment, their thinking was predetermined . . . when they were faced with . . . protecting . . . the rational core of the national interest." In brief, Morgenthau calculated that the rational char-

4. Hans J. Morgenthau, *The Impasse of American Foreign Policy* (Chicago, 1962), 56–58. Vol. II of Morgenthau, *Politics in the Twentieth Century*; Morgenthau, *Dilemmas of Politics*, 69.

acter of the national interest could be detected and understood by thinking as the statesman must have thought and by theorists "putting their
thoughts into the context of their personalities and social environment."[5]

With regard to the variable elements of the national interest, identifying the content and range of a nation's goals becomes more problematic. Morgenthau pointed to the difficulty of measuring accurately all the
crosscurrents of personalities, public opinion, sectional interests, partisan
politics, moral folkways, and transnational loyalties that impact on the
formulation of a nation's interest at any one time. The national interest
can function as a meaningful standard in foreign policy only if nations
and statesmen impose some hierarchical and rational order upon the values that make up the national interest and among the limited resources
committed to them. Against those critics who claim that he treated the
national interest as a purely self-evident diplomatic norm, Morgenthau's
position was clear: "While the interests which a nation may pursue in its
relation with other nations are of infinite variety and magnitude, the resources which are available for the pursuit of such interests are necessarily limited in quantity and kind." In fact, Morgenthau's position parallels
the essence of Walter Lippmann's classic observation that a workable foreign policy "consists in bringing into balance, with a comfortable surplus
of power in reserve, the nation's commitments and the nation's power."[6]

The precondition for this rational assessment, according to Morgenthau, "is a clear understanding of the distinction between the necessary and variable elements of the national interest." Especially in democratic countries, where the variable elements of the national interest tend
to be the subject of contentious debate, those advocating an extensive
conception of the national interest often present certain variable elements
as though their attainment were necessary for a nation's survival and
well-being. For example, a nation's security may be invoked to rationalize
unqualified support for such variable foreign-policy aims as the rearma-
ment of Germany, the rollback of communism, or the defense of Nationalist China. In making a distinction between the necessary and the desirable in foreign policy, a rational conception of the national interest
requires that all external objectives (actual or potential) be subjected

5. Morgenthau, *The Decline of Democratic Politics*, 92.
6. Morgenthau, *Dilemmas of Politics*, 69; Walter Lippmann, *U.S. Foreign Policy:
Shield of the Republic* (Boston, 1943), 8.

to scrutiny and assigned an approximate place in the scale of national values.[7]

Morgenthau reviewed both objective and subjective forces shaping the perception and actual conduct of American national interest in world affairs for over two centuries. His approach to the historical record of American diplomacy exhibited a number of recurrent themes that can be briefly identified. First, he emphasized that history represented an essential foundation for the study of international politics and foreign policy; indeed, historic events important for an understanding of international politics are generally manifestations of social and political forces that reflect the timeless principles of human nature. Second, his attempt to outline distinctive "phases" of American diplomatic history was largely based on the extent to which policy-makers justified American conduct abroad by reference to the permanent and variable elements of the national interest. In this respect, he took exception to those who sought to characterize the American national purpose as exempt from the self-interested pursuit of power and national advantage that shape the struggles of international life. Third, the national interest as a guide for foreign policy must be balanced, Morgenthau argued, by a realization of both qualitative and quantitative changes in world politics since the beginning of the twentieth century. Finally, in judging the prospects of a democratic foreign policy, he pointed to the relevance of the domestic political order (*e.g.*, public opinion, foreign-policy bureaucracy, relations between the executive and legislative branches) and its meaning for the limits and opportunities of American power in world affairs.

Morgenthau focused upon opposing realist and idealist conceptions of international politics in American experience. For example, the idea that "a nation can escape . . . from power politics into a realm where action is guided by moral principles rather than by considerations of power is deeply rooted in the American mind."[8] Standing for moral purposes beyond the state (*e.g.*, freedom and order, liberty and justice, economic growth and social equality), Americans have typically regarded the struggle for power as a social aberration—the result of ignorance, faulty institutional arrangements, or the suppression of the public voice. From

---

7. Morgenthau, *Dilemmas of Politics*, 74.

8. Morgenthau, *In Defense of the National Interest*, 23; "Outline and Notes for Contemporary Diplomatic Problems," 1950 (TS in Morgenthau Papers, Box 76), 1–10.

Washington's warning against "inveterate antipathies against particular nations and passionate attachments to others" to Wilson's Fourteen Points, the nation's identity was deeply involved with the assertion of universal human rights and political liberties. For well over a century of relative isolation from world politics, Americans resorted to that mixture of self-righteousness and genuine moral fervor in the expectation that their lofty moral example would shed enlightenment abroad. Commenting on the American inclination to invoke abstract moral principles to justify concrete national interests, Morgenthau wrote: "Wherever American foreign policy has operated, political thought has been divorced from political action. Even where our long range policies reflect . . . the true interests of the United States, we think about them in terms that have . . . a tenuous connection with the policies pursued. We have acted on the international scene, as all nations must, in power-political terms; but we have tended to conceive of our actions in non-political, moralistic terms."[9]

Morgenthau noted that it took over a century after the founding of the Republic for the illusion of American moral superiority to give way to a more sobering estimate of the nature of conflict and the causes of war in international politics. His belief in the enduring importance of power and self-interest in American foreign policy was based on the notion that "underneath this political dilettantism, nourished by improvidence and a sense of moral mission, there lives an almost instinctive awareness of the perennial interests of the United States."[10] On the basis of these two opposing conceptions, Morgenthau identified three periods of American foreign policy: (1) the realistic—thinking and acting in terms of power; (2) the ideological or utopian—thinking in terms of moral principle but acting in terms of power; and (3) the moralistic—thinking and acting in terms of moral principle. The division of American diplomatic history, however, referred only to general tendencies and did not preclude the simultaneous influence of different perspectives within the same period.

The classic age of American statecraft owed its existence to those qualities of political thought, historical perspective, and common sense that the first generation of Americans applied to government and foreign

9. *Ibid.*, 7.
10. *Ibid.*, 4.

affairs. Believing themselves to be the beneficiaries of the *novus ordo seclorum* imprinted on America and the world, the Founding Fathers were practical philosophers who succeeded in translating principles of transcendental justice into terms of personal and property rights. The constitutional debate between Federalist and Anti-Federalist factions touched upon the operative moral and political choices shaping the diplomacy of the young Republic.[11] Morgenthau praised the Federalist leadership of the 1790s for recognizing that the security of the United States was predicated upon the kind of power relationships that America would establish with other nations. In his "Pacificus" and "Americanus" essays, Hamilton defined the limits and responsibilities of American power in the context of Washington's proclamation of neutrality in the War of the First Coalition against revolutionary France. Thomas Jefferson and his Anti-Federalist supporters opposed the proclamation and sided with France by appealing to three standards derived from moral principles—faithfulness to treaty obligations, gratitude to France for its aid during the American Revolution, and the general affinity of republican institutions. Believing that the rule of morality is not the same between nations as between solitary individuals, Hamilton countered these claims by a direct appeal to the interest of the United States: "There would be no proportion between the mischiefs . . . to which the United States would expose themselves, by embarking in the war, and the benefit which the nature of their stipulation aims at securing to France. . . . Self-preservation is the first duty of a nation; and though in the performance of stipulations regarding . . . war, good faith requires that its ordinary hazards . . . be fairly met . . . yet it does not require that extraordinary and extreme hazards should be run."[12]

Hamilton's emphasis on American national interest was rooted in the conviction that the United States would gain little and risk everything by siding with France against almost all of Europe. Throughout the nineteenth century, Morgenthau stressed that Federalist principles and perceptions continued to express the underlying national interests and objec-

11. See Hans J. Morgenthau, "The Philosophy of American Foreign Policy," 1952–55 (TS in Morgenthau Papers, Box 76). For an authoritative account of diverse conceptions of law and ethics shaping the early American diplomatic heritage, see Daniel G. Lang, *Foreign Policy in the Early Republic: The Law of Nations and the Balance of Power* (Baton Rouge, 1985).

12. Morgenthau, *In Defense of the National Interest*, 14–15.

tives of the United States: military and political predominance in the Western Hemisphere; a balance of power in Europe; a balance of power in Asia based on an independent China; and an adequate military structure to protect such limited interests abroad. Fortunately, what the American moral mission demanded "was by a felicitous coincidence identical with what the national interest seemed to require."[13]

The ideological phase of American foreign policy began with Jefferson's accession to the presidency and lasted until the Spanish-American War at the close of the nineteenth century. In many public utterances, Jefferson's dedication to abstract morality contributed to his contempt for the European balance of power and support for the egalitarian aspirations associated with the French and American revolutionary causes. In opposition to Hamilton's distinction between the morality of states and the morality of individuals, Jefferson held to a uniform standard and wrote that the moral duties that exist between individuals in a state of nature "accompany them into a state of society, and the aggregate of the duties of all the individuals composing the society constitutes the duties of that society towards any other; so that between society and society the same moral rules exist as did between individuals composing them. . . . Compacts . . . between nation and nation are obligatory on them by the same moral law which obliges individuals to observe their compacts."[14] However, in his private letters during the final decade of the Napoleonic Wars, Jefferson's international thought pointed to the ever-changing distribution of power in the world rather than immutable moral principles. Speaking in 1812, when Napoleon was at the pinnacle of his power, Jefferson said: "We . . . ought to pray that the powers of Europe be so poised and counterpoised . . . that their own security may require the presence of all their forces at home, leaving the other quarters of the globe in undisturbed tranquility."[15] It was only after 1815, when Napoleon's defeat removed the French threat to the European balance, that Jefferson allowed himself to indulge in the cultivation of moral principles divorced from political exigencies.

13. Graebner, "Morgenthau as Historian," in Thompson and Myers (eds.), *Truth and Tragedy*, 73.

14. Thomas Jefferson, "Opinion on French Treaties," in Paul Ford (ed.), *The Works of Thomas Jefferson* (New York, 1905), VII, 285–86.

15. Graebner, "Morgenthau as Historian," in Thompson and Myers (eds.), *Truth and Tragedy*, 73–75.

Along somewhat different lines, John Quincy Adams represented "the classic example of the political moralist in thought and word, who cannot help being a realist in action." He judged the differences between the American colonies and Great Britain to be a struggle between right and wrong; similarly, during his tenure as secretary of state and president, the security objectives of the United States were often defined by arguments of a legal and democratic nature. Adams' contribution to American foreign policy—freedom of the seas, the Monroe Doctrine, and Manifest Destiny—constituted the harmonious synthesis of power and principle in the American political tradition. During the Adams Administration, the legal principle of freedom of the seas became a weapon to safeguard American independence from the British fleet; the principles of anti-imperialism and nonintervention in the Monroe Doctrine were a negative condition for the enduring greatness of the United States; and the idea of Manifest Destiny became a moral justification for the westward expansion of the United States.[16]

The third, and more moralistic, phase of American diplomacy began with American involvement in the Spanish-American War and reached its zenith in the political thought of Woodrow Wilson. Seeing the hand of God in America's decision to annex the Philippines, William McKinley, ignorant of the bearing of this step on the national interest, committed American power beyond the confines of the Western Hemisphere. Whereas McKinley expected and found no guidance in America's traditional national interests, Wilson's thought not only rejected the national interest but was explicitly opposed to it on moral grounds. As early as 1913, Wilson alluded to the moral failure of the national interest in world affairs: "We dare not turn from the principle that morality and not expediency . . . must guide us and that we will never condone inequity because it is . . . convenient to do so. . . . It is a very perilous thing to determine the foreign policy of a nation in . . . terms of national interest. It not only is unfair to those with whom you are dealing, but it is disregarding as regards your own actions."[17]

In his political actions during the Great War, however, Wilson could no more ignore the national interest than could Jefferson. Morgen-

16. Morgenthau, *In Defense of the National Interest*, 22–23.

17. Thomas A. Bailey, *A Diplomatic History of the American People* (New York, 1946), 604.

thau wrote: "It was only the objective force of the national interest, which no rational man could escape, that imposed the source of America's . . . danger upon him as the source of his moral indignation." In conceiving of American national interest in moral and legal terms, Wilson led the United States to war, not to secure the balance of power, but to protect international law and morality. Wilson failed at Versailles because he faced the Allied powers with moral principles to the neglect of the nation's historic interest in the politics of Europe. British Prime Minister Lloyd George observed: "The Americans appeared to assume responsibility for the sole guardianship of the Ten Commandments and the Sermon on the Mount; yet when it came to a practical question of . . . responsibility, they absolutely refused to accept it."[18]

Morgenthau's outlook on American foreign policy during the interwar years examined the impact of two forms of utopianism—isolationism and internationalism. By proclaiming the self-sufficiency of the United States in the Western Hemisphere and neglecting the rivalries of European nations, isolationists deluded themselves into believing that they were working for the restoration of the earlier realistic tradition of American diplomacy. The fallacy of isolationism, Morgenthau suggested, was in viewing isolation as a fact of nature, where freedom from entanglement in Europe followed from the mere act of abstention. By contrast, the early political realists treated isolation as an objective of policy, resulting from both political conditions outside the Western Hemisphere and policies contrived and executed in their support. Indeed, "isolationism empties of all . . . political content the realistic political principle of isolation and transforms it into the unattainable parochial ideal of automatic separation."[19]

When internationalism triumphed in the late 1930s, it did so by reviving the moral horizon Wilsonianism. The relevance of the balance of power and spheres of influence for American national interest were rejected and subordinated to illusory expectations regarding the promotion of democratic ideals throughout the world. In short, the debate between isolationism and internationalism in the 1930s turned on whether the United States had a moral obligation to promote peace by joining the

18. Morgenthau, *In Defense of the National Interest*, 25; Morgenthau, *Politics Among Nations*, 144.
19. Morgenthau, *In Defense of the National Interest*, 28–30.

League of Nations or whether it was morally incumbent on the United States to oppose fascism in Europe and uphold international law in Asia. Both world views, Morgenthau asserted, are united by the conviction "that the United States has no interest in any military or political configurations outside the Western Hemisphere. While isolationism stops here, Wilsonianism asserts that the American national interest is not somewhere in particular, but everywhere, being identical with the interests of mankind itself."[20]

Morgenthau was also critical of the moral postulates shaping American policies during and immediately after World War II. For Roosevelt, the war was being fought for humanitarian ideals, formulated in the Four Freedoms and the Atlantic Charter, and unrelated to the distribution of power that the United States had a vital interest in shaping through the strategy and tactics of the Allied war effort. Fortunately, the moralizing rhetoric of the Roosevelt Administration coincided with America's traditional national interest "due to the impact of a national emergency upon innate common sense, and to the strength of the national tradition that holds in its spell the actions of those who deny its validity in words." Beyond the goal of "unconditional surrender" of the Axis powers, Americans looked to a brave new world free of war and the struggle for power. Returning from the Moscow Conference in 1943, Secretary of State Cordell Hull declared that "there will no longer be need for spheres of influence, for alliances, for balance of power, or any other of the special arrangements through which, in the unhappy past, the nations strove to safeguard their security or promote their interests."[21] Finally, America's commitment to the unconditional surrender of the Axis powers overshadowed any responsible planning in anticipation of such developments as the occupation of a divided Germany, unity of the Atlantic alliance, and Soviet power in Eastern Europe. In anticipating a new postwar utopia free from power politics, America confronted a new, more formidable threat to its security as soon as the old one had been subdued.

Morgenthau's writing on the role of the national interest following the Second World War stressed the limits of power and exposed "the inner weaknesses of American foreign policy, both in its overall con-

20. *Ibid.*
21. *Ibid.*, 31; Morgenthau, *Truth and Power*, 76.

ceptions and its responses to the concrete issues of the day."[22] Of particular importance here are the historical and moral transformations of the modern state system, in addition to noting how these changes impacted upon the permanent and variable interests of American foreign policy during the postwar era. Until World War II, the United States could pursue its national interests within the framework of the traditional state system. Since the sixteenth century, this system was characterized by conflicts among several European nations of approximately equal strength. Nations promoted their interests by joining alliances and coalitions to surpass the strength of would-be aggressors and equalize the balance of power. What transpired in Africa or Asia simply mirrored the underlying struggles for power among major European powers. Since the beginning of this century, the Eurocentric state system has been so transformed that today hardly anything is left of it.

Following World War II, four basic changes in the traditional Western state system had radical consequences for the national interests of nations both within and outside Europe.[23] First, what was once a European political system has been transformed into a world system where all the nations of the world have become active and vocal participants in the struggle for power. Second, the system has been transformed qualitatively in that Europe has lost its political predominance in the world. Third, the traditional balance-of-power system composed of a multiplicity of states with approximately equal strength has been replaced by a bipolar system of world power. In terms of the "high politics" of war and national security, there is no combination of other nations that could challenge the strength of either superpower. Fourth, the demise of Europe as the center of political power has transformed relations between Europe and the developing world. The collapse of colonial empires foreclosed the opportunity for European powers (including the United States and Soviet Union) to seek profitable overseas expansion without necessarily interfering with each other's interests. Of considerable importance and frequently overlooked by his critics, however, is how Morgenthau linked the political transformation of the structure and function of international relations to revolutionary developments in the fields of technology and morality.

22. Morgenthau, *The Impasse of American Foreign Policy*, 2.
23. *Ibid.*, 56–67.

A succession of technological revolutions during the first half of the twentieth century—in transportation, communication, and warfare—has transformed the natural and social environment of man almost beyond recognition and has radically changed man's experience of himself. The machine age has lightened immensely the intellectual and moral obligation of keeping one's self and dependents fed, clothed, and protected from the natural elements—which endeavors a century and a half ago absorbed the vital energies of man. Although science and technology elate man with the promise to transform *homo faber*, the maker of tools, into *homo deus*, the maker of worlds, they also depress him. The transforming power of technology and the cognitive power of science, as Morgenthau suggested, are "being paid for not only with the threat of nuclear extinction but also with the actual destruction of the natural environment upon whose preservation the continuation of human life depends." As science has produced the technological instruments of totalitarian control and destroyed that realm of inner freedom through which the individual experiences his autonomy as controlling, the individual "is the hapless object of these technological developments and political possibilities. He is reduced to shaking his fists in impotent rage at those anonymous forces which control a goodly fraction of his life but which he cannot control. In order to restore at least an illusion of control, he can go on strike, indulge in wanton destruction, or resort to individual or mass violence. Or he can join the forces of control, vicariously enjoying their power."[24]

Concomitant with the revolution in modern technology has been the erosion of pragmatic political norms and moral principles that have influenced the modern statesman's choice of methods in the conduct of war and diplomacy. International morality was, throughout the seventeenth and eighteenth centuries, the concern of the personal sovereign and of a relatively small and homogeneous group of aristocratic rulers. The moral duties of this international aristocracy were by necessity of a supranational character. National standards of allegiance were qualified by the classical and Christian principles of natural law. Individual statesmen felt themselves to be personally responsible for compliance with the moral rules of conduct, for it was to them as rational human beings that this moral code was addressed. Gibbon's notion of Europe as "one great

24. Morgenthau, *Science: Servant or Master?* 2–4.

republic" was built upon a legacy of family ties, a common language (French), a common style of life, and accepted standards of what a gentleman could and could not do for himself and the state. Foreign policy was a limited means to a limited end. The restraining influence of the moral climate coincided with conflict and competition for such limited goals as possession of a province, a frontier, or a succession to a throne. Of this system little is left today.

The French Revolution of 1789 marks the beginning of a new epoch in history that witnessed the gradual decline of cosmopolitan international society and the restraining influence of morality on foreign policy. The fragmentation of a formerly cohesive system of sovereigns into a multiplicity of morally self-sufficient national communities is indicative of the profound change that in recent times has transformed the relationship between supranational and national ethics.[25] Important here is how Morgenthau differentiates between traditional forms of nationalism and the twentieth-century phenomenon of "nationalistic universalism." For the nationalism of the nineteenth century, the nation is the ultimate goal of political action beyond which there are other nationalisms with equally justifiable goals. In addition, the international conflicts in which traditional nationalism was invoked involved two elemental encounters: conflicts between a nationality and an alien master, and conflicts between national groups over respective spheres of dominion. Moralists who accepted the primacy of the nation hoped, as late as the First World War, that a society of satisfied nations would find in the legal and moral principles of national self-determination the means for their own preservation.

The nationalistic universalism of the present age was heralded by Woodrow Wilson's war "to make the world safe for democracy." Like the Crusades of the Middle Ages, those who typified Wilson's international philosophy promoted one moral system for the rest of the world.

> They proved that the inequities of the adversary had been present all along as implications of a national philosophy and culture, and that the triumph of their own party was necessary in the ethical scheme of the universe. . . . Bergson discovered that the war was a

25. Morgenthau, "Philosophy of International Relations," July 2 and 28, 1952 (TS in Morgenthau Papers, Box 81), 3–5, 41–46; *Politics Among Nations*, 242–45; *In Defense of the National Interest*, 61.

conflict between "life and matter," with the Entente Powers ranged on the side of life and the Central Powers defending matter. Scheler proclaimed that English philosophy and character were alike manifestations of cant; Santayana wrote of "egotism in German philosophy." . . . Then, as if to make a permanent record of the prostitution of the philosophic art, the victorious governments issued to each soldier in their armies a bronze medal with the inscription, "Great War for Civilization."[26]

During the 1930s, the philosophy of National Socialism was proclaimed as the new moral code that would supplant the "vicious creed of bolshevism and the decadent morality of democracy." The Nazi menace, in the minds of many on the side of the United Nations, was challenged by the universal democratic message embodied in the principles of the Atlantic Charter and the Yalta Agreement. The emergence of a new Cold War enjoined the two remaining moral systems claiming universal validity, democracy and communism, in a competition for the dominion of the world. The nationalistic universalism of the present period is not connected with any one particular nation and has become a kind of secular religion, universal in its interpretation of the nature and destiny of man and in its messianic promise of salvation for all mankind.[27] In short, what is distinctive about the present age is not the political conflict between two great powers or the ideological conflict between two philosophies or ways of life. What is new, however, is the identification of one with the other.

In view of these revolutionary developments in international politics, Morgenthau maintained that the United States had one primary national interest in its relations with other nations—the security of its territory and political institutions. Beyond this basic requirement, however, the United States had a number of secondary or variable interests in the world, such as promotion of peace and security everywhere, support for democratic governments, the containment of communist governments and movements, the relief of poverty, hunger, and disease. In seeking to

26. Max H. Fish (ed.), *Selected Papers of Robert C. Binkley* (Cambridge, Mass., 1948), 328; *Politics Among Nations*, 253–56.

27. For an informative assessment of the politics and philosophy of modern mass ideological movements, see Eric Voegelin, *Science, Politics, and Gnosticism* (Chicago, 1968).

impose a measure of rational order on the values that make up the national interest, Morgenthau warned that these variable objectives are subject to two important limitations. They should never be pursued at the expense of the primary interest of national security, and they can be pursued only within the narrow limits of available wisdom and power.[28]

The primary interest of national security in the postwar period required the United States to reaffirm its traditional commitments of maintaining American superiority in the Western Hemisphere and preserving a balance of power in Europe and Asia. Regarding Soviet-American rivalry in the early postwar years, "the basic objective of our policy is to contain . . . the Soviet Union within the limits . . . established by the lines of military demarcation at the end of the Second World War." Morgenthau heralded the initial formulation of containment, the Truman Doctrine, and the Marshall Plan as evidence of America's pragmatic ability to act decisively in the face of an obvious peril. Yet the creative improvisation distinguishing American foreign policy in the spring of 1947 was short-lived. Ever since the Korean War, he argued, successive presidential administrations "transformed military containment and foreign aid, devices which in 1947 successfully met specific situations, into remedies of absolute validity, adequate for any and all international exigencies." Commenting on the new challenges to American foreign policy in the 1950s and 1960s, he wrote: "The great innovations of 1947 became the routine responses of the fifties and sixties. . . . [They were] unable to meet the need for new policies, as presented . . . by Khrushchev's new foreign policy, or the opportunities for such policies, as presented . . . in the Hungarian Revolution of 1956, the disintegration of the colonial empires . . . and the pre-revolutionary state in which much of Latin America finds itself."[29]

Perhaps the central tenet of Morgenthau's criticism of United States foreign policy since the end of World War II was that American responses abroad dissolved "into a series of stereotyped reactions, organically connected neither with each other through an over-all design nor with the interests of the nation." American policy has "aimed at standing still" and preserving an indefensible status quo in the nations of Africa and Asia. When military containment shifted to Asia after the Korean War,

28. Morgenthau, *A New Foreign Policy for the United States*, 240.
29. Morgenthau, *The Impasse of American Foreign Policy*, 1–2, 9.

Morgenthau stressed the limits of military power, both as an instrument of policy and as an analytical tool for understanding the realities of international life. Reacting to the Cold-War rhetoric of John Foster Dulles, Morgenthau voiced a concern that would recur frequently in his subsequent writing on America's diplomatic and military response to the challenge of revolutionary and communist movements throughout the world. Specifically, the profound neglect of political consequences associated with the globalization of military containment was compounded by the adverse effects of the traditional American inclination for exploiting universal moral and legal formulas as a substitute for the responsible exercise of power. Morgenthau's staunch criticism of United States involvement in Vietnam was based on the American government's neglect of a proper conception of the national interest, defined in terms of the balance of power.[30] Not only did he judge the conflict as only marginally related to American security, but he also found the logic of containment of dubious value in seeking to resolve a national revolution on the periphery of Asia. In an essay written before the Cold War, Morgenthau referred to those qualities of political and ethical judgment that stand in vivid contrast to more indiscriminate forms of opposition to communism: "Practical political action is not often a subject for authoritarian moral judgments of a universal scope. Those who act in the political field must deal with the possible, not with the ideal; they must try to get the relatively good, the lesser evil; they cannot without frustration reject whatever is not wholly good; they cannot be satisfied with proclaimed ends but must deal with actual means."[31]

The Projection and Balance of Power in Politics and Foreign Policy

Equally important for Morgenthau's theory of international politics is the concept of power. In speaking of power, Morgenthau meant

30. Hans J. Morgenthau, "Globalism: Johnson's Moral Crusade," *New Republic*, July 3, 1965, pp. 19–22; "Johnson's Dilemma: The Alternatives Now in Vietnam," *New Republic*, May 28, 1966, pp. 12–16; "What Ails America?" *New Republic*, October 28, 1967, pp. 17–21.

31. Hoopes, *The Devil and John Foster Dulles*, 118. See also Thompson, "The Cold War: Morgenthau's Approach," in *Moralism and Morality in Politics and Diplomacy*, 93–107.

"man's control over the actions and minds of other men." On numerous occasions, he took exception to the popular misconception that political power represents nothing more than tactics of physical coercion or the organized use of violence. When applied to the level of man's political existence, he wrote: "Power is a psychological relation between those who exercise it and those over whom it is exercised. It gives the former control over certain actions of the latter through the impact which the former exerts on the latter's mind. This impact derives from three sources: the expectation of benefits, the fear of disadvantages, the respect or love for men or institutions."[32]

The actual instrumentalities of power are variable, encompassing orders, threats, authority, charisma, or any combination of these. As a universal phenomenon covering all social relationships, power is no less manifest when it is disciplined by moral ends (or constitutional safeguards) than when it appears as an untamed force finding its sole justification in its own strength and aggrandizement. For Morgenthau, the moral dilemma of all political action is that man cannot help but sin when he acts in relation to his fellow man; he may be able to minimize the sinfulness of social action, but he cannot escape it. At the international level, the relatively constant relationship between power and national interest is the basic datum for purposes of theoretical analysis and political practice. According to Morgenthau, the struggle for power in service of a nation's interest crystallizes into three basic patterns: to keep one's power (policy of the status quo); to increase one's power (policy of imperialism); and to demonstrate one's power (policy of prestige).[33] He contended that the struggle for power could be waged by two different means: diplomacy and military force. When nations militarily compete for power, they engage in an armaments race or war. Alternatively, sustained peaceful interactions among them contribute to a process of institutionalized diplomacy.

Morgenthau's typology of national power included both tangible and intangible components. Foremost among the former are geography,

32. Morgenthau, "Notes on Political Theory" (TS in Morgenthau Papers, Box 80), 3–20; *Politics Among Nations*, 13.

33. Alfred J. Hotz, "Morgenthau's Influence on the Study of International Relations," in Thompson and Myers (eds.), *Truth and Tragedy*, 317–18. See also Morgenthau, *Politics Among Nations*, 27–32, 36.

natural resources, industrial capacity, military preparedness, and population. Important intangible factors include national morale, national character, quality of diplomacy, and quality of government. In an age haunted by the specter of global nuclear devastation, he criticized attempts to stress military force or material strength over more intangible facets of national power. Especially during the 1960s and 1970s, Morgenthau pointed to the increasing ideological embodiment of power in world politics and wrote: "The ideological contest between hostile philosophies, social and political systems . . . will ultimately not be decided by political, military . . . and economic interventions of the contestants in the affairs of other nations, but by the . . . virtues and vices of their respective political, economic, and social systems. Throughout its history, this has been the source of America's ideological strength and attractiveness." [34]

Commenting on the transformation of American foreign policy since the end of the Second World War, Morgenthau singled out the quality of a nation's diplomacy as perhaps the most important factor in calculating national power: "The quality of a nation's diplomacy combines those different factors into an integrated whole . . . and awakens their slumbering potentialities by giving them the breath of actual power. . . . By giving direction to the national effort, it will . . . increase the independent weight of certain factors, such as industrial potential, military preparedness . . . and morale." Morgenthau believed that "the United States must resort to the time-honored diplomatic method of fashioning a legal and viable community of interests" to secure the coherence of the Western alliance, accommodate the economic and political development of Germany and Japan, and counter communist control of colonial revolutions throughout the Third World. [35]

Morgenthau's belief that postwar developments required the vigorous application of traditional diplomatic practices followed, in large part, from the revolutionary impact of nuclear weapons on the use of force in international politics. Prior to 1945, conventional weapons could be used as a rational instrument of foreign policy. As a rule, the statesman

34. Morgenthau, *A New Foreign Policy for the United States*, 243; *Politics Among Nations*, 112–49.
35. Morgenthau, *Politics Among Nations*, 140–41; *The Restoration of American Politics*, 207.

in the prenuclear age could reasonably calculate whether he could achieve his objectives by peaceful diplomatic options of whether he had to rely upon force in the threat or actuality or war. The threat and counterthreat of force could always be put to the test of actual performance. After the acquisition of unlimited nuclear power by both the United States and the Soviet Union, however, Morgenthau observed: "The rational relationship that existed, prior to 1945, between force as a means and the ends of foreign policy does not apply to nuclear weapons. . . . If they were used as instruments of national policy, nuclear weapons would destroy the tangible objectives of policy and the belligerents as well. In consequence, they are not susceptible to rational use as instruments of national policy." [36]

Because a subsequent chapter examines Morgenthau's position on the nuclear debate in greater detail, it will be sufficient to note here his argument that the stabilization of deterrence is impossible without resorting to conventional diplomatic and military methods. In the 1960s and 1970s, he was extremely critical of American strategists who tried to hammer out methods of waging nuclear war in the conventional manner so that nuclear war would produce conventional (*i.e.*, rational) and tolerable consequences. That America could fight a limited nuclear war in conventional fashion was the arguable premise of such proposals as the "clean" H-bomb, tactical nuclear war, graduated deterrence with "firebreaks," and counterforce strategy. [37]

An important corollary of Morgenthau's conception of power is the principle of the balance of power. In his view:

A configuration, such as the balance of power, is a general social phenomenon to be found on all levels of social interaction.

The balance of power, far from being just an arbitrary device of diplomats and Machiavellian scholars, is the very law of life for independent units dealing with other independent units—domestic or international—that want to preserve their independence.

The aspiration for power on the part of several nations, each trying either to maintain or overthrow the status quo, leads of necessity to

36. Morgenthau, *A New Foreign Policy for the United States*, 208.
37. *Ibid.*, 215.

a configuration . . . called the balance of power and to policies aimed at preserving it.[38]

Over the years, Morgenthau's analysis has emphasized the main patterns of the balance of power, the different methods of the balance of power, the changing structure of the balance of power, and the inflexibility of the new balance of power.

Morgenthau identified the period between the Treaty of Westphalia and the First World War as the classic period of the balance of power in Europe. Though the balancing process was maintained by a variety of devices (*e.g.*, divide and rule, compensations, armaments, and alliances), its operation served dual purposes. In general, the balance strategy succeeded in preserving the existence of all the major European powers from the end of the Thirty Years' War (1648) until the partitions of Poland at the end of the eighteenth century; in addition, the balance policy succeeded in preventing any one state from achieving universal domination. As Morgenthau suggested, however, "universal dominion by any one state was prevented only at the price of warfare, which from 1648 to 1815 was virtually continuous and in the twentieth century . . . twice engulfed . . . the whole world."[39]

On the basis of the historical evidence, Morgenthau identified at least five requisite conditions for the successful function of the classic balance of power.[40] First, there was a sufficiently large number of independent states to make alliance formation and dissolution readily possible. Second, European diplomats shared in a common political culture that permitted a moral consensus regarding the rules of the game to be observed in both peace and war. Third, the international system was limited to a geographically confined area of the globe. Societies in the Middle East, Africa, and Asia were important only insofar as they fit within the objectives of European foreign policies. A fourth requirement was the availability of a weapons technology that inhibited quick mobilization for war, prevented the pursuit of prolonged wars, and reduced the prospects of wars of annihilation. Fifth, there was freedom of action for the

38. Morgenthau, *Dilemmas of Politics*, 41, 258; *Politics Among Nations*, 167.
39. Morgenthau, "Outline and Notes for Contemporary Diplomatic Problems" (TS in Morgenthau Papers, Box 76), 19–25; *Politics Among Nations*, 202.
40. Morgenthau, *Politics Among Nations*, 167–224, 338–54.

central decision-makers of the states in the system. These elites were largely unaffected by the dictates of public opinion, the need to consider ideological values, or the domestic costs of foreign-policy commitments.

In conjunction with these primary conditions, several other aspects of the classic balance of power can be identified. As a rule, Great Britain played the traditional role of the "balancer" as it threw its support toward one or another coalition to assure that no one bloc achieved predominance. In addition, the balance of power was regularly interpreted as a mechanical, self-regulating principle (*i.e.*, a system-derived impulse toward stability that occurred automatically). Furthermore, alliances in the classic balance of power were not based on friendships or permanent loyalties, but on ever-changing interests and capabilities. Morgenthau wrote: "The balance of power of that period was amoral rather than immoral. The technical rules of the art of politics were its only standard. Its flexibility was the result of imperviousness to moral considerations, such as good faith and loyalty, a moral deficiency which to us seems deserving of reproach."[41]

The century and a half from 1815 until the Second World War saw the gradual extension of the European balance of power into a worldwide system. After 1945, the European balance became a mere function of the worldwide balance, of which the United States and the Soviet Union constituted the main weights. Moreover, local or regional power balances throughout the world have become "theaters" where the contest between the two great protagonists is fought. Morgenthau referred to three important structural changes in the traditional, or classic, balance of power.

First, the reduction in the number of states able to play a major role in international politics has deprived the balance of power of much of its flexibility and uncertainty. The flexibility of the classic balance of power resulted from the unreliability of alliances, which made it imperative for the major actors to be cautious and limited in their moves. The disparity in power between major and minor nations is so pronounced that the latter have lost their ability to tip the scales or provide effective barriers to the limitless aspirations for power.

Second, no nation or combination of nations can be expected to perform Great Britain's traditional role of "balancer" in the bipolar

41. *Ibid.*, 190; *In Defense of the National Interest*, 41.

distribution of power. Following the Second World War, Morgenthau doubted whether any third force (*e.g.*, de Gaulle's France, a united Europe, or nonaligned Third World) was similarly detached and strong enough to exert a decisive influence on the foreign policy of either superpower.

Third, the disappearance of the colonial frontier throughout the twentieth century has rendered the classic balance of power obsolete. Prior to the First World War, great powers could deflect their rivalries from their mutual frontiers to the politically empty spaces of Africa or Asia. Nations sought power through acquiring territory, then considered the symbol and substance of power. As the balance of power became worldwide, however, the dichotomy between the center and the periphery disappeared. Commenting on American diplomacy in the decades after World War II, Morgenthau argued that the globalization of the Truman Doctrine transformed the traditional balance of power into a universal ideological struggle for the minds of men. In the developing world, the issue is not primarily the projection of diplomatic leverage or the conquest of territory, but rather a struggle between conflicting ideologies and ways of life.[42]

Morgenthau's assessment of the balance of power and its applicability to postwar international politics is both enigmatic and ripe with ambivalence. Admittedly, he acknowledged that the proliferation of nuclear capability has led to a much more complex distribution of global power. However, "the instability of the international balance of power," he believed, "is due not to the faultiness of the principle but to the particular conditions under which the principle must operate in a society of sovereign nations."[43] Paradoxically, Morgenthau discussed the eclipse of the classic balance of power and simultaneously affirmed that the underlying principles involved in maintaining the balance of power remained valid throughout time.

Although convinced that the principle of balance of power can be found at all levels of social interaction, Morgenthau is less instructive regarding its application and value in postwar global affairs. His own inventory of the limitations and weaknesses of the concept is divorced

42. Morgenthau, *Politics Among Nations*, 190, 342–45.
43. *Ibid.*, 167. See also Cecil V. Crabb, Jr., and June Savoy, "Hans J. Morgenthau's Version of *Realpolitik*," *Political Science Reviewer*, V (Fall, 1975), 206–209.

from any sustained discussion of how the balance may be expected to operate in light of developments that point to its obsolescence. Four basic limitations may be cited. First, the idea of the balance of power is a metaphor taken from the field of mechanics, suggesting that mutual interactions among independent parts can be exactly determined by means of an objective mathematical formula. However, any such mechanical equilibrium must possess a recognizable quantitative criterion by which power can be compared. What makes the balance of power inherently uncertain, Morgenthau believed, is the relative imprecision involved in calculating such intangible components of power as national morale, quality of diplomacy, and character of government. "It is impossible for the observer of the contemporary scene to assess even with approximate accuracy the relative contributions these elements may make to the power of different nations," he said.[44] For the statesman, then, the rational calculation of the relative capabilities of several nations often takes the form of educated guesses that can be validated only in retrospect.

Second, Morgenthau believed that "the uncertainty of all power calculations not only makes the balance of power incapable of practical application but leads . . . to its very negation in practice." Even during the heyday of the classic balance of power, the concept was open to at least two interpretations. It could signify either *equality* of power (*e.g.*, as Britain or the United States tried to maintain in Europe) or *superiority* of power (*e.g.*, as the United States sought in the Western Hemisphere since the early nineteenth century). Morgenthau recognized, however, that the objective of complete balance or equivalence in power is a dubious prospect for any nation. Because no nation can be certain that its calculation of the distribution of power at any one time is correct, policymakers tend to err on the side of preserving an ample margin of safety in amassing the power necessary to counter the power of rivals. "Since no nation can foresee how large its miscalculations may be, all nations must seek the maximum of power attainable under the circumstances. . . . The limitless aspiration for power, potentially always present . . . in the power drives of nations, finds in the balance of power a mighty incentive to transform itself into an actuality."[45] By equating the balance with supe-

44. Morgenthau, *Politics Among Nations*, 204.
45. *Ibid.*, 204–208.

riority, preventive war between nations becomes a natural tendency of the balance of power. In fact, Morgenthau conceded that most of the wars fought since the beginning of the modern state system have their origin in the balance of power.

Third, the difficulties involved in calculating the relative power of other nations have made the invocation of the balance of power one of the favored ideologies in international politics. In his discussion of the national interest, Morgenthau noted how the power drives of nations take hold of ideal principles and transform them into ideologies in order to disguise and rationalize themselves. As Morgenthau noted, nations interested in preserving a particular distribution of power "make their interest appear to be an outgrowth of the fundamental, universally accepted principle of the modern state system." Commenting on how ideology accentuates the difficulties inherent in the mechanics of the balance of power, he wrote: "The contrast between . . . the pretended aspiration for balance and the actual aim of predominance . . . which . . . is of the very essence of the balance of power, makes the latter in a certain measure an ideology. . . . The balance of power thus assumes a reality and a function that it actually does not have."[46]

Finally, the contemporary balance of power is without the restraining influence of an underlying moral-ethical consensus among nations regarding the appropriate means and ends of foreign policy. In the period of the classic balance of power, international politics became an aristocratic pastime, a sport of princes, all recognizing the same rules of the game and playing for the same limited stakes. As described by Gibbon in *The Decline and Fall of the Roman Empire*, the struggle for power on the international scene was in the nature of "temperate and undecisive contests." But from Morgenthau's perspective, the increasingly ideological character of world politics has deprived the balance-of-power mechanism of all normative restraint. In a revealing passage, he concluded: "The struggle for the minds of men, advancing rival claims to universal dominion on the part of different nations, has dealt the final . . . blow to that social system of international intercourse within which for almost three centuries nations lived together in constant rivalry, yet under the roof of shared values and universal standards of action. . . . Beneath

46. *Ibid.*, 211–13.

the ruins of that roof lies buried the mechanism that kept the walls of the house of nations standing: the balance of power." [47]

The Imperatives of Diplomacy and Statesmanship

"Nothing is as fatal to a nation," wrote Edmund Burke, "as an extreme of self-partiality, and the total want of consideration of what others will naturally hope and fear." No counsel of prudence could be more significant for an age in which modern technology, especially in the form of nuclear weapons, portends the growing obsolescence of the nation-state as the final unit of international organization. Few surveys of Morgenthau's realism and international theory give sufficient attention to how and why he related the national interest and projection of American power to the traditional methods of diplomacy and personal attributes of statesmanship. Seeking to outline the preconditions for permanent peace, Morgenthau accounted for both the modern disparagement of diplomacy as well as the prospects for its revival under the conditions of contemporary world politics. Of central importance is the way he related the functions of diplomacy, conducted in defense of the national interest, to the "extraordinary moral and intellectual qualities that all the leading participants must possess." [48]

The conduct of a nation's foreign policy by its diplomats is for national power in peace what military strategy and tactics by its military leaders are for national power in war. Morgenthau treated diplomacy as a symptom of the struggle for power among sovereign states that try to maintain orderly and peaceful relations among themselves; the traditional methods of diplomacy have grown ineluctably from the objective nature of things political and can be disregarded only at the risk of failure. Diplomacy of high quality will bring "the differing elements of national power to bear with maximum effect upon those points in the international situation which concern the national interest most directly." The success of foreign policy may be jeopardized if the diplomat fails to calculate properly the national objectives in light of the power actually or

47. Edward Gibbon, *The Decline and Fall of the Roman Empire* (New York, 1932), II, 93–95; Morgenthau, *Politics Among Nations*, 337.

48. Edmund Burke, "Remarks on the Policy of the Allies with Respect to France," in *The Works of the Rt. Honourable Edmund Burke* (Boston, 1889), IV, 447; Morgenthau, *Politics Among Nations*, 547.

potentially available for the pursuit of these objectives, the goals of rival nations in terms of the power available to achieve these goals, the extent to which competing interests may be reconciled or deflected to common ground, and the range of appropriate means for the realization of particular objectives. In seeking to secure the interests of his nation and the interests of peace, the diplomat must also "use persuasion, hold out the advantage of compromise, and impress the other with the military strength of his country."[49]

The decline of the traditional methods of diplomacy is essentially the result of a complex of factors.[50] Whereas in times past statesmen had to rely on ambassadors to communicate with other foreign leaders, modern means of transportation and communication have made personal contacts among national leaders routine. Opposition to diplomacy has also grown from an intellectual attitude hostile to the very idea of foreign policy as an independent sphere of thought and action. Nineteenth-century liberals relegated foreign policy and diplomacy to the residue of a feudal age. In Bentham's words, "Nations are associates and not rivals in the grand social enterprise." Similarly, Cobden wrote: "At some future election we may . . . see the test of 'no foreign politics' applied to those who offer to become the representatives of free constituencies." Sir Henry Wotton's classic reference to the diplomat as "an honest man sent abroad to lie for his country" was reflected in Woodrow Wilson's unwillingness "to trust to the council of diplomats the working out of any salvation of the world from the things which it has suffered." Yet history has thus far supported George Canning's warning in 1823 that "the general acquisition of free institutions is not necessarily a security for general peace."[51]

Two additional phenomena must share responsibility for the decline: the trend toward public parliamentary procedures instead of traditional diplomatic negotiations, and the very nature of world politics in the second half of the twentieth century. Attempts to set up the United Nations as an alternative to the traditional methods of diplomacy have

49. Morgenthau, *The Restoration of American Politics*, 198–99; *Politics Among Nations*, 517–19.

50. Hans J. Morgenthau, "Dilemma of the Summit," *New York Times Magazine*, November 11, 1962, p. 118.

51. Jeremy Bentham, *Emancipate Your Colonies* (London, 1830); Morgenthau, *Politics Among Nations*, 35, 525; *Scientific Man*, 65.

been largely ineffective. For example, the objective of this new type of diplomacy is not so much the resolution of outstanding issues dividing member states, but outvoting a rival bloc by the necessary two-thirds majority in the General Assembly. Furthermore, the public nature of these deliberations obscures the extent to which the United Nations and traditional diplomacy are not mutually exclusive categories between which members must choose. Morgenthau pointed out that the United Nations Charter itself refers at different places to the successful operation of diplomacy as the essential precondition for its success. Conceiving of the United Nations as simply a new setting for the old techniques of diplomacy, Dag Hammarskjöld observed: "Conference diplomacy may usefully be supplemented by more quiet diplomacy within the United Nations, whether directly between representatives of Member Governments or in the contacts between the Secretary-General and Member Governments. . . . Within the framework of the Charter there are many possibilities . . . for variation of practices. . . . With only slight adjustments, discussions of major issues of a kind that have occurred outside the United Nations could often be fitted into its framework, thus at the same time adding to the strength of the world organization and drawing strength from it." [52]

Of perhaps more importance in explaining the decline of diplomacy in the traditional manner has been the emergence of a Cold War based upon two incompatible conceptions of the postwar world. Morgenthau noted two factors that distinguish the conflict between the United States and the Soviet Union from the many hostile confrontations history records. The first was the inability of either superpower to pursue conciliatory policies through compromise, which might have led to the settlement of the outstanding issues. Both sides, imbued with the crusading spirit and new moral force of nationalistic universalism, became the proprietors of two gigantic power blocs and faced each other with unyielding opposition. A second factor was the necessity for both sides to protect and promote their interests through unilateral action on the opponent's will by all means available—diplomatic, military, economic, subversive—short of the actual use of force. The very conditions of the Cold War transformed diplomacy into "a mere auxiliary of a war waged against the enemy, not for the purpose of accommodating conflicting in-

52. Morgenthau, *Politics Among Nations*, 474.

terests, but for the triumph, however verbal, of one nation over another."[53] Although diplomacy can be used for the settlement of limited conflicts, it can at best do nothing more than mitigate the clash of rival political philosophies and the competition of incompatible ways of life.

Morgenthau's belief that the practical art of diplomacy continues as an indispensable obligation for nations and statesmen grew out of his conviction that the methods of the Cold War were inappropriate for a new age marked by greater flexibility between the two leading power blocs. The ideological conduct of foreign policy in a rigid, bipolar world was being challenged by four major developments: the extent to which second-rank powers were less dependent on the superpowers; the rise to prominence of Germany and Japan; the problem of nuclear proliferation; and the force of revolutionary politics throughout the developing nations of Africa, Asia, and Latin America. "A nation which under present conditions is either unwilling or unable to take full advantage of the traditional methods of diplomacy condemns itself either to the slow death of attrition or the sudden death of atomic destruction."[54] For Morgenthau, diplomacy was viewed as perhaps the last best alternative in a troubled world where strategies of the national interest and balance of power rest precariously on a foundation of unstable and always-changing values.

It is with no small amount of irony, not to mention intellectual misfortune, that many accounts of Morgenthau's work in the current literature of international relations neglect the vital relationship between the first and last chapters of *Politics Among Nations*. To the six principles of political realism must be added the nine rules of diplomacy that have a special bearing upon the contemporary situation. Not only do these rules repudiate the allegation that Morgenthau treated the concepts of power and interest as static categories of analysis; in addition, they reveal a sensitive mind, alert to the temptations of power and cognizant of how discriminating moral judgments impact upon the implementation of a nation's interest. According to Morgenthau, the elements of a peace-preserving diplomacy must adhere to the following requirements.[55]

1. *Diplomacy must be divested of the crusading spirit.* Neither the United States nor the Soviet Union can afford to define the objectives of

53. Morgenthau, *The Restoration of American Politics*, 205–206.
54. Morgenthau, *A New Foreign Policy for the United States*, 208.
55. Morgenthau, *Politics Among Nations*, 539–48.

their foreign policy in terms of a world-embracing political religion. Morgenthau warned that the two political religions of our age have taken the place of the two great Christian denominations of the sixteenth and seventeenth centuries. A century of unprecedented devastation and bloodshed in the Wars of Religion was the painful legacy of sovereigns who sought to impose their faith on the rest of the world. Only if both superpowers rid themselves in time of the universalistic aspirations "can a moral consensus, emerging from shared convictions and common values, develop—a moral consensus within which a peace-preserving diplomacy will have a chance to grow."

2. *The objectives of foreign policy must be defined in terms of the national interest and must be supported with adequate power.* National security, conceived of as integrity of the national territory and its institutions, serves as the irreducible minimum that diplomacy must defend with adequate power. Yet, that Morgenthau understood well both the changing and normative aspects shaping the definition of a nation's security is attested to by his observation on the conduct of diplomacy in the nuclear age: "Until the advent of that age, a nation could use its diplomacy to purchase its security at the expense of another nation. Today, short of a radical change in the atomic balance of power in favor of a particular nation, diplomacy, in order to make the nation secure from nuclear destruction, must make them all secure." [56]

3. *Diplomacy must look at the political scene from the point of view of other nations.* The revolutionary impact of nuclear weapons meant that nations must define their interests in restrictive and transcendent terms. With an eye toward both the militarization and globalization of Cold-War hostilities, Morgenthau warned that peace is jeopardized when each side challenges the other throughout the world and the ambition of both is inspired by the crusading zeal of a universal mission. Defining their national interests in terms of national security would allow each side to "draw back from outlying positions, located close to, or within, the sphere of national security of the other side, and retreat into their respective spheres, each self-contained within its orbit." Such an approach would entail widening the distance that separates both spheres of national security and clarifying respective spheres of influence so "that to touch or even to approach it means war."

56. *Ibid.*, 541.

4. *Nations must be willing to compromise on all issues that are not vital to them.* Both morality and expediency require that nations differentiate between permanent needs of national security and secondary, or variable, interests that are a product of ever-shifting internal and external circumstances. Compromise on secondary issues presents the diplomat with the difficult task of trying "to keep in balance interests that touch each other at many points and may be intertwined beyond the possibility of separation." For example, any decision to supply friendly Arab regimes with military equipment has to be judged within the context of other objectives of American policy, such as preservation of Israel's security, self-determination for the Palestinians, access to vital resources in the region, and navigation rights in the Persian Gulf. The difficulty in distinguishing vital from nonvital issues can be seen vividly in the postwar pattern of Soviet-American competition for power and influence throughout the developing world. In a passage that could apply equally to the 1979 Soviet invasion of Afghanistan or American mining of Nicaraguan harbors in 1984, Morgenthau observed: "It is hardly a less immense task to keep the other side's influence as small as possible in the regions close to one's own security zone without absorbing those regions into one's own orbit." The inability of either the United States or the Soviet Union to embrace a workable diplomatic solution in the context of military intervention can be explained in part by continuing uncertainty about the necessary and variable elements of the national interest.

5. *Give up the shadow of worthless rights for the substance of real advantage.* Compromise is rarely possible among nations that seek to promote specific political interests by resorting to a diplomacy couched in legalistic and propagandistic terms. The defense of rights and abstract legal principles throughout the annals of diplomatic history has too often been oblivious to the consequences such insistence may have on the nation and mankind. From the tragic fate of the Melians recorded by Thucydides to the Wilsonian principle of self-determination invoked by Hitler for the destruction of Czechoslovakia, legal and political norms have no reality apart from distinctive cultural and national traditions within which they are applicable. The diplomat's choice, according to Morgenthau, "is not between legality and illegality, but between political wisdom and political folly."

6. *Never put yourself in a position from which you cannot retreat without losing face and from which you cannot advance without grave*

risks. Diplomatic failure has often been the price paid by those countries who confound the pretense of legal right with the actuality of political advantage in seeking to promote their own interests. Classic examples include Napoleon III on the eve of the Franco-Prussian War and the policies of Austria and Germany prior to World War I. American involvement in Indochina over a fifteen-year period was indicative of this principle in two respects. The rapid escalation of American intervention and support for South Vietnam left the United States unable to retreat from its position without incurring a serious loss of prestige among allies. In addition, Presidents Johnson and Nixon were unable to advance from that position through bombings, as well as secret military engagements into Cambodia, without inviting serious political risks that ultimately led to American withdrawal and the collapse of South Vietnam.

7. *Never allow a weak ally to make decisions for you.* At issue here is the problem of a stronger nation losing its freedom of action by identifying its national interests with those of a weak ally. The latter, confident of the support from a powerful friend, can formulate and implement foreign-policy objectives of its own choosing. The stronger nation may then be compelled to support specific actions that have little bearing on the original purpose of the alliance and may be deemed vital only by the weaker partner. For example, the Baghdad Pact, SEATO, and the Eisenhower Doctrine represented open-ended alliances. They had three characteristics in common: complementary interests tending toward transformation into incompatible ones, a radically unequal distribution of benefits, and an ideological emphasis. Frequently united by nothing more than an anti-communist ideological commitment (and this in view of the remoteness of the *casus foederis*), alliance membership for nations in Asia and the Middle East required no common objective, policy, or action. Many uncommitted nations joined in these alliances primarily because of the economic, military, and political support they received from the United States. More recent examples of how the policies of a weaker ally impacted adversely on the interests of the United States can be seen in the consequences following the overthrow of the Shah of Iran and the Marcos regime in the Philippines.

8. *The armed forces are the instrument of foreign policy, not its master.* Whatever the objectives of a nation's foreign policy, they always entail control of the actions of others through influence over their minds.

The nature of foreign policy and the conduct of war, although both may serve the national interest, differ in their immediate objectives, in the means they employ, and in the modes of thought they bring to bear upon their respective tasks. The military mind operates between the absolutes of victory and defeat, and relies on methods that are simple and unconditional in order to bring the greatest amount of violence to bear upon an enemy's vulnerable points. The mind of the diplomat, more complicated and subtle, must rely upon that patient, intricate, and discreet maneuvering in order to meet the other side on the middle ground of a negotiated compromise. Morgenthau consistently reminded American policy-makers that the *political* objective of military preparations is to make the application of force unnecessary by inducing a potential enemy to desist from the use of military force. An example of this failure was the initiative taken by Secretary of State Dulles to extend the policy of containment, originally applied to Europe, systematically to the Middle East and Asia through a network of alliances. The substitution of military for diplomatic methods, then as well as now, will hardly be sufficient to meet such issues as sources of continuity and change in the political and military power of the Soviet Union, modernization and political development in the Third World, and the extent to which American economic security is dependent on changes in the international political economy.

9. *The government is the leader of public opinion, not its slave.* Morgenthau pointed to the "existential incompatibility" between the democratic requirements of consensus and consent of the governed and the prerequisites of a sound foreign policy. Writing with regard to the preferences of democratic public opinion in the United States, Tocqueville observed:

> Foreign politics demand scarcely any of those qualities which are peculiar to a democracy: they require, on the contrary, the perfect use of almost all those in which it is deficient. Democracy is favorable to the increase of the internal resources of the state; it diffuses wealth and comfort, promotes public spirit, and fortifies the respect for law in all classes of society: all these are advantages with only an indirect influence over the relations which one people bears to another. But a democracy can only with great difficulty regulate the details of an important undertaking, preserve in a fixed design, and

work out its execution in spite of serious obstacles. It cannot combine its measures with secrecy or await their consequences with patience.[57]

The dilemma is tragic in that it can never fully be resolved. The American president must perform the two historical functions of his office: to be the educator of the people and the conciliator of seemingly irreconcilable positions. This obligates the chief executive "to impress upon the people the requirements of a sound foreign policy by telling them the facts of political life" and to build on a compromise "that leaves the essence of sound foreign policy intact while assuaging domestic opinion." It is worth noting that Morgenthau penetrated to the moral core of decision making in a democratic society. The normative order of a democracy must rest with both the majority and minority acting on the conviction that they are right, "a conviction tempered by the awareness of the possibility that they might be mistaken." Morgenthau asserted: "If both the majority and the minority remain within this relativistic ethos of democracy, while at the same time respecting those absolute, objective principles that are beyond the ken of that relativism, the vitality of their contest will accrue to the vitality of democracy. Otherwise, they will strain the delicate ties that keep a democratic society together, and they will risk destroying it while trying to keep it alive."[58]

Attempts to evaluate Morgenthau's philosophy of realism and world politics by the prevailing orthodoxy of behavioral science have floundered upon an intellectual disposition unable or unwilling to grasp the misery and grandeur of human existence. The quality of a nation's diplomacy, in addition to the requirements of leadership in foreign affairs, cannot be comprehended adequately by the principles of scientific reason. From the deeds of the great diplomatists throughout the ages— men like Richelieu, Callières, Mably, John Quincy Adams, Cambon, Jusserand, Harold Nicolson—the vocation of politics achieves coherence by the wisdom born out of the experience of insecurity and heroic fulfillment of human possibilities. The enduring value of Morgenthau's inter-

57. Alexis de Tocqueville, *Democracy in America* (New York, 1945), I, 234–35. See Hans J. Morgenthau, "Who Pays for Foreign Policy?" 1975 (TS in Morgenthau Papers, Box 108), 1–3.

58. Morgenthau, "Notes on Political Theory" (TS in Morgenthau Papers, Box 80), 8; *Politics Among Nations*, 146–47.

national thought may be explained in good measure by his command of the statesman's historic task of seeking victory while situated at an uneasy juncture between fate and freedom, necessity and chance.

No amount of tangible facts imparted through education can substitute for the type of experience that pushes great men to the limits of their human possibilities. The rationality of the statesman must find its way in the struggle between moral and social forces that operate both within and between members of society. In the words of Goethe: "While trying to improve evils in men and circumstances which cannot be improved, one loses time and makes things worse; instead, one ought to accept the evils . . . as raw materials and then seek to counterbalance them."[59] Morgenthau was too well versed in diplomatic history and political ethics to attempt the hopeless task of providing an operational formula of statesmanship (*i.e.*, where reason, conceived as empirical science, can supply the rules of human conduct by showing the different results correlated with different actions). "In this labyrinth of unconnected causal connections man discovers many little answers but no answer to the great questions of his life, no meaning, no direction."[60]

According to Morgenthau, the rationality of the statesman grows out of the eternal laws by which man moves in the social world. The validity of those laws, the Aristotelian truth that man is a political animal, does not derive from objective facts from whose uniformity the physical sciences derive their laws. The mark of the great philosopher is that through his insight and wisdom he can elevate his experiences into the universal laws of human nature. The mark of the great statesman is the recognition that "in the contingencies of the social world [are] the concretizations of eternal laws." Yet for the statesman there is no escape from politics or the necessity of political philosophy. Neither philosophy nor action can free the statesman from the "inescapable tension between reason and experience, between theoretical and practical knowledge." As Morgenthau wrote: "The philosopher . . . knows more than the king, . . . [but the philosopher] cannot act according to his knowledge. The king, even if he knew all the philosopher knows, would still not know for certain what action the concrete situation requires. No theoretical knowledge but only the experience of acting can teach him that. Yet even that

59. Morgenthau, *Scientific Man*, 218.
60. Morgenthau, *Scientific Man*, 218.

experience will teach him only how to avoid the repetition of yesterday's blunder, not how to not commit a new one tomorrow."[61]

Perhaps no other American leader exemplified the challenge and crisis of statesmanship better than Abraham Lincoln. In a number of essays on Lincoln's political ethics and religious outlook, published posthumously as *The Mind of Abraham Lincoln: A Study in Detachment and Practicality*, Morgenthau wrote about those qualities of Lincoln's mind and character that illuminate the very nature of the human condition. In appraising the nature of Lincoln's greatness, Morgenthau deferred to Emerson's definition of a great man as: "He is great who is what he is from nature and never reminds us of others." Such men, Emerson advised, "speak to our want" and teach others what it means to be a man and how to act as one. Although indifferent to religion as dogma and organization, Lincoln was "aware of the existential human condition from which the religious impulse made rational in dogma and visible in organization, springs: the finiteness of man in knowledge and action." Thus there appears the *aristeia* of man, "his heroic struggle to be . . . more than he is and to know that he is and can be more than he is." For Lincoln, the sense of insecurity and powerlessness was expressed in his private *Meditation on the Divine Will* written in 1862: "In great contests each party claims to act in accordance with the will of God. Both *may* be, and one *must* be wrong. God can not be *for* and *against* the same thing at the same time."[62]

61. Morgenthau, *Dilemmas of Politics*, 321.

62. Roy P. Basler (ed.), *The Collected Works of Abraham Lincoln* (New Brunswick, N.J., 1953), V, 403–404; Hans J. Morgenthau and David Hein, *Essays on Lincoln's Faith and Politics* (Lanham, Md., 1983), 3–4; Morgenthau, *Scientific Man*, 222–23.

CHAPTER FOUR

Realism and Moral Choice in American Foreign Policy

Morgenthau's political realism and its normative rationale represent a forceful testament to both power and interest backed by power as the crowning essence of international politics. Critics of his political philosophy are quick to deplore what is perceived to be an admixture of Machiavellian and Hobbesian sentiments limiting, or perhaps sacrificing, the positive force of moral conviction in a tragic, demonic social drama from which man has no escape. From this vantage point, Morgenthau is often viewed as a modern apostle of *raison d'état*. As a leading theorist of international relations has written: "From Machiavelli to Meinecke and Morgenthau the elements of the approach and reasoning remain consistent." Describing Morgenthau's approach in *Politics Among Nations*, another scholar concluded that he "argues for the primacy of *realpolitik* over morality in the affairs of state." These summary observations suggest that Morgenthau approached the moral dilemma in foreign policy as a contest between principle and expediency, morality and immorality. The logical consequence of framing the debate in these terms is to equate realism with the belief that "the state is exempt from morality, but also that if the state does rely on morality, morality will fail to protect it."[1]

This chapter substantiates how Morgenthau's interest in the empirical dimensions of state behavior was matched by his unyielding focus on the proper relations between power, or the national interest, and mo-

---

1. John A. Vasquez (ed.), *Classics of International Relations* (Englewood Cliffs, N.J., 1986), 2; Waltz, *Theory of International Politics*, 117.

rality. His assessment of *raison d'état* grew out of a framework of moral reasoning based upon the experience of tragedy and guilt in man's political existence. Morgenthau helped to broaden the philosophical base of realism by judging the normative roots of the American diplomatic tradition according to both the creative and the destructive forces in human nature. His appreciation of America's liberal-democratic ideals and the relation of those values to United States foreign policy led him to recoil from the ethical dualism evident in European *raison d'état*. No less for the practitioner than the prophet, a meaningful standard of political action derives from the challenge and limitations in relating absolute or universal norms to the contingencies of particular political events. In regard to his international thought, Morgenthau's realism is conspicuous by its appreciation of, even if it did not fully transcend, the tension between the national interest and dedication to principles of justice and established mutualities in the community of nations. In his first comprehensive treatise on American foreign policy, Morgenthau wrote: "The choice is not between moral principles and the national interest, devoid of moral dignity, but between one set of principles divorced from political reality, and another set of . . . principles derived from political reality."[2]

Ethics and the Limits of Historical Justice

Reinhold Niebuhr, in *The Structure of Nations and Empires*, raised the very questions that have shaped man's relentless quest to find the truth about himself and society.[3] Is there any consistency or perennial force in man's search for community? Is there a permanent pattern in the anatomy of community that may be found in such diverse communities as the tribe, city-state, or the ancient or modern empire? Morgenthau, like Niebuhr, insisted that any valid conception of political ethics must acknowledge the intellectual and moral predicament that prevents man from completely understanding and adequately judging both history and himself. The complexities and ambiguities of the human factor in politics and history call into question the interplay of rational and contingent elements. The statesman, conscious of history, must be aware of the malleability of the human will; yet he must also be cognizant of

2. Morgenthau, *In Defense of the National Interest*, 34.
3. Reinhold Niebuhr, *The Structure of Nations and Empires* (New York, 1959).

the limitations of rational suasion and the need for objective barriers to human will.

Man's doubt about the meaning of history stems from the difficulty of differentiating between what is typical and perennial and what is unique and ephemeral in varying historical situations. As Montaigne wrote: "As no event and no shape is entirely like another, so also is there none entirely different from one another: an ingenious mixture on the part of Nature. . . . All things hold together by some similarity; every example is halting, and the comparison that is derived from experience is always defective and imperfect. And yet one links up with the comparisons at some corner. And so do laws become serviceable and adapt themselves to every one of our affairs by some wrested, forced, and biased interpretation." All events are unique in that they happen in a certain way only once and never before or since; yet the very possibility of theory, as well as the existence of objective standards of political truth, depends upon the rational perception of social forces that are a by-product of human nature and that, under similar circumstances, manifest themselves in comparable respects. The contingencies of the present and of the future array themselves in a limited number of typical patterns. Morgenthau alluded to the German situation in 1932, which contained essentially three germinal developments: parliamentary democracy, military dictatorship, and Nazism. The eventual outcome depended upon contingent elements of the situation that could not be foreseen. Although always taking exception to rationalistic blueprints of the social world, Morgenthau believed that the choices of statesmen and nations are "not devoid of a measure of rationality if approached with the expectations of Macbethian cynicism."[4]

The intellectual difficulty that stands in the way of any theoretical understanding of the social world is matched by the fundamental moral dilemma in which history involves man. The "moral ambivalence" of the actor on the political scene is expressed in several key respects. Morgenthau referred to "the tendency of man to claim for his position in history more in terms of moral dignity than he is entitled to, and to grant his fellows less than is their due."[5] Whatever man does or intends to do

4. Jacob Zeitlin (ed.), *The Essays of Michel de Montaigne* (New York, 1936), III, 270; Morgenthau, *Scientific Man*, 149–51; *The Decline of Democratic Politics*, 8.
5. Morgenthau, *The Decline of Democratic Politics*, 13.

emanates from himself and refers again to himself; the very act of acting destroys our moral integrity. Upon leaving the realm of his thought and pure intentions, the individual is involved in the sin and guilt of politics because he violates a basic tenet of Western morality—to respect man as an end in himself and not to use him as a means to an end.

Moreover, the corruption of individual judgment may be explained by the ideological function morality performs. This task is essentially different from the two other interrelated functions of morality: (1) limiting the interests that power seeks and the means that power employs to that end; and (2) approving certain ends and means that not only become politically feasible but also acquire a positive moral value. Yet civilization requires more than these negative or positive functions; it also requires "the mitigation of the struggle for power by glossing over power interests and power relations and making them appear as something different than what they actually are." Ideologies, as Morgenthau wrote in *Politics Among Nations*, render involvement in the contest for power psychologically and morally acceptable to the actors and their audience. In a revealing passage from *War and Peace*, Tolstoy wrote:

> When a man acts alone, he always carries with him a certain series of considerations that have, as he supposes, directed his past conduct, and that serve to justify to him his present action, and to lead him to make projects for his future activity.
>
> Assemblies of men act in the same way, only leaving to those who do not take direct part in the action to invent consideration, justifications, and projects concerning their combined activity. . . .
>
> They remove moral responsibility from those men who produce the events. At the time they do the work of the brooms that go in front to clear the rails for the train: they clear the path of men's moral responsibility. Apart from those justifications, no solution could be found for the most obvious question that occurs to one at once on examining any historical event; that is, How did millions of men come to combine to commit crimes, murders, wars?[6]

In university lectures on the philosophy of international relations, Morgenthau devoted considerable attention to how morality in politics

6. *Ibid.*, 59; Leo Tolstoy, *War and Peace*, trans. Constance Garnett (New York, 1966), Epilogue, Pt. 2, Chap. 7.

and diplomacy is shaped by competing historical world views. Up until the nineteenth century, there were two basic philosophies of history accepted in the Western world—the cyclical and the transcendental.[7] The cyclical conception of history, typical of ancient Greek and Roman thought, treated civilizations like organisms with cycles of birth, decay, and death. There is no end or inherent meaning to the historic process of one civilization replacing another. A modern restatement of this position can be seen in Spengler's *Decline of the West*.

The transcendental school believes in a determining link between the moral law under which the historic process develops and the actual historic process itself. This is the conception most clearly developed in Christian theology. There exists a necessary discrepancy between the postulates of morality and the empirical patterns of history. St. Augustine, for example, saw in history the conflict between the City of God (*civitas dei*) and the City of Man (*civitas terrena*), a conflict that would continue until the Day of Judgment when Christ would appear again to judge both the living and the dead. Man's temporal affairs constitute that stage of history within which man demonstrates his sinfulness. Christianity teaches that man is the creature of God, that he is essentially a spiritual being with a nature and destiny that transcends time and space. Morgenthau alluded to the historiography of Arnold Toynbee as encompassing both cyclical and transcendental features. For Toynbee, "the decline of civilization has a relation to, and a moral meaning concerning, the movement of man from his moral destiny, and the flowering of civilization is the result of man's awareness and attraction to his spiritual destiny."[8]

By the nineteenth century, a new conception of history found acceptance in Western culture and is characterized by the philosophy of Rousseau, Hegel, and Marx. The contribution of these thinkers, as Morgenthau noted, is especially important for modern solutions to the moral dilemma in politics and foreign affairs. What unites these different thinkers is their common acceptance of a moral meaning within history. This conception is anticipated by Rousseau, fully developed by Hegel, and applied by Marx to the modern political and economic scene. The great achievement of Rousseau is the attempt to remove the moral qualities of

7. Hans J. Morgenthau, "Philosophy of International Relations," July 23, 1952 (TS in Morgenthau Papers, Box 81), 57.
8. *Ibid.*, 58.

the historic process from the transcendental sphere of religion to the historic process itself. The concept of the "general will" becomes the measure of morality and justice within the state. For Rousseau, any discord between the will of the majority and the requirements of ethics is inconceivable, because the general will, the sense of moral standards, reveals itself in the will of the majority.

Hegel's philosophy starts from the assumption that the real is rational and the rational real. The task of the philosopher is to "recognize reason as the rose in the cross of the present and thereby to enjoy the present, that is the rational insight which reconciles us to the actual."[9] Hegel conceived of history as a process for the unfolding of the world spirit, of the rational and good in history. The process of unfolding proceeds in stages from the conflict between dialectical opposites until the world spirit becomes conscious of itself and history reaches an end. Progress is logically required and is an inevitable attribute of the historical process. Comparing the idealism of Hegel to the historical realism of the Christian tradition, Morgenthau understood that this profound difference has enormous consequences for our thinking on political and social affairs, our conception of the nature of man, his destiny, and the problems of moral philosophy.

Whereas Hegel found reality in the self-realization of the world spirit, Marx found it in the materialization of society. What moves the world is not self-realization of the spirit in reality, but material conditions in society. Morgenthau alluded to the dual nature of rationality in Marx's philosophy. First, there is a dialectical process, defined in terms of class struggle, which links one period of history with another. Second, there is a rational nexus within each historical epoch connecting all forms of existence with the existing forces of production and distribution of valued resources. Marx's notion of "superstructure," encompassing all outward forms of cultural expression from music and literature to politics and foreign policy, received meaning from materialist forces that determine the economic arrangements of a society. The concept of dialectical materialism enabled Marx to project a classless society as the rational and necessary objective shaping the historic process. The same eschatological hope, based upon the same intellectual procedure, is to be found in the

9. Hegel, *Philosophy of Right*, 12.

Marxian conception of the revolutionary war that will do away with class war and with the international war arising from it.[10]

According to Morgenthau, the underlying philosophy of history separating the classical and Christian traditions from modern liberal and socialist viewpoints has direct consequences for the role and meaning of ethics in political life. For Plato and Aristotle, the harmony between the absolute laws of morality, of which politics is a part, and human life in general is expected only by accident or the grace of God. From the horizon of Christian faith, man cannot attain moral perfection in this world; "the best he is capable of is to conceive its meaning, to achieve through an isolated act of goodness a tiny fragment of it, and make aspiration toward it the guiding principle of a whole life." Both Marxism and nineteenth century liberalism are alike in the temptation to see in revolution or social reforms that path to an imminent end to all of history. Whereas liberalism expects the disappearance of war from the uniformity of governments based on the principle of democratic nationalism, Marxism connects the same hope with the universal acceptance of the socialist pattern. As Morgenthau observed: "The very ideal of world revolution as the final struggle to end all struggles, is in its unhistoric abstractness the perfect counterpart of the national and democratic wars and revolutions, whose successful conclusion will bring about lasting peace."[11]

With reference to the field of political ethics, the modern conception of history finds no unbridgeable gap between what actually is and what ought to be. Progress is expected not only in technology and the rational control of the natural world, but also within the moral controls of the historical process. Moral deficiencies are understood as only falling short of the ultimate consummation that will inevitably come about. The corruption of human nature becomes a quantitative matter to be corrected by the inevitable accumulation of more and more knowledge. The very field of politics thus becomes a kind of atavistic residue from a pre-rational period. It follows that moral deficiencies are really rational deficiencies in two different senses: either in the sense that the human mind has not been trained or informed about what man ought to do, or in the sense that man has not learned the correct manipulation of social situa-

10. Morgenthau, *Scientific Man*, 52–53.
11. Morgenthau, *The Decline of Democratic Politics*, 375.

tions in conformity with the objective laws of history. The moral problem is deprived of its autonomy and becomes a mere scientific problem in the social sphere.

The classic example of this approach in the international sphere is the reliance upon technology to diminish international tensions and improve the prospects for peace. The nineteenth century developed a "science of peace" as a separate branch of scientific knowledge. The traditional notion of a "natural frontier" based on strategic and political considerations was challenged by various attempts to define a "scientific frontier." The Congress of Vienna, upon Metternich's suggestion, appointed a statistical commission charged with treating territories by the "objective" standard of number, quality, and type of populations. Morgenthau cited Disraeli's Mansion-House speech on November 9, 1878, in which the Prime Minister justified the Second Afghan War by saying that the frontier of India was "a haphazard and not a scientific one." In an unprecedented level of international activity following the First World War, governments and private groups competed with each other in organizing peace conferences, in encouraging innovative teaching and research, and in publishing hundreds of volumes to cure the ills of humanity in a scientific way. More recently, Morgenthau warned: "The scientific theories of our day pretend to be capable of manipulating with scientific precision a society of sovereign nations who use weapons of total destruction as instruments of their respective foreign policies. . . . They create the illusion of the viability of the nation-state in the nuclear age. If statesmen should take these theories at their pseudo-scientific word and act upon them, they would fail, as the statesmen of the interwar period failed when they acted upon the progressivist theories of their day."[12]

If man has learned anything from history, it is the fact that the very same political and moral problems with which humanity was concerned in antiquity continue to challenge the modern mind: the limits and obligations of freedom; the need to balance requirements of justice and order; and the meaning of equality within a scheme of ordered liberty. Furthermore, the perennial nature of these philosophical questions can be attributed to an eternal battle within the soul of man—the inspiration of

12. Hans J. Morgenthau, "Science of Peace: A Rationalist Utopia," *Social Research*, XLII (Spring, 1975), 23–25; *The Decline of Democratic Politics*, 66.

man to transcend his own natural limitations and, thereby, the experience of falling short of what he wants and believes he ought to accomplish. It is this ability to visualize a state of affairs—one that does not exist in reality but is a product of the creative inspiration of man—that influences the attitudes and actions of men. Man's ability to conceive of human relations based on perfect love far exceeds his ability to transform that longing into reality. The inevitability of failure of one's expectations is inherent in the tragic character of human existence. Believing that evil lies in the very fact of power itself, Morgenthau summarized in lecture the ethical problem in human existence:

> In the exercise of divine power . . . you assume full knowledge of the moral law, and the use of power only for the purpose of fulfilling the moral law. But in no human situation can you have assurance as to what the moral law is, nor can you be sure that the power will be used exclusively for the purpose of fulfilling the moral law. . . . From the point of view of individual morality, you may defend the proposition that all that counts is good intentions. But we are not dealing here with the problems with which Kant dealt, but with the problems of social philosophy. Here the intent of the actor is almost irrelevant.[13]

Man can never view the moral predicament of man in politics and history with the same objectivity that is applicable to the world of inanimate nature. The moral limitation upon his understanding of history is hubris—pride in his intellect, pride in his goodness, pride in the collectivity with which he identifies himself. In the field of foreign policy, nations define their conflicts with others not by interest and power determined by circumstances, but by moral values determined by abstract principles. Citing the failure of American policies toward the Soviet Union after the Second World War, Morgenthau described how "Yalta" became a popular symbol, "not of the legal ratification of errors of military and political judgment, but of a moral deception that the wicked perpetrated upon the good." Sir Winston Churchill represented, in Morgenthau's estimation, an unrivaled example of a modern statesman able to "remember the past in order to learn how to act aright in matters

13. Hans J. Morgenthau, "Philosophy of International Relations," August 6, 1952 (TS in Morgenthau Papers, Box 81), 49.

political and military." Beyond his belief that the war was a military means to a political end, Churchill exemplified the intellectual and moral disposition of the great leader "able to see a problem in its true proportions . . . to see without the passions of pride, of hatred, and of contempt." Churchill was one of the few to "master the paradox of wanting passionately to win over an enemy to whom he feels . . . superior, and of having to view his relations with the enemy with the detachment and objectivity of a scholar."[14]

The Ethics of Politics and Foreign Policy

Although critics and commentators have singled out numerous problems in Morgenthau's theory of international politics, few have wrestled with the more challenging issue of the philosophy or conception of political ethics underlying the theory. This neglect is particularly acute in light of Morgenthau's unequivocal rejection of classical *raison d'état* as a basis for calculating the moral dignity of American national interest in world affairs. It is a distortion and gross oversimplification of Morgenthau's work to conclude that he epitomizes the European legacy of *realpolitik*, with its intrinsic denial of ethical constraints upon the statesman. Admittedly, the lessons of Machiavelli and Hobbes were not lost upon Morgenthau in his appraisal of human nature and the origin of conflict in civil society. With Plato and Aristotle, however, he argued vigorously that the ineradicable moral impulse of man to submit political action to ethical evaluation is not preempted by the primacy of self-interest and power at all levels of human conduct. Morgenthau reminded his readers that the popular juxtaposition of the Machiavellian and the moralist is "inadequate to do justice to a political situation in which on either side good and evil, wisdom and error, are inextricably blended and intertwined."[15]

The allegation that Morgenthau's philosophy decouples moral choice from the struggle for power misrepresents his abiding concern for those ethical vitalities—the compelling force of judgments that give value and meaning to life—that distinguish the human condition in all its conflictual and cooperative dimensions. Moreover, the argument that his ap-

14. Morgenthau, *The Decline of Democratic Politics*, 338.

15. Hans J. Morgenthau, "The Moral Dilemma in Foreign Policy," in *The Yearbook of World Affairs, 1951* (London, 1951), 13.

proach to political ethics is secondary to, or a derivative of, the objective force of power and ineluctable logic of self-interest is equally indefensible. As a philosopher, Morgenthau understood that the array of institutions and regulations by which any society seeks the minimum stability and order for its own government depends upon ethical assumptions about the basis of individual and group behavior. The ethics of realism speak not to the inevitable triumph of power over principle; rather, the goals and purposes of power in man's collective existence evolve from competing conceptions of justice and virtue. As a political theorist, Morgenthau agreed with Aristotle's description of political science as an "architectonic" discipline aiming at the whole of human good, not just for isolated individuals but for all the members of a community.

Throughout his career, Morgenthau devoted considerable attention to rival ethical perspectives in both classical and modern political philosophy. Central to his own thinking was the conviction that moral self-awareness is inseparable from man's impulse to transcend his natural limits by seeking power and dominion over others.

> Those critics of mine who believe I have no moral concern for politics are mistaken; they are bound to be mistaken because they identify morality with politics; they find morality in politics. Anybody who attempts to demonstrate that he finds a discrepancy between morality and politics is misunderstood. It is as if the test of morality were to gloss over the gap between what men do and what they ought to do in order to identify morality with reality. . . . This is the position in which I find myself with regard to the problem of morality. People arrive at the conclusion that I am not concerned with the problem of morality. The truth is that I am too much concerned with it. [16]

Critics who equate this outlook with the cynicism of Machiavelli, or suggest that it ventures little beyond a "might makes right" defense, exhibit little regard for the care and subtlety with which Morgenthau treated a classic paradox in Western political philosophy. The existential fact of power engenders within human consciousness "that revolt against power which is as universal as the aspiration for power itself." To placate the opposition that emerges when the *animus dominandi* is recognized

16. Hans J. Morgenthau, "Philosophy of International Relations," July 28, 1952 (TS in Morgenthau Papers, Box 81), 42, 49–50.

for what it is, those who wield power for political purposes invoke ideologies to conceal their aims. The aspiration for power is couched in rationalizing language in harmony with the precepts of morality and justice. "Hypocrisy," as Niebuhr observed, "becomes an inevitable by-product in the life of men and nations which retain some loyalty to moral principles, but whose actions do not fully conform to those principles." [17] On numerous occasions, Morgenthau acknowledged that power is a crude and unreliable instrument for limiting the aspirations for power in both domestic and international politics. In addition, he never suggested that the international scene ought to be equated with the state of nature described by Hobbes as a war of every man against every man. Before turning to Morgenthau's reflections on the ethics of *raison d'état*, brief mention should be made of his approach to the norms and rules governing the exercise of power in politics and foreign policy.

Throughout the history of Western civilization, the teachings of Machiavelli and Hobbes have "lacked the intellectual and practical influence that has made such philosophies as St. Augustine's and Locke's potent forces" in relating the rights and aspirations of the individual to the purposes of civil society. Citing attempts by Nietzsche, Mussolini, and Hitler to glorify the struggle for power and absence of restraint as an ideal of society, Morgenthau's judgment was clear-cut: "But in the long run philosophies and political systems that have made the lust and struggle for power their mainstays have proved impotent and self-destructive. Their weakness demonstrates the strength of the Western tradition that seeks, if not to eliminate, at least to regulate and restrain the power drives that would otherwise tear society apart or deliver the life and unhappiness of the weak to the arbitrary will of the powerful." These normative systems have operated on the basis of one fundamental principle: "Superior power gives no right, either moral or legal, to do with that power all that it is physically capable of doing." The exercise of power is, therefore, "subject to limitations, in the interest of society . . . and in the interest of individual members, which are not the result of the mechanics of the struggle for power but are superimposed on that struggle in the form of norms or rules of conduct." [18]

17. Reinhold Niebuhr, "The Moral Issue in International Relations," n.d. (TS in Morgenthau Papers, Box 79), 5; Morgenthau, *Politics Among Nations*, 225.
18. Morgenthau, *Politics Among Nations*, 226.

Morgenthau observed that the expression of self-interest and power in politics is subjected to normative restraint on the basis of three distinctive types of rules of conduct: ethics, mores, and laws. For example, the injunction "Thou shalt not kill" may be applicable to any of the three categories depending upon the type of sanctions used by society to punish the offender. An ethical sanction occurs when an individual experiences pangs of guilt and remorse for murdering another. A sanction peculiar to mores is evident when society responds to the taking of human life through demonstrations, boycotts, and social ostracism. Legal norms are invoked when society reacts to criminal offenders by rational procedures of law enforcement and adjudication. Civilization is built upon these continuous reactions of individuals to the pressures exerted by society in behalf of objective standards designed to keep the aspiration for power within socially tolerable bounds. Democratic nations, in particular, seek to mitigate more violent forms of conflict by relying on such "civilized substitutes" as competitive examinations, competition for social distinctions, and periodic elections for public and private office.[19]

Morgenthau believed that "the history of political thought is the history of the moral evaluation of political power." The test of a principle of morality always lies in a situation of conflict, where one principle of morality stands opposed to another and the ensuing struggle decides which interpretation shall prevail. This is true of individual life; a principle of egotistical morality, for example, will be opposed by a principle of unselfish, communal morality. The conflict between both helps to define operative standards of individual moral behavior. This same dialectical experience is repeated on the international scene. The statesman confronts a conflict between what may be required by the ethics of national conduct and principles of morality that are viewed as binding for the conduct of all men regardless of nationality. This conflict, as Morgenthau argued, in no way diminishes the reality of man's encounter with a hostile environment in which he experiences a universal obligation to mankind. Morgenthau found proof for this moral attachment, despite the stronger binding force of national as opposed to international ethics, in numerous actions: the termination of the terrible killing in war once the end of self-defense is achieved; the widespread condemnation of "ag-

19. Hans J. Morgenthau, "Lectures in International Politics," 1946 (TS in Morgenthau Papers, Box 78), 1–13.

gressive" war; the soldier in combat who tries to distinguish between combatants and civilians; and the work of numerous humanitarian organizations such as the Red Cross and relief agencies of the United Nations. In an interesting observation to his students, Morgenthau once observed that the Cold War between East and West is as much a conflict of ethics as of power.

> You have today at least two, keeping in mind the distribution of power, systems of ethics which oppose one another: the Western, traditional Christian one, and the Russian system. . . . I am not here advocating the idea of an inescapable ideological conflict between Russia and the Western world, but I think it would be an illusion to overlook the fact that certain things which we regard as ethical are regarded as non-ethical by the Russians; that there exists a cleavage not only on certain political interests but also with regard to certain basic principles of morality and conduct in general.[20]

Morgenthau frequently cited the problem of Germany, as seen by both Germans and the rest of the world, as a vivid example of the influence of ethics on world politics. Of particular value is his assessment of the political legacies of Bismarck and Hitler, both often associated with the heritage of *raison d'état* and influential in shaping policies designed to avoid "encirclement" of Germany by its neighbors to the east and west. Bismarck, regardless of particular immoral acts committed on a treacherous diplomatic chessboard, "rarely deviated from the basic rules of the game which had prevailed in the society of Christian princes of the eighteenth century." Although the destruction of Germany's opponents may have been politically desirable, Bismarck's defensive-minded diplomacy "confronted the proximity of Russia and France as a condition of Germany's political existence" and "tried to turn it to Germany's advantage by maintaining closer relations with Russia and by isolating France." Hitler, by contrast, was free of Bismarck's moral scruples and treated the physical destruction of Germany's eastern and western neighbors as an expedient political technique devoid of ethical significance.[21]

Morgenthau cited two basic possibilities for judging the relation-

20. Hans J. Morgenthau, "The Evil of Politics and the Ethics of Evil," *Ethics*, LVI (October, 1945), 1.
21. Morgenthau, *Politics Among Nations*, 232–33.

ship of ethics to power in world affairs. One option, like Rome's solution of the Carthaginian problem, is for a nation to fulfill its power aspirations by "the appropriate means without regard for any transcendent moral considerations." A second approach is typified by a foreign policy that "actually sacrifices the national interest where its consistent pursuit would necessitate the violation of a moral principle, such as the prohibition of mass killings in times of peace." The conflict between these two alternatives was dramatically illustrated by Churchill's reaction to Stalin's proposal for the postwar punishment of Germany at the Teheran Conference in 1943. Against Stalin's suggestion that the fifty thousand officers and technicians of the German General Staff be rounded up and shot at the war's end, Churchill responded: "The British Parliament and public will never tolerate mass executions. . . . I would rather be taken out into the garden here and now and be shot myself than sully my own and my country's honour by such infamy."[22]

Morgenthau's preoccupation with the role and consequences of power in political life has been a persistent inquiry into the practical wisdom of the prudent statesman who aspires to political success but must also operate within a framework of national values and traditions. For our purposes, it is instructive to concentrate on his treatment of the national interest as a problem in political ethics. The lingering remnants of idealism and utopianism in United States diplomatic history reinforced Morgenthau's conviction that American statesmen have persistently misunderstood the nature of foreign policy and its moral significance. In particular, American moral judgment has been corrupted by imagining that the tension between foreign policy and morality, always evident in immediate experience, could easily be made to disappear in favor of more nonviolent, harmonious forms of international cooperation. This is illustrated by the American temptation to visualize the foreign-policy process in mutually exclusive terms: "On the one side, there is the realist, the Machiavellian bargainer, who conceives of foreign policy . . . in terms of power and for whom the end . . . justified the means employed; on the other side, there is the moralist . . . whose ability to bargain is . . . circumscribed . . . by his insistence upon principles which must be reflected in the bargain but cannot be made its object."[23] From the horizon of politi-

22. Winston L. S. Churchill, *Closing the Ring* (Boston, 1951), 373–74. Vol. V of Churchill, *The Second World War*. See Morgenthau, *Politics Among Nations*, 234.
23. Morgenthau, *Dilemmas of Politics*, 249.

cal ethics, this false dichotomy points to the dilemma of trying to reconcile the statesman's obligation to protect the interests of the national community and his loyalty to values and ideals transcending the national community. Fundamental to Morgenthau's effort to bridge this gap are his critique of *raison d'état* and his "sense of transcendence" regarding the moral input into foreign policy.

In an essay prepared for *The Yearbook of World Affairs* in 1951, Morgenthau wrote explicitly about the issue of moral principles versus reason of state—"the issue which Machiavelli had raised into the full consciousness of the Western world and which . . . has never ceased to trouble its conscience." The Anglo-American approach to foreign affairs has more often emphasized the deliberate moral choices and universal principles of conduct underlying the expression of national interest. A classic statement within this tradition can be found in William Gladstone's pamphlet "Bulgarian Horrors and Russia in Turkestan," which, in 1876, judged the obligations of British interests in the following terms: "My hope . . . is twofold. First, that, through the energetic attitude of the people of England, their Government may be led to declare distinctly, that it is for the purposes of humanity alone that we have a fleet in Turkish waters. Secondly, that fleet will be so distributed as to enable its force to be most promptly and efficiently applied, in case of need, on Turkish soil, in concert with the other Powers, for the defense of innocent lives, and to prevent the repetition of those recent scenes, at which hell itself might almost blush."

At the Paris Peace Conference in 1946, former Secretary of State James F. Byrnes observed the difficulty encountered by American diplomats in explaining to their Soviet counterparts "that there were some questions which . . . involved principle and could not be settled by bargaining."[24] English and American thinkers, therefore, applied a philosophy of choice to both internal and external politics.

Morgenthau acknowledged that Meinecke's *Die Idee der Staatsräson* provided the classic account of the philosophic polemics shaping the Continental debate between the Machiavellians and anti-Machiavellians. Throughout the centuries, proponents of *raison d'état* argued that this principle was the ruling force undergirding all state conduct. Sir

---

24. Morgenthau, "The Moral Dilemma in Foreign Policy," in *The Yearbook of World Affairs, 1951*, pp. 22–23.

Herbert Butterfield, in an essay entitled "The Relations Between Morality and Government," described the ambiguity and inconsistency surrounding the use of the concept throughout history. Up until the time of Machiavelli, the term served as a characterization of the state as "a power apparatus." After 1600, "reason of state" could refer at times to statecraft in general and at other times to the founding, maintenance, strength, security, and expansion of the state. *Raison d'état*, interpreted as a form of diplomacy, may also suggest that all major decisions in foreign policy will be dictated by external circumstances beyond human control, statesmen and people alike being absolved as a consequence from all moral responsibility. The quest for moral guidance would be cast aside to give free play to expediency and the concern for power. Morgenthau took exception to an implicit political assumption of *raison d'état*—that there is morality on one side and immorality on the other. He asserted: "Even most of the Machiavellians, coming to the defense of the despised master, did not dare prove that the doctrine of political realism, as it stood, could be morally justified, but rather endeavored to demonstrate that Machiavelli did not mean what he seemed to say, that his position was to be explained by the conditions of the time. . . . Yet the equation of political moralism with morality and of political realism with immorality is itself untenable."[25]

The philosophy of *raison d'état*, Morgenthau asserted, is betrayed by the error of differentiating the political sphere from the private for purposes of ethical evaluation. In matters of foreign policy, the state is subject to no rule of conduct but the one that is dictated by its own self-interest. *Salus publica suprema lex*. Ethical prohibitions, as proponents of *raison d'état* believed, are vitiated by the statesman's obligation successfully to pursue national goals, defined in terms of power, in a world devoid of substantive multinational norms. Although an individual's moral nature may be reflected in private life, political life is free of such ethical limitations and is immoral by nature. This dual standard of morality was strikingly formulated by one of the greatest Italian statesmen, Cavour, when he said: "If we had done for ourselves what we have done for Italy, what scoundrels we would have been."[26]

25. *Ibid.*, 34–35. Butterfield's critique of *raison d'état* is developed by Thompson, *Moralism and Morality in Politics and Diplomacy*, 46–49.
26. Morgenthau, *The Decline of Democratic Politics*, 314; Cavour quoted in Morgenthau, "The Evil of Politics and the Ethics of Evil," 4.

Herein lies a profound misconception that assumes a fundamental difference between the actions of individuals and the actions of statesmen acting for their own nations. The difference in relations between individuals within states and between states is more a matter of degree than kind. What changes for the nature and role of moral judgment on either level is not the action itself, but the social environment within which these norms must function. One obvious example of this structural difference can be noted in the case of faithfulness to treaty obligations. The norm *pacta sunt servanda* (*i.e.*, treaties voluntarily entered into are binding) is typically less effective than the ethical and political sanctions affecting private contracts. A contract of civil law, for example, uses standardized language whose legal meaning can usually be determined by objective, universally recognized standards. An international treaty, on the other hand, may be disguised with diplomatic language so that its wording is indicative only of what it does not mean. "This dichotomy," as Morgenthau pointed out, "stands or falls depending on the existing conditions of peace and order that exist on both planes." For example, individual actions in an unintegrated society in the midst of either revolution or civil war approach the usual conditions on the international scene. In no uncertain terms, Morgenthau summarized his objection to *raison d'état* by saying: "The importance of this conception has been literary rather than practical. . . . Political philosophy from the Greeks to our time has started with the assumption that man in the political sphere is not allowed to act as he pleases and that his action must conform to a standard higher than . . . success. It has even made this conformity the test of legitimate political power. . . . As the *lex Salica* put it: 'King thou will be if thou follow the law. If thou do not follow the law, thou will not be king.'"[27]

Morgenthau's rejection of the dual moral standard embodied in *raison d'état* raises the more problematic issue of his own conception regarding the moral basis of all political conduct. "The commands of morality," he acknowledged, "are absolute and must be obeyed for their own sake." On the subject of the professor's philosophical obligation in both the classroom and political arena, he spoke frequently of an "organic relation between transmitting knowledge and an objective, immu-

27. Morgenthau, *Scientific Man*, 176; Hans J. Morgenthau, "Philosophy of International Relations," n.d. (TS in Morgenthau Papers, Box 81), 19–20.

table truth." The scholar's life "is a profession which requires the dedication and ethos of the whole man." On the question of whether morality is always relative, the ever-changing result of environment and circumstances, Morgenthau left little doubt about his ethical convictions. His observations on the Van Doren scandal at Columbia in 1959 deserve to be quoted at length.

> How do you explain that the moral ideas of Plato and Pascal, of Buddha and Thomas Aquinas are . . . acceptable to our intellectual understanding and moral sense? If the historic systems of morality were not erected upon a common foundation of moral understanding and valuation, impervious to the changing conditions of time and place, we could [not] understand any moral system but our own. . . . It is only because we as moral beings have something in common with all other men—past and present—that we are able to understand . . . the core of the moral systems of others.

That quality that all men have in common as moral beings is an existential reach for transcendence as a condition of fulfilling their own humanity. Morgenthau cited the passage from the Scriptures: "He that findeth his life shall lose it; and he that loseth his life for my sake shall find it." [28]

Although never denying that normative systems of thought frequently function as subterfuges to rationalize an individual's lust for power, Morgenthau took seriously the role of morality in conflicts of power: "Political ethics is . . . the ethics of doing evil. . . . Neither science nor ethics nor politics can resolve this conflict between politics and ethics into harmony. . . . To know with despair that the political act is inevitably evil, and to act nevertheless is moral courage. To choose among several expedient actions the least evil one is moral judgment." [29]

For Morgenthau, the popular juxtaposition of "power" politics and "moral" politics is fundamentally mistaken. The supposed opposition between man and society is "a mere figure of speech" in that "it is always the individual who acts, either with reference to his ends alone or with reference to the ends of others." Morgenthau suggested that the differ-

28. Morgenthau, *The Purpose of American Politics*, 355–58.
29. Roger L. Shinn, "Realism and Ethics in Political Philosophy," in Thompson and Myers (eds.), *Truth and Tragedy*, 96.

ence in moral character between a private, as over against a political, action is a relative one and is devoid of the absoluteness that contemporary doctrine attributes to it. Commenting on the ethical quality of political conduct, he wrote: "The political actor has . . . a general moral responsibility to act wisely . . . and for him expediency becomes a moral duty. . . . What is here done with good intentions but unwisely and . . . with disastrous results is morally defective, for it violates the ethics of responsibility to which all action affecting others and . . . political action *par excellence* is subject."[30]

Many students of Morgenthau's thought have understandably found a troubling ambivalence in his relationship of interest and principle. For example, one critic notes that "the overall impact of Morgenthau's writing is to maintain a separation of the political sphere and the moral sphere, though judgments are made about the immorality of politics." At times, his terminology tends to portray the moral dilemma of politics in rather extreme terms. Surely, Morgenthau's objective to affirm, yet limit, the boundaries of moral choice in public life appears suspect in light of such categorical observations as:

> The invocation of moral principles for the support of national policies is always and of necessity a pretense.

> It is impossible . . . to be a successful politician and a good Christian.

> There is no escape from the evil of power regardless of what one does. Whenever we act with reference to our fellow men, we must sin. . . . The political act is inevitably evil.[31]

The unqualified character of these "musts" and "inevitables" left Morgenthau vulnerable to the accusation of surrendering to Machiavellian cynicism.

Morgenthau's sometimes-extreme accentuation of the "autonomy

30. Morgenthau, *Scientific Man*, 186; "The Evil of Politics and the Ethics of Evil," 11.

31. Morgenthau, *Scientific Man*, 196–202; "National Interest and Moral Principles in Foreign Policy," 11; "The Influence of Reinhold Niebuhr in American Political Life and Thought," in Harold R. Landon (ed.), *Reinhold Niebuhr: A Prophetic Voice in Our Time* (Greenwich, Conn., 1962), 105; Ronald Stone, *Reinhold Niebuhr: Prophet to Politicians* (Lanham, Md., 1981), 202.

of politics" and "paramountcy of the national interest" in foreign policy must also be evaluated within the context of his stern denunciation of legalistic and moralistic approaches to international politics. In taking strong exception to the pretentious idealism of these approaches, he seemed to jeopardize his own case for the morality of political action. Elsewhere in his writing, however, Morgenthau was more restrained and informative about the ethical failure of political idealism and the link between morality and public policy. From an ethical standpoint, the idealist in politics erred in assuming "that the principles of morality have the same substantive quality as . . . the principles of politics, economics, or law."[32] In the arena of international politics, the idealist jeopardizes the national interest by promoting world-embracing principles that are too vague and general to provide guidance to policy (*e.g.*, "defend and promote democracy" or "freedom and the rights of man").

Noteworthy in this respect was a televised debate in January 1974 between Morgenthau and Daniel Berrigan on the subject of Israeli power and the rights of Palestinians and other Arab states in the Middle East. At issue, according to Berrigan, was America's moral obligation to resist Israel as "an imperial nation embarked on an imperial venture." Morgenthau responded that it is one thing to raise certain questions in the abstract—especially theological, ethical questions—and it is something else altogether to raise the same questions in the concrete context of a particular political and military situation. In Morgenthau's judgment, Berrigan's ethical deficiency consisted of starting from a basic assumption of the Judaic-Christian tradition—that the world is evil, that violence is evil—and then picking out a particular manifestation (*i.e.*, the actions of Israel) and equating it with the devil as such. The requirements of political justice, by contrast, would have required Berrigan to compare the evil he saw in Israeli policies with the corruption and immorality around Israel and then arrive at an assessment that the church fathers call a Conclusion of Prudence. The lack of moral discrimination only strains relations, worsens conflicts of interests by investing them with moral content, and results at the end in a moral crusade.[33]

32. Morgenthau, *Dilemmas of Politics*, 253.
33. "Daniel Berrigan and Hans Morgenthau Discuss the Moral Dilemma in the Middle East," *Progressive*, XXVIII (March, 1974), 31; Robert C. Good, "The National Interest and Political Realism: Niebuhr's Debate with Morgenthau and Kennan," *Journal of Politics*, XXII (1960), 602.

Although the idealist dichotomizes and ultimately substitutes the principles of morality for those of politics, Morgenthau refused to consider morality as just another branch of human activity, coordinate with other substantive intellectual disciplines. To the contrary, morality "is superimposed upon them, limiting the choice of ends and means and delineating the legitimate sphere of a particular branch of action altogether." This restraining function is especially important in the political sphere, he argued, "for the political actor is peculiarly tempted to blind himself to the limits of his power and to overstep the boundaries of both prudence and morality." Even the most ruthless political leader must pay tribute (however hypocritical) to moral standards by justifying his actions in ethical terms. Based on this logic, Morgenthau could label *raison d'état* a "figure of speech": "The moves and countermoves in the struggle for . . . power must be intelligible as a dialectic movement toward the realization of justice. However devoid of positive ethical significance the individual act may be, it is bound to be less than completely evil . . . for the necessity of justifying it in ethical terms carries with it the obligations for even the most cynical actor to choose his measures so that they, however evil, will coincide at . . . some point with the standards of ethics." [34]

Realism and a Framework of Moral Reasoning

The widely held assumption that Morgenthau has simply updated Hobbes does him serious injustice. He was aware of this popular fallacy and acknowledged: "Disregarding the voluminous evidence, some of them have picked a few words out of their context to prove that realism in international affairs is unprincipled and contemptuous of morality." Particularly troubling for some critics was his reference to the dictum of Hobbes that "there is neither morality nor law outside the state." Not so widely reported was his observation that "universal moral principles, such as justice and equality, are capable of guiding political action to the extent that they have been given concrete content and . . . [are] related to political situations by society." Indeed, Morgenthau has always maintained that the actions of states *are subject to universal moral principles*.

34. Morgenthau, "The Evil of Politics and the Ethics of Evil," 5; *Dilemmas of Politics*, 253–54.

Summarizing Lincoln's religious philosophy, no less than the fundamental moral predicament of the statesman in foreign affairs, Morgenthau wrote: "Man is a forlorn actor on the stage of the world; for he does not know the nature of the plot and the outcome of the play written by an inaccessible author." Yet, with a memory that spans the ages, man is also a "confident and self-sufficient actor; for he knows that there is a script, however . . . unknowable its content, and he can do more than act out what he believes the script to require."[35] It is possible to identify five basic themes or concepts on the basis of which Morgenthau's ideas on international morality differed from those of Hobbes.

1. *Cosmic Humility.* Although Morgenthau considered national interest as the perennial standard by which foreign policy must be judged and directed, he also affirmed the requirement of cosmic humility with regard to the moral evaluation of states. Such a standard obliges the realist to view the moral significance of political action as a product of the ineluctable tension between the moral command and the requirements of political success. "To know that states are subject to the moral law is one thing; to pretend to know what is morally required of states in a particular situation is quite another." Throughout history, statesmen have often yielded to the temptation of identifying the moral aspirations of a particular nation with the moral laws that govern the universe. In this regard, Morgenthau wrote: "The lighthearted equation between a particular nationalism and the counsels of Providence is morally indefensible . . . for it is liable to engender the distortion of judgment which, in the blindness of crusading frenzy, destroys nations and civilizations—in the name of moral principle, ideal, or God himself."[36]

Morgenthau's concern for the ideological concealment and justification of necessity was given classic expression in the thought of John Adams, who wrote: "Power always thinks it has a great soul and vast views beyond the comprehension of the weak and that it is doing God's service when it is violating all His laws. Our passions . . . possess so much metaphysical subtlety . . . and overpowering eloquence that they insinu-

35. Morgenthau, *Dilemmas of Politics*, 80–81; Morgenthau and Hein, *Essays on Lincoln's Faith and Politics*, 16. See also George Liska, "Morgenthau vs. Machiavelli: Political Realism and Power Politics," in Thompson and Myers (eds.), *Truth and Tragedy*, 104–11.

36. Morgenthau, *Politics Among Nations*, 11.

ate themselves into the understanding and conscience and convert both to their party." [37]

In one respect, therefore, the gap between moral principle and political expedience functions as a brake on the temptation to pretense and hypocrisy.

2. *Morality as a System of Restraints.* Any discussion of the role of international ethics must guard against two extremes: either overestimating the influence of ethics upon international politics or underestimating the reality of moral choices that deny that statesmen are moved by anything but ideological or material motivations. Morgenthau's awareness of the "irremediable gap" between "the moral ideal and the facts of political life" was also qualified by his belief that there are moral absolutes that are not to be trespassed under any circumstances in the pursuit of national interest. "Moral rules do not permit certain policies to be considered at all from the point of view of expediency." Into this category, Morgenthau included policies of mass extermination, torture, and the killing of civilian populations in war. Critics raise a legitimate point of debate by referring to Morgenthau's often categorical formulation of the moral dilemma in all political action. What is the significance, for example, of "moral absolutes that are not to be trespassed under any circumstances" when Morgenthau speaks of the "objective" requirements of the national interest in the following terms: "Whenever the appeal to moral principles provides guidance for political action in international affairs, it destroys the very moral principles which it intends to realize." Paradoxically, it is this "irremediable gap" that Morgenthau wished to transcend when he wrote: "Certain things are not to be done on moral grounds, even though it would be expedient to do them. Such ethical inhibitions operate in our time on different levels with different effectiveness. Their restraining function is most obvious and most effective in affirming the sacredness of human life in times of peace." [38]

In relating moral restraints to politics, Morgenthau echoed Burke's vision of prudent statesmanship. The role of prudence for Morgenthau, as for Burke, was that of adjusting principle to circumstance. "There can be no political morality without prudence . . . without consideration of the political consequences of seemingly moral action." Prudence, there-

37. *Ibid.*, 90.
38. Morgenthau, *Politics Among Nations*, 231.

fore, becomes an important procedural standard if policy ends are to be made consistent with policy means. A continuing challenge for the ethics of American realism is the extent to which the resort to prudence enables the statesman to narrow or bridge the gap between the parochial and general interest. Niebuhr, for example, argued that "any kind of prudence which estimates common problems from the perspective of a particular interest will define the interest too narrowly." Moral reasoning in international politics, he suggested, must "draw upon another moral and spiritual resource to widen the conception of interest. . . . The sense of justice must prevent prudence from becoming too prudential in defining interest." [39]

3. *Morality and the Pragmatic Anglo-American Tradition.* Morgenthau's emphasis on prudence in policy making was paralleled by his preference for the pragmatic qualities of the Anglo-American political tradition. In contrast to the philosophic polemics characterizing the debate between *raison d'état* and moral principles on the European continent, the political theory of the English-speaking peoples developed "not in comprehensive systematic efforts but in a series of debates concerned with the practical merits of limited concrete issues." As a series of cases debated in the forum of public opinion, the Anglo-American approach exhibited the belief in the infinite variety and random nature of reality, the idea of historical progress and the scientific search for truth as a cooperative social endeavor, the preference for empirical procedures aiming at immediate practical results over theoretical consistency, the ability to see in any concrete issue the instance of a general proposition rather than empirical proof for *a priori* abstractions, and the prominence of public debate determining a decision in light of the rational merits of the case. In international politics, universal norms must always be filtered through circumstances of time and place that limit their application. In his "Fragment of an Intellectual Biography," Morgenthau summarized his position by saying: "This aversion to a dogmatism that sacrifices pragmatic effectiveness for logical or ideological consistency has remained a persistent element of my intellectual attitude." [40]

4. *Foreign Policy and Transcendent Principles.* Often neglected by

39. Good, "The National Interest and Political Realism: Niebuhr's Debate with Morgenthau and Kennan," 601; Morgenthau, *Dilemmas of Politics*, 84.

40. Morgenthau, "Fragment of an Intellectual Biography," in Thompson and Myers (eds.), *Truth and Tragedy*, 67; *Dilemmas of Politics*, 251.

international relations scholars also was Morgenthau's own "sense of transcendence"; this served both to illuminate and to complicate his thinking on foreign policy norms. Perhaps one reason why this particular theme has failed to stimulate much debate is that Morgenthau's transcendent frame of reference is somewhat vague, more implicit than explicit, and without clearly defined roots in any philosophical or theological system. Nowhere does he explicitly develop a transcendent international political ethic or a normative calculus by which to rank and evaluate alternative ethical objectives in world politics. By neglecting to develop further the transcendent source of applicable universal norms in foreign policy, his "sense of transcendence" tends to function as an indiscriminate standard of analysis; at most, it provides a negative judgment on sinful man while failing to affirm the positive moral potential of the prudent statesman. For those detractors who indict Morgenthau as a modern spokesman for *raison d'état*, his insistence on the limitations of morality in politics takes precedence over the fact that he could never fully escape the judgment made by transcendent norms upon every politically expedient act. The difficult question for students of foreign policy concerns the extent to which Morgenthau introduced norms to direct and judge interest from a moral vantage point beyond the operative political reality of the nation. In other words, is the parochial national interest the ultimate and exclusive standard from which all principles derive?

Despite Morgenthau's observation that moral principles must be derived from political practice and not imposed on it, one could plausibly argue that his discussion of the national interest could not help but invoke transcendent norms as a distinctive force in the life of nations. In denying the application of any criteria for judging state behavior, other than those derived from political necessity, the realist must end up a cynic. Yet Morgenthau was anything but a confirmed cynic, even if he never explained fully how or why such norms entered into his view of the national interest. Two vivid examples will illustrate the presence of this ambiguity in his thinking.

In seeking to defend the primacy of the national interest in foreign policy, Morgenthau repeatedly objected to the pretentious hypocrisy of America's presumed innocence and virtue. Yet, ironically, his objection to moral pretense in foreign policy seemed to infer a standard of evaluation beyond any particular conception of the national interest. One scholar, documenting Morgenthau's transcendent frame of reference, suggested: "The charge of hypocrisy is a moral charge not a political judgment. It is to protest that a man [or nation] is not what he pretends to be, and . . . is not as moral as he pretends to be. If the only standard for judging the behavior of states were national interest, one would not likely accuse the pretentious statesman of hypocrisy, a term laden with moral censure."[41] If the charge of hypocrisy were to be interpreted as an expedient political action, then one would have expected Morgenthau to accept the adherence to moral claims, like the wielding of the sword, as justifiable when it was in the national interest to do so. From a purely political standpoint, the pretense to virtue in statecraft would more likely be condemned, not by reference to moral hypocrisy, but as an imprudent act of sheer political stupidity. In other words, without recourse to moral judgments transcending interest, Morgenthau's position would be compatible with *raison d'état*. Not only would moral claims be fabricated by the state (as in Hobbes), but their intrinsic value would be reduced to a formula of expedient assumptions rationalizing political decisions (as in Machiavelli).

Similarly, Morgenthau's emphasis on the paramount importance of diplomacy as an element of national power displayed a curious mix of propositions, again based on both political self-interest and transcendent moral principles. On the one hand, diplomacy must reflect (even as it tries to moderate) antagonistic interests in a world devoid of any moral consensus on operative international norms. "Diplomacy, however morally unattractive its business may seem to many, is nothing but a symptom of the struggle for power among sovereign states." At the same time, however, Morgenthau never envisioned diplomacy as merely an inventory of amoral methods capable of being placed in the service of any system of values. Morgenthau treated diplomacy itself as a kind of norm, directed by certain motives toward certain goals: "The objective of foreign policy is relative and conditional: to bend, not to break, the will of the other side . . . in order to safeguard one's own vital interests without hurting those of the other side. The methods of foreign policy are relative

41. For an analysis of Morgenthau's reliance upon universal political norms, see Good, "The National Interest and Political Realism: Niebuhr's Debate with Morgenthau and Kennan," 609–12.

and conditional: not to advance by destroying the obstacles in one's way, but to retreat before them . . . to soften and dissolve them . . . by means of negotiation and pressure."[42] Yet these diplomatic norms are anything but self-evident in Morgenthau's reliance upon the national interest as a moral-free guide to foreign policy. Morgenthau's idea that the national interest demands a moderate and restrained diplomacy to help create an international society conducive to democratic values did not escape the "invocation of moral principle" so much as it invested the national interest with moral content.

These examples culminate in a conception of national interest that embodied a notion of purpose that, by its nature, must transcend pure self-interest. How is one to account for this implicit normative dimension in the workings of the national interest, in light of Morgenthau's periodic tendency to recoil from universal principles in foreign policy? Undoubtedly, a number of his more extreme statements were perhaps chosen for their cutting edge in a polemical contest with the idealists. A good case, however, can be made for the contention that these bold affirmations of the national interest purged of pretentious moral content do not fairly represent Morgenthau's thought. Indeed, Morgenthau made it clear that he had no objection to residual ethical considerations limiting the statesman's duty to promote national security. Instead, he took exception to the idealistic tradition of applying universal moral principles to the actions of states without due regard for the political effects of avowedly moral action. Summarizing Morgenthau's outlook on the moral requirements of foreign policy, one commentator has observed: "More than Niebuhr, Morgenthau is inclined to say that politics . . . involves a choice of lesser evils. These are fateful choices that involve not so much the balancing of rights against rights as judgments about which course of action is least likely to bring harmful results."[43]

In seeking to fashion an acceptable political ethic, Morgenthau emphasized two ways in which transcendent norms influence the pursuit of narrow self-interest. First, these principles serve as the relevant, objective, and constant goal of political life. "Both individual and state must judge political action by universal moral principles, such as that of liberty." Admittedly, this theme is not always present or stated unequivocally in

42. *Ibid.*; Morgenthau, *Politics Among Nations*, 530.
43. Thompson, "Moral Reasoning in American Thought on War and Peace," 393.

his published work. Furthermore, given the absence of a moral consensus in world politics, Morgenthau provided little indication of the type of new policies or instrumentalities that could generate mutual moral sympathies regarding transnational political issues. In a statement distinguished not only for its candor but also by a lingering moral hope for mankind, he wrote: "As there can be no permanent peace without a world state, there can be no world state without the . . . community-building processes of diplomacy. For the world state to be more than a dim vision, the accommodating processes of diplomacy . . . must be revived. Whatever one's conception of the ultimate state of international affairs may be, in the recognition of that need and in the demand that it be met, all men of good will can join."[44]

Second, Morgenthau's sense of transcendence relied on universal moral principles to expose and moderate the temptation to hypocritical pretense in foreign policy. At this level, morality functioned more as a judgmental restraint than a controlling end-in-view. The prudent statesman capable of distinguishing between "the misery of politics" and the realm of universal ethical norm is less apt to commit the sin of the fascist mind: the equation of "political and military success with moral superiority."[45] Therefore, the absolute principle (or, at least, its recognition) prevents acts of gross immorality, while at the same time identifying every political act as in fact political and inconsistent with the moral law. Morgenthau never wavered from the belief that "all human actions in some way are subject to moral judgment. We cannot act but morally because we are men. . . . But man, exactly because his imagination soars above natural limits and his aspirations aim at certain objectives that are not naturally limited, must submit *as man* to moral limitations that may be larger or more narrow as the case may be, but which exist."[46]

A number of concluding observations can help illuminate several unresolved issues and continuing topics of debate in Morgenthau's conception of political ethics. Reconciling the requirements of political necessity and moral judgment depends upon distinguishing between the absolute good that is everywhere the same, and the relative good

44. Morgenthau, *Politics Among Nations*, 9, 547.
45. Good, "The National Interest and Political Realism: Niebuhr's Debate with Morgenthau and Kennan," 612.
46. Hans J. Morgenthau, *Human Rights and Foreign Policy* (New York, 1979), 1.

that is merely good under particular circumstances. Morgenthau believed that the very existence of political conflicts points to an "irreducible minimum" of psychological aspirations that all men share because of a common human nature. These include such objectives as freedom and self-expression, power and social distinction. From this psychological foundation arises an "edifice of philosophic valuations, ethical postulates, and political aspirations." The fact that these standards of political action and moral evaluation are shared only on the verbal level is indicative of the considerable variance in conditions under which men strive to satisfy their desire for freedom and power. In an essay distinguishing between philosophic and political standards of action, Morgenthau alluded to the role of universal and relative conceptions of morality: "While philosophically the similarities of standards are considerable throughout the world—most philosophies agree in their evaluation of the common good, of law, peace and order, of life, liberty, and the pursuit of happiness—moral judgments and political actions show wide divergences. . . . Justice and democracy come to mean one thing here, something quite different there. A move on the international scene decried by one group as immoral and unjust is praised by another as the opposite."[47]

The success of political ideologies will be determined, not by the number and importance of abstract truths and moral values in the message, but by its ability to provide some immediate satisfaction to deeply felt intellectual and political needs. In terms of the execution of American foreign policy, Morgenthau frequently chided policy-makers for allowing such moral and philosophic abstractions (*e.g.*, global crusades for democracy and human rights) to impede the objective investigation of what other people want. This, perhaps more than any other miscalculation, explains the miscarriage of American power and moral purpose in the Vietnam War.

Morgenthau spoke of the relativization of justice as a precondition for a heightened ethical awareness and relativization of power in world politics. National conceptions of justice, in order to be effective in restraining the machinations of power in foreign policy, must build upon

47. Hans J. Morgenthau, "A Positive Approach to a Democratic Ideology," *Proceedings of the Academy of Political Science*, XXIV (January, 1951), 79–81.

normative precepts applicable to fluctuating conditions and circumstances. The fragmentation of a once-cohesive international society into a multiplicity of morally self-sufficient communities, which no longer operate according to either Christian or secular cosmopolitan precepts, is the manifestation of a profound change that has transformed the relationship between universal moral commands and competing systems of national ethics. Today's ethics of nationalistic universalism, far from limiting the struggle for power on the international scene, "gives that struggle a ferociousness and intensity not known to other ages." Compromise, the virtue of the old diplomacy, becomes the treason of the new; "for the mutual accommodation of conflicting claims, possible or legitimate within a common framework of moral standards, amounts to surrender when the moral standards themselves are the stakes of the conflict."[48]

If Morgenthau's position continues to raise doubts about the moral significance of political action, this is largely attributable to the relationship between his estimate of man's nature and the use of transcendent norms in political analysis. Up to a point, Morgenthau's view of human nature paralleled Reinhold Niebuhr's depiction of man's tragic situation. For Morgenthau, "the lust for power" was a "ubiquitous empirical fact." In a revealing passage, he noted: "For no social action can be completely free of the taint of egotism which, as selfishness, pride, or self-deception, seeks for the actor more than is his due." Niebuhr objected to Morgenthau's rather fatalistic formulation of man's moral predicament because it ignored the potentially creative presence of the human will. To will evil, Niebuhr believed, implied the freedom to will the good. The biblical concept of human will provided Niebuhr with a responsible basis for maintaining that man is in part free, and in part bound by necessity; as sinful, yet knowing himself to be a sinner; as capable of justice, yet inclined to injustice.[49]

Furthermore, Morgenthau's pessimistic view of man raises an additional difficulty. The pervasive evil in human nature and politics rendered his formal ethic so transcendent that it could not easily function

48. Hans J. Morgenthau, "Philosophy of International Relations," n.d. (TS in Morgenthau Papers, Box 81), 28–31; *Politics Among Nations*, 252–56.
49. Reinhold Niebuhr, "Christianity and Communism: Social Justice," *Spectator*, November 6, 1936, pp. 802–803.

as a vital force directing man's creative energies in an imperfect world. Morgenthau asserted that "all nations stand under the judgment of God," but he also acknowledged that God's will is "inscrutable to the human mind." Morgenthau believed that operative political norms are ultimately derived from transcendent ethical principles; however, he was less helpful on how, and to what degree, these principles are capable of guiding political action when distorted by the institutions of sinful man. Because his concept of moral principle was so transcendent, morality could operate only as a restraint on political man by saving him from hypocrisy (*i.e.*, by demonstrating to him that he is not God).[50]

The normative foundations of Morgenthau's world view point to an inevitable ambiguity, because the factors of interest and power, which are regarded as an irrelevance in pure morality, must be tentatively admitted to the realm of social morality. He realized that a narrow preoccupation with self-interest in the affairs of men and nations ultimately would be a source of discord; however, the presumptuous deprecation of self-interest runs an equally grave risk of ignoring those forces and aspirations that are necessary to prevent the harmony of the whole from destroying the vitality of the parts. Along similar lines, the risks and danger of power must be accommodated and channeled for two constructive purposes: to assure a proper counterweight against power in the interest of justice and to provide for the coercion that is necessary for the order and stability of any community. Moral reasoning in international politics, he believed, obliged the pragmatic statesman to reconcile competing moral values flowing from divergent interpretations of a nation's interest in a particular situation and at a particular time. Morgenthau pointed to the intellectual legacy of Burke, who wrote: "Nothing universal can be rationally affirmed on any moral or any political subject. Pure metaphysical abstraction does not belong to these matters. The lines of morality . . . admit of exceptions; they demand modifications. These exceptions and modifications are not made by the process of logic, but by the rules of prudence. Prudence is not only the first in rank of the virtues political and moral, but she is the director, the regulator, the standard of them all."[51]

50. Good, "The National Interest and Political Realism: Niebuhr's Debate with Morgenthau and Kennan," 613.

51. Morgenthau, *Dilemmas of Politics*, 84.

Morgenthau's analysis of the ethical problem in international relations points to the inability of a government morally to transcend what the nation regards as its interests. Yet even a prudent expression of self-interest in the nuclear age can promise little unless leaders confront the ultimate question of how the good of the nation may fit into a more general and universal scheme of values.

CHAPTER FIVE

Morgenthau and Contemporary Foreign-Policy Developments

Our focus now turns to Hans J. Morgenthau's outlook on several major foreign-policy issues of the last decade that have generated considerable debate among scholars and public officials. To evaluate Morgenthau only at the level of formal theory or political philosophy ignores his role as a political activist who sought to "speak the truth to power." His opposition to the credo of *raison d'état* formed the organic basis for recommending operative restraints and obligations indispensable for the successful defense of American national interests in world affairs. Realism did not require Morgenthau to ignore international developments—particularly in view of nuclear-weapons technology—that rendered the nation-state, as well as the traditional balance of power, virtually obsolete. As public commentator, Morgenthau stressed limitations on the uses of power and inveighed against its inordinate exercise over a range of cases, from the relatively minor Quemoy-Matsu crisis to the Vietnam War. Specific attention is devoted to Morgenthau's views on such topics as international law and world government, nuclear war and disarmament, intervention and the projection of American military and political power in the Third World, and the promotion of human rights in foreign policy.

International Law and Organization

Numerous scholars have looked to the modern science of international law as a substitute for, or as a restraining influence upon, the competition for power and military advantage in world affairs. What George Kennan has termed the "legalistic-moralistic approach" encompasses the optimistic belief that international law, if codified to include the political relations of states, could do away with the balance of power, spheres of influence, and policies seeking national aggrandizement. Having authored a doctoral dissertation on the judicial function in international politics, Morgenthau retained a lifelong interest in its nature and limitations. Typical of his intellectual inclination, he probed beyond selected cases and events to lay bare the operative philosophical world view shaping both the interpretation and application of legal principles in the relations of sovereign states.

The development of international law since the last decades of the nineteenth century is characterized by assumptions rooted in the positivist doctrine of law. In general, positivist philosophy limits the true objects of scientific knowledge to phenomena that can be verified by observation and excludes all issues of an *a priori*, metaphysical nature. The legal positivist restricts his attention to rules enacted by the state and excludes all law not found in the statute books or recorded in court decisions. Summarizing the positivist doctrine of law, Morgenthau wrote: "Positivist jurisprudence . . . separates the law from other normative spheres, that is, ethics and mores . . . and from the social sphere, comprehending the psychological, political, and economic fields. . . . It proceeds on the assumption that law, as it really is, can be understood without the normative and social context in which it actually stands."[1]

According to Morgenthau, the positivist doctrine of law culminates in a threefold misconception of the nature of international law. First, the antimetaphysical assumptions ignore the fact that legal rules always refer to ethics and mores for the determination of their meaning. "At the foundation of any legal system there lies a body of principles which incorporate the guiding ideas of justice and order to be expounded by the rules of law." Morgenthau pointed to such concepts as "the binding force of international law" and "sovereignty" as legal principles whose foundation is to be found, not in the "positive" law itself, but only outside it.[2]

Second, in the international field, positivism commits the methodological error of neglecting the sociological context of economic interests,

1. Morgenthau, *Dilemmas of Politics*, 217.
2. *Ibid.*, 218.

social tensions, and aspirations for power. These underlying factors function as "the motivating forces in the international field and . . . give rise to the factual situations to be regulated by international law." In the domestic arena, the self-sufficiency of the written law could be maintained because the correspondence between legal concepts and sociological context was often a temporary fact in a stabilized society. As Morgenthau noted, the positivist method of formalist and conceptualist interpretation of domestic law produces inadequate results when applied to a society of a distinctively different nature. In the decentralized international milieu, the presumption of self-sufficient law is vitiated by complex sociological relationships that are unique and atypical in nature. He wrote: "Where the experience of international law showed that an individual situation required an individual interpretation of the legal rule, the positivist method could not fail to disregard all individual aspects of the factual situation and concentrate on the general working of the legal rule which, by virtue of its logical self-sufficiency, was to contain all elements necessary for its understanding; and to this the sociological context could contribute nothing."[3] For Morgenthau, therefore, international law involving political agreements among states expresses certain interests and rights subject to change and the most contradictory interpretations.

Third, the statist monism integral to positive law excludes from the domain of international law all rules whose validity cannot be traced to written official documents. The axiom of legal self-sufficiency is confronted with two problems for which the positivist doctrine of international law has no solution. On the one hand, all rules embodied in written documents are not valid international law; and, on the other hand, there are valid rules of international law other than rules outlined in written documents. Legal positivism has provided no objective standard by which to differentiate between *seemingly* and *actually* valid rules of international law.

Despite his intellectual quarrel with the modern "science" of international law, Morgenthau never doubted either the existence of international law or its tangible contribution in specifying the rights and duties of states in relation to each other. The rules of international law for the modern state system were established by the Treaty of Westphalia (1648).

3. *Ibid.*, 222.

Upon this foundation, contemporary international law has added thousands of treaties, hundreds of decisions of international tribunals, and innumerable decisions of domestic courts. He wrote: "These treaties and decisions regulate . . . the relations between nations arising from . . . the variety of international contacts, which are the result of modern communications, international exchange of goods and services, and the great number of international organizations in which most nations have cooperated for the furtherance of their common interests." Morgenthau conceded that during the four hundred years of its existence international law has, in most respects, been scrupulously observed. Lack of public confidence in international law has often resulted from the dubious efficacy of such grand designs as the Kellogg-Briand Pact, the Covenant of the League of Nations, and the Charter of the United Nations. These instruments, however, are "not typical of the traditional rules of international law concerning, for instance, the limits of territorial jurisdiction, the rights of vessels in foreign waters, and the status of diplomatic representatives."[4]

In the final analysis, Morgenthau described international law as "a primitive type of law" similar to that prevailing "in certain preliterate societies." The primitive character of international law is, in large measure, the inevitable result of the decentralized structure of international society. An international society composed of sovereign states is devoid of any central law-enforcing authority. International law, Morgenthau contended, owes its existence to two factors, both decentralized in nature: identical or complementary interests of individual states and the distribution of power among them. Finding the substance of international law in the interplay of contingent, objective social forces, he wrote: "The cry . . . for order under law as an alternative to the international anarchy of our age is reasonable under the assumption that the international sphere already contains the social elements making for order and peace."[5]

On the subject of international organization, Morgenthau recounted the political and moral shortcomings behind idealistic aspirations for world government; in addition, he examined the requirements of American national interest in terms of effective participation in a

4. Morgenthau, *Politics Among Nations*, 272–73.
5. Morgenthau, *Scientific Man*, 117.

universal political forum such as the United Nations. He noted that contemporary proposals for world government frequently contain an element of "perfectionist escapism." The perfectionist believes that, by a sheer act of will on the part of the individual either through social reform or education, man can be changed and made to abandon the evils of politics and the lust for power out of which those evils grow. "The technological . . . potentialities of the age have . . . made world government a rational necessity, but they have not made it a panacea for the evils and liabilities of politics." Proponents of world government, from Woodrow Wilson to Cordell Hull, have consistently operated on the misconception that mere membership and support of international organization provides a viable alternative to the traditional methods and practices of international politics. Rather than signaling the eclipse of power politics or ushering in a new age of global collaboration, the United Nations "simply provides a new medium for the traditional methods of international politics and adds a new instrument for the pursuance of traditional objectives." [6]

Morgenthau pointed to several major factors inhibiting the function of the United Nations as an effective supranational institution. First, the intention of the UN Charter was capable of realization only if the wartime unity of purpose continued in times of peace. The charter makes the harmonious cooperation of the great powers the guiding principle of the United Nations and obliges the great powers to exercise a limited world government. However, the permanent discord among its most powerful members is the overriding fact that from the very outset has paralyzed the UN as a political organization. Morgenthau continued to believe that a lessening of Cold War hostilities depended less on popular resolutions and more on the ability of the leading protagonists to accomplish two objectives: the ideological decontamination of their respective national interests and the willingness to rely upon traditional methods of diplomatic negotiations, accommodation, and compromise. [7]

Second, the absence of unity among the major powers severely im-

6. Morgenthau, *Truth and Power*, 124–26; *The Impasse of American Foreign Policy*, 107–11; *The Restoration of American Politics*, 273–77.
7. Hans J. Morgenthau, "US and UN," *Foreign Policy Bulletin*, XXXIII (September, 1954), 5.

pairs the resort to the police measures of collective security. The charter's provision for a great-power veto eliminates any possibility of applying collective security methods against a permanent member of the Security Council. Faced with the risk of war from a coerced settlement, all nations are guided in their decisions by what they see as their national interests. In addition, Morgenthau noted that the enforcement of an international legal order and protection of the international status quo present a police force with problems quite different from those the national police has to solve. What is at stake in world, as opposed to domestic, affairs is not the defense of the legal order and the political status quo against piece-meal violations, but the very survival of the legal order itself. An international police force can contribute to the goals of an international organization only in the measure that its legal preferences and political sympathies happen to coincide with the policies of the international organization they are called upon to support. Within the United Nations, these forces have typically reflected both the composition and the military character of the two-thirds majorities of the General Assembly to which they owed their existence. For example, in 1950 only sixteen members of the UN provided armed forces of any kind against North Korea, and of these only the United States, Canada, Great Britain, and Turkey can be said to have supplied more than token forces. What remained the distinctive feature of the UN force in the Congo was the numerical majority of contingents from African nations that had a special interest in the pacification of the Congo without the intervention of non-African nations. An international police force, as Morgenthau suggested, "cannot be more reliable and efficient than the political interests and military capabilities of the nations supporting it allow it to be."[8]

Morgenthau urged the United States to approach the United Nations in a pragmatic spirit, using it for purposes to which its methods seem to be best adapted. The United Nations, created to express the common interests of mankind, has over the years been inhibited in this capacity by a number of structural and procedural defects: the immobilization of the Security Council because of great-power conflicts; the political and ideological fragmentation of the General Assembly through

8. Hans J. Morgenthau, "The Political Conditions for an International Police Force," *International Organization*, XVII (January, 1963), 399–402.

voting procedures that give all nations the same numerical weight; and the residual strength of national sovereignty, which mitigates the force of supranational sympathies.[9] Yet Morgenthau urged the United States to "resist these crippling tendencies" by making "judicious use of the organization through its general policies" and promoting institutional reform. In the context of a nation's moral obligation to mankind, he once wrote: "A new American foreign policy, intent upon broadening and strengthening the area of common interests and aware of the threat to world peace and order emanating from the balkanization of large sectors of the political world, must pay special attention to the unused potential of the United Nations." He identified two positive functions that the UN could perform. At a minimum, the United Nations provides novel opportunities for the amicable resolution of secondary conflicts in which the vital interests of the great powers are *not* at stake. In disputes affecting the primary interests of the major powers, the contribution of the UN lies in the area of procedure, in providing unobtrusive diplomatic options contributing to the mitigation of international conflict. Especially during a period of strained relations, the various special agencies of the United Nations make it possible for diplomatic representatives to remain in personal contact at a time of crisis (*e.g.,* the use of the UN for settlement of the Berlin blockade in 1948–1949).[10]

In addition, national policies channeled through the United Nations must be presented in such a manner as to solicit the approval of other nations having different interests and policies. To some degree, this will entail some amount of ideological justification of particular policy goals that can be associated with vague supranational sentiment. Yet Morgenthau consistently reminded policy-makers and ambassadors that national policy can prevail in the UN only if it is defined in terms transcending a parochial national interest and encompassing the interests of those nations whose support it seeks. "By defining those interests in terms of the United Nations, the United States will strengthen the free world, the United Nations, and itself." In the nuclear age, nations can no longer afford to protect and promote their separate interests through the tradi-

9. Hans J. Morgenthau, "The U.N. of Dag Hammarskjöld Is Dead," *New York Times Magazine,* March 14, 1965, pp. 32, 37–39.

10. Morgenthau, *A New Foreign Policy for the United States,* 244; *Politics Among Nations,* 473–75; *The Impasse of American Foreign Policy,* 110–11.

tional use of force without risking their own destruction. They require, Morgenthau believed, a supranational authority that will do for them what they cannot afford to do.[11]

The Ethics and Strategy of Nuclear War

The crisis of contemporary governments—regardless of their type, composition, or ideology—lies in their inability to govern in accord with the three requirements of legitimate government. The sovereign nation-state is no longer able to protect the lives, guarantee the liberty, or facilitate the pursuit of happiness of their citizens. This is the case, Morgenthau believed, because "these operations are hopelessly at odds with the requirements and potentialities of modern technology and the organization it permits and requires." In regard to national security, the people are virtually helpless in the face of the ultimate abuse, their own destruction. A government armed with nuclear, and even nonnuclear, weapons holds the life of its citizens in precarious balance. Weapons designed to promote the objective of stable mutual deterrence also serve as a "provocation to a prospective enemy similarly armed, and that dialectic of defense-deterrence, threat and counterthreat, seeks and assures the destruction of all concerned."[12] Universal destructiveness is pushed to the extreme in the nuclear field, where effectiveness is the equivalent of total destruction, obliterating the conventional distinction between defense and offense, victory and defeat. Human existence, then, becomes a function of the will of two unprecedentedly mighty governments who have the power to destroy utterly their respective populations. Unlike many experts in the field of national security, Morgenthau wrote about this novel phenomenon in terms of both the objectives of strategic doctrine as well as the ethical and philosophical challenge to human existence posed by the existence of nuclear weapons.

What Einstein said decades ago is still applicable today: "The unleashed power of the atom bomb has changed everything except our way of thinking." Before turning to Morgenthau's assessment of the assump-

11. Morgenthau, "US and UN," 6.

12. Hans J. Morgenthau, "Decline of Democratic Government," *New Republic,* November 9, 1974, pp. 14–16.

tions and doctrines shaping the use of force in American foreign policy, it is important to consider how he viewed the impact of nuclear weapons upon the intellectual, moral, and social condition of man. Influential for Morgenthau's thinking was the central theme outlined by Karl Jaspers in *The Future of Mankind*. According to Jaspers, the salvation of mankind depends upon an awareness of the likelihood of total destruction and of the possibility of salvation through a radical transformation of man himself. He wrote: "An effective awareness of the possibility of total perdition is the only way by which the presently probable might become finally improbable. . . . The threat of total extinction points to thoughts about the meaning of our existence. The atom bomb cannot be adequately comprehended as a special problem. . . . Mere intellectual speculation about it does not mean absorption into the reality of one's life—and the life of man is lost without a change. . . . It is not enough to find new institutions; we must change ourselves, our characters, our moral-political wills."[13]

Jaspers advocated nothing less than the development of "a new man after the model of the *homo novus* of the Renaissance who, by virtue of the novelty of his qualities, will be able to cope with the novelty of the nuclear age." Morgenthau contrasted this line of reasoning with a school of thought, exemplified by Edward Teller and Herman Kahn, that believes nuclear war is but a quantitative extension of conventional violence. "War," argued Kahn, "is a terrible thing, but so is peace. The difference seems in some respects to be a quantitative one."[14] A more contemporary expression of this approach is favored by advocates of the nuclear utilization theory. Proponents of NUTs emphasize the use of nuclear weapons should the calculus of deterrence fail. These "conventional" orientations assume that civilized life will go on after a nuclear war as it has gone on after most conventional wars of the past. Morgenthau certainly agreed that we see little change in the political or ethical motives of man; at the same time, however, change is no less desirable "in every man's manner of living. Every little act, every word, every attitude in millions . . . of people matter. What happens on a large scale is

13. Hans J. Morgenthau, "Fighting the Last War," *New Republic*, October 20, 1979, p. 15; Karl Jaspers, *The Future of Mankind* (Chicago, 1958), 3, 6, 22–24.

14. Morgenthau, *Science: Servant or Master?* 113; Herman Kahn, *On Thermonuclear War* (Princeton, 1960), 46. See also Edward Teller and Allen Brown, *The Legacy of Hiroshima* (Garden City, N.J., 1962).

but a symptom of what is done in the privacy of many lives. The man who cannot live with his neighbor . . . by his conduct, which even behind locked doors, is never wholly private—keeps peace from the world. He does, in miniature, what on a large scale makes mankind destroy itself. Nothing that man is and does is quite without political significance." [15]

In terms of the human condition, the nuclear age has changed man's relation to himself by giving death a new meaning. Morgenthau's argument rests broadly on the proposition that the meaning of life reflects the individual's awareness and response to the inevitability of death. In death, man confronts the negation of what is the specifically human in his existence: the consciousness of himself and the world; the remembrance of things past and to come; and a creativeness in thought and action that aspires to, and approximates, the eternal. Throughout history, man has responded to the anxiety of his own existential finitude by aspiring to transcend death in one of three ways: by making himself the master of death (by committing what Nietzsche called "suicide with a good conscience"); by believing in the immortality of his person (*e.g.*, the separation of body and soul in the afterlife); and by replacing the belief in the immortality of the person with attempts to assure the immortality of the world he leaves behind (*e.g.*, the creation of religion, art, and reason that survive the creator).[16] Morgenthau pointed to a number of important ramifications following from nuclear death understood as the irrevocable end of man's existence.

Nuclear war, as the mass destruction of persons and things, destroys the meaning of death by depriving it of its own individuality. There can be no Leonidas falling at Thermopylae or Socrates submitting to the verdict of the corrupt Athenian assembly. In addition, nuclear destruction destroys the experience of immortality by making both society and history impossible. What would matter in the simultaneous destruction of people and nations would be the quantity of the killed, not the quality of one man's death over against another. Finally, the reality of nuclear death becomes a meaningless absurdity for a secular age, which has lost all faith in individual immortality in another world and yet is aware of the impending doom of the world through which it tries to perpetuate itself

15. Hans J. Morgenthau, "An Atomic Philosophy," *Saturday Review*, February 10, 1961, p. 18.
16. Morgenthau, *The Restoration of American Politics*, 19–21.

here and now. It is against this backdrop, this inability to grasp how nuclear death transforms the meaning of human existence, that Morgenthau criticized the modern inclination to talk about defending civilization against communism as the Greeks talked about defending their civilization against the Persians. "To die with honor is absurd if nobody is left to honor the dead."[17]

For nearly forty years both the United States and the Soviet Union have pursued the rational goal of deterrence with the irrational means of an unlimited nuclear arms race. The restraints that the fear of mutual destruction has imposed upon the foreign policies of the Soviet Union and the United States are based upon the expectation of annihilation in the event of a military confrontation. They depend upon what Churchill described as a "balance of terror" in which one country, after having suffered unacceptable damage from a nuclear attack by an adversary, would still be able to retaliate with strategic forces and inflict unacceptable damage on an aggressor. Peace, therefore, is inseparable from the psychological assumption that nuclear war would be a genocidal and suicidal absurdity.

Morgenthau warned, however, that the indefinite persistence of this conviction may be threatened in the event that (1) either superpower develops a first-strike capability to destroy enough of an opponent's nuclear arsenal to render a second strike academic; or (2) either superpower deploys a defensive system that might reduce the damage from a nuclear exchange to tolerable proportions. What matters, as Morgenthau suggested, is not whether these assumptions are correct, but that they *might* be held. These developments shift the strategic debate from the prerequisites of mutual deterrence to a nation's ability to wage a successful nuclear war. The restraints that upheld deterrence would become irrelevant. Avoidance of a nuclear war becomes meaningless for nations who are convinced they can win a nuclear war either through a debilitating first strike or an impenetrable defense.

Morgenthau never doubted or disavowed the contribution of strategic or tactical nuclear weapons for the promotion and defense of American global interests. Yet, for some three decades, he expressed grave reservations about the conventional thinking shaping the evolution of United States strategic doctrine. The tendency to model and justify

17. *Ibid.*, 23–25.

nuclear strategy in conventional terms was implicit in the early formulation of "massive retaliation" and it was subsequently refined in the 1960s and 1970s by counterforce strategies based on the principle of "mutual assured destruction." Underlying all conventional estimates of nuclear policy is "a theory of nuclear war which assumes nuclear war to be just another kind of violence, greater in magnitude but not different in kind from the types of violence with which history has acquainted us." From this theoretical assumption, it follows that the United States need not limit itself to avoiding a nuclear confrontation; in addition, the United States must also prepare to survive it. Furthermore, Morgenthau warned of the inescapable link between the continuation of a costly nuclear arms race and the commitment to a counterforce strategy that purports to offer controllable war-fighting options by means of more accurate nuclear weapons. He wrote: "Under the assumptions of that strategy, a dynamic relationship exists between the number of targets presented by one side and the number and quality of weapons directed at those targets by the other. Given a static number of targets, an increase in the number and quality of counter-force weapons will improve the prospects of counter-force strategy. . . . Both sides, then, have an incentive to increase targets and counter-force weapons indefinitely." [18]

From the beginning of history until 1945, a great power could rationally choose to wage all-out war against another power for political ends, as long as the calculus of risk and advantage seemed favorable. By definition, a "weapon" is a tool for executing the tactics and strategy of battle. A "war" is fought for the attainment of political goals. In Clausewitz's terms, it is "politics by other means." The availability of nuclear weapons, however, results in two extraordinary paradoxes that stem from the destructiveness of these weapons. First, a quantitative increase in strategic weaponry does not necessarily correlate with an increase in national power. [19] Once a nation acquires the capability of destroying all enemy targets chosen for destruction, taking all contingencies into consideration, additional nuclear weapons will not increase its power.

Second, Morgenthau pointed to the inverse relationship between

18. Hans J. Morgenthau, "The Four Paradoxes of Nuclear Strategy," *American Political Science Review*, LVIII (March, 1964), 31; *The Restoration of American Politics*, 19–21.

19. Morgenthau, *Politics Among Nations*, 122.

the degree of destructiveness of these weapons and their rational usability. Between two major nuclear actors with rough equivalence in destructive potential, mutual threats tend to cancel each other out. Because
the destruction of one actor would call for the simultaneous destruction
of the other, both superpowers can afford to disregard the threat on the
assumption that both nations will act rationally. According to Morgenthau, "it is only the assumption that the nations concerned might act
irrationally by destroying each other in all-out . . . war that the threat of
nuclear war is credible." For example, the credible resort to nuclear
threat was exemplified by the Soviet Union during the Suez Crisis (1956)
and by the United States in the Berlin Crisis (1961). More recently, in
discussing America's response to the Soviet invasion of Afghanistan and
the seizure of hostages in Iran, Morgenthau noted that policy-makers
"have ruled out from the very outset . . . that resort to that medium of
action in international relations which has always been regarded as the
ultima ratio regum, the last resort of kings." In short, Morgenthau drew
a sharp distinction between the threat and actual use of force: "While the
threat of force can be used as a rational instrument, the actual use of that
force remains irrational; for the threatened force would not be used for
the political purpose of influencing the other side but for the irrational
purpose of destroying the other side with the attendant assurance of one's
own destruction." [20]

Morgenthau believed that the security of the United States, threatened by the exposure of American territory to nuclear destruction, required a dual emphasis on "the novel methods of deterrence and arms
control." The management of nuclear power confronted policy-makers
with two interrelated problems: the abatement of the nuclear arms race
and the prevention of nuclear proliferation. As long as both the United
States and Soviet Union competed for new weapons, he saw little possibility in preventing lesser powers from following suit. Moreover, energetic diplomatic initiatives designed to curtail the nuclear arms race are
justified because the indiscriminate destructiveness of nuclear weapons
overwhelms all possible objectives of a rational foreign policy. "If they
are used as instruments of national policy, nuclear weapons would de-

20. *Ibid.*, 29–30. See also Hans J. Morgenthau, "The Danger in Iran," 1980 (TS in
Morgenthau Papers, Box 110), 3–4; "What Presidential Candidates Might Think About,"
1976 (TS in Morgenthau Papers, Box 108), 1–7.

stroy the tangible objective of policy and the belligerents as well." In consequence, Morgenthau wrote: "What the nuclear powers have . . . been doing pragmatically—that is, to refrain from the use of nuclear weapons—they ought to now do . . . as a matter of principle: to eliminate nuclear weapons from their regular armory, so that they will not be used as instruments of national policy, and assign to them . . . the function of a deterrent, to be used only in suicidal desperation." [21]

Denying the rational usability of nuclear weapons in world politics, Morgenthau identified three specific consequences for the conduct of American foreign and military policy. First, because nuclear threats are inherently lacking in political credibility, they ought to be eliminated from standard diplomatic practice.[22] He argued that nuclear force was credible only in terms of maintaining a residual second-strike deterrent capability. Morgenthau more often seems to admit a distinction between nuclear threats designed to serve diplomatic-political gains using tactics of intimidation or blackmail (noncredible) and the perception *qua* threat in the mind of the decision-maker that can and has shaped the manner in which both superpowers have preserved a system of mutual deterrence based on a devastating second-strike capability.

Second, because nuclear weapons contribute little to the normal exercise of national power, policy-makers should give greater attention to the development of nonnuclear instruments of national power. Commenting on the American reluctance to exercise the nuclear option in foreign policy, Morgenthau noted that "other nations, especially the Soviet Union, take advantage of this unilateral restraint . . . and the United States has great difficulty in defending . . . its interests with anything short of force." Nuclear weapons in the hands of both superpowers "only provide assurance that national interests can be supported with the conventional diplomatic and military methods." [23]

Third, the availability of long-range communication, delivery, and transportation systems has radically altered the importance of the control of territory for national power. For example, "the conjunction between the large radius of nuclear destruction and the relatively small size of their territories imposes a . . . handicap upon the ability of . . . traditional na-

21. Morgenthau, *A New Foreign Policy for the United States*, 13, 208.
22. *Ibid.*, 29.
23. Morgenthau, *Politics Among Nations*, 114.

tion states, such as Great Britain and France, to make a nuclear threat credible."[24]

Morgenthau remained skeptical of broad-gauge disarmament strategies and expressed only cautious optimism at the prospects of nuclear-arms control. Yet his healthy skepticism was tempered by an appreciation for the fundamental differences between conventional and nuclear disarmament. He viewed disarmament as the reduction or elimination of armaments for the purpose of limiting the destructive and anarchical tendencies of international politics. Beginning with the Russian proposals of 1816, attempts at controlling conventional arms have been few and have been achieved only under two extraordinary conditions. First, arms reduction was agreed on by a limited number of nations and was largely local in character. Second, the agreed-upon ratio of armaments reflected either the absence of competition for power or temporary preference for regulated, rather than unregulated, competition for power in the form of armaments acquisition. By contrast, all attempts at general disarmament (*e.g.*, the two Hague Conferences, the Geneva Conference of 1932, and the disarmament commissions of the United Nations) have been conspicuous failures. They could not have succeeded even under the most favorable circumstances because the continuation of the contest for power among the nations concerned made agreement on the ratio of armaments impossible.

At the root of these failures, Morgenthau believed, was the modern philosophy of disarmament, which starts from the assumption that men fight wars because they have arms. Idealistic proponents of disarmament have postulated a correlation between the possession of arms and the larger issues of war and peace. Morgenthau judged that such thinking treats the symptom, while leaving the underlying ills essentially intact: "What makes for war are the conditions in the minds of men which make war appear the lesser of two evils. In those conditions must be sought the disease of which the desire for . . . arms is but a symptom. . . . It is indeed possible to outlaw nuclear weapons, but it is not possible to outlaw the technological knowledge . . . to make them. It is for this obvious reason that the prohibition of particular weapons has generally not been effective in war." At best, Morgenthau considered disarmament or the limitation of armaments as "an indispensable first step in a general settlement

24. Morgenthau, *A New Foreign Policy for the United States*, 242.

of international conflicts." Disarmament can contribute to general pacification and can ease the financial burden of a costly arms race *only* when there is a "mutually satisfactory settlement of the power contest."[25] Disarmament, then, will reflect the measure of political understanding nations are able to achieve.

An entirely different situation prevails with regard to the reduction of nuclear weapons. Nuclear-arms control and disarmament are based upon a community of interests of nations that have achieved the ability to destroy each other many times over even under the worst of circumstances. Conventional disarmament is a by-product of a military economy of scarcity, where there are always more possible targets than weapons. Any agreement to control these weapons would signify the end of competition for military advantage. Nuclear weapons operate within a military economy of abundance, where there are more nuclear warheads available than there are targets against which those weapons could be used. This distinction between conventional and nuclear weapons is what makes nuclear disarmament practically possible. Neither the Soviet Union nor the United States gains anything militarily or politically by increasing its might beyond this already unprecedented level of destruction. Morgenthau cited the remarks of Henry Kissinger during a press conference in 1974: "What in the name of God is strategic superiority? What is the significance of it . . . at these levels of numbers? What do you do with it?"[26]

Whereas disarmament seeks to reduce or eliminate armaments, arms control aspires to regulate the armaments race for the purpose of increasing military stability. Concerning the indispensability of the latter, Morgenthau wrote: "A realistic evaluation of the world scene has convinced me . . . that if the nuclear armaments race cannot be brought under control before any number of nations will have nuclear weapons, only a miracle will save mankind." Moreover, the only conceivable alternative to pursuing an arms race by conventional modes of thought "requires the quantitative and qualitative stabilization of nuclear armaments." Such restrictions on armaments can conceivably encompass international, mutual, or unilateral controls. Morgenthau decried the tendency of policy-

25. Morgenthau, *Politics Among Nations*, 389–90, 397–401.
26. Hans J. Morgenthau, "Fighting the Last War," *New Republic*, October 20, 1979, p. 16; "The Dilemma of SALT," 1979 (TS in Morgenthau Papers, Box 109), 1.

makers and strategists to link arms control calculations exclusively to the increasing weapons level of a potential adversary. Instead, a rational approach to arms control involves "stopping one's nuclear armaments at the point where they provide an invulnerable . . . deterrent and cutting them back to that point in so far as they have exceeded it." Provisions in the SALT agreements of 1972 and 1979 prohibiting the deployment of ABMs (antiballistic missiles) and placing numerical limitations on different types of offensive nuclear weapons constitute a success in the field of nuclear-arms control. In practice, however, arms control is based on "the stability of nuclear technology; for it is only on that assumption that the nations concerned can afford to desist from competition." In view of its dependence on technological stability, "nuclear arms control . . . is likely to remain both limited and temporary." [27]

American Foreign Policy and Strategies of Intervention

Often in contrast to other American realists, Morgenthau was much more outspoken on the specific problems confronting United States foreign policy in the Third World. For some three decades after World War II, he cited a combination of intellectual and political miscalculations, the net effect of which has been to weaken American power and influence in many parts of the developing world. The examples of Korea, Taiwan, Cuba, and South Vietnam provide vivid testimony of "our inability to achieve our political purposes even with an abundance of material means." [28] The vivid contrast between America's power resources and publicly stated foreign-policy commitments derived, in no small part, from a basic misconception about the nature and types of intervention that have become increasingly important since the Second World War.

Morgenthau viewed the concept of intervention as an inevitable and ever-present political reality commensurate with the struggle for power on the international scene. Intervention, through either the withholding of benefits or the inflicting of disadvantages, is a general designation for the various forms of competition and cooperation characterizing the interplay of conflicting national interests in world politics.

27. Morgenthau, *Politics Among Nations*, 403; *The Restoration of American Politics*, 162.
28. Morgenthau, *The Restoration of American Politics*, 275.

Certain states, as Thucydides observed in ancient Greece, have always found it advantageous to intervene in the domestic affairs of other states in behalf of their interests. Other states can be counted upon to oppose such interventions while not ruling out, at some future point, intervention in behalf of their own interests.

Since the time of the French Revolution of 1789 and the rise of nation-states, statesmen and legal scholars have assumed the unavailing task of trying to designate objective criteria by which to distinguish legitimate from illegitimate intervention. The French Constitution of 1793 contains a passage stating that France will "not interfere in the domestic affairs of other nations and will not tolerate interference by other nations in their affairs." With some irony, Morgenthau noted that this declaration ushered in an era of intervention on the widest possible scale. Following the Congress of Vienna in 1815, the concept of intervention and norm of nonintervention served, at one time or another, the various political desiderata of most of the major European powers. A number of states relied upon the principle to insulate themselves from interference by the traditional monarchies of the Holy Alliance. Great Britain, for example, opposed the Russian reaction to liberal movements across Europe as well as attempts to intervene in Spain in 1820 and Hungary in 1848. Yet, as Morgenthau pointed out, the British intervened in behalf of nationalism in Greece and in behalf of the conservative status quo in Portugal because its interests seemed to require it.[29]

The obeisance with which nations have publicly endowed the rule of nonintervention has become even more significant with the development of a worldwide balance-of-power system following the two world wars of the twentieth century. Great and small powers alike cited the merits of the 1965 United Nations General Assembly "Declaration on the Inadmissibility of Intervention in the Domestic Affairs of States and the Protection of Their Independence and Sovereignty." The key passage stipulates that "no state has the right to intervene, directly or indirectly, for any reason whatever, in the internal or external affairs of any other state" and that "no state shall organize, assist, foment, finance, incite or tolerate subversive, terrorist or armed activities directed toward the violent overthrow of another state, or interfere in the civil strife of another

29. Hans J. Morgenthau, "To Intervene or Not to Intervene," *Foreign Affairs*, XLV (April, 1967), 425–26.

state." Yet Morgenthau emphasized that the history of international and regional instability since World War II merely confirms that "there is nothing new either in the contemporary doctrine opposing intervention or in the pragmatic use of intervention on behalf of interests of individual nations."[30] Thus, the American presence in Vietnam or the Dominican Republic in the 1960s, no less than the Soviet invasion of Czechoslovakia in 1968, appears as a mere continuation of a tradition that was well established in the nineteenth century.

Although the political justification of, and opposition to, the practice of intervention remains a well-established instrument of diplomacy, Morgenthau cited a number of fundamental differences between interventions of the past and those of the present. These differences have "altered the techniques of contemporary intervention, have drastically reduced the traditional legal significance of the consent of the state intervened against, and have affected in a general way the peace and order of the world."[31] Briefly summarized, these developments point to important changes in the structure of international politics and the processes of foreign policy during the postwar era.

The Process of Decolonization. Although the number of sovereign nations has more than doubled since 1945, many of the new states in the developing world are not viable political or economic entities. Many former colonies, in order to subsist, depend heavily on the assistance provided by the former colonial powers and the leading superpowers. Intervention by other nations has often been a precondition for their survival. Exposure to political pressures from the supplying governments forces the recipient to keep open alternative sources of assistance by playing one supplying government against another. Egypt's expulsion of the Soviet presence in 1971 and its subsequent consolidation of political and economic ties with the United States are perhaps the most dramatic example of this pattern. Intervention, therefore, becomes a political calculation as important for the donor as the host country.

The Revolutionary Age of International Politics. Morgenthau observed that the present age resembles the period of history just after the Napoleonic Wars in that new and old nations alike are threatened by revolution or are at one time or another in the throes of it. The uncertain

30. *Ibid.*
31. *Ibid.*

path of modernization and political development for many of these developing countries has created a revolutionary environment within which the great powers are tempted to intervene for political purposes. For example, the United States and Western allies have not been slow to intervene on the side of factions that oppose the instability fostered by communist resistance. Alternatively, the Soviet Union and People's Republic of China, both claiming leadership of the world's working and oppressed classes, have intervened in behalf of subversive agents all over the world.

Intervention by Proxy. The modalities of intervention have been influenced profoundly by the preeminent revolutionary feature of the postwar period—the recognition by the nuclear armed giants that a direct military confrontation would carry unacceptable risks. The concept of peaceful coexistence does not rule out the inevitability of conflict and competition for power and prestige between the superpowers. Since the principle was first formulated by Khrushchev in 1956, the Soviet Union and United States have waged a Cold War based on strategies of containment and expansion below the nuclear threshold. In addition to competing for influence upon a foreign government in more traditional ways, the major powers have opposed each other surreptitiously through the intermediary of factions and political alignments shaping the domestic conflict of weak nations. Morgenthau disputed the popular fallacy, a pervasive ideological misconception, that the United States has always intervened on the side of the government and the Soviet Union on the side of the opposition. "It is characteristic of the interplay between ideology and power politics," to which consideration will be given in the pages to follow, "that this has not always been so."[32]

Intervention and Ideological Universalism. What gives many modern examples of intervention their revolutionary character is how the national interests of states have become imbued with world-embracing ideological content. Ideology has become an independent motivating force in a Cold War where the leading protagonists have become "fountainheads of two hostile and incompatible . . . systems of government and ways of life, each trying to expand the reach of its respective political values and institutions and to prevent the expansion of the other."[33] Intervention and the projection of power is a natural by-product in a con-

32. *Ibid.*, 428.
33. *Ibid.*, 428–29.

flict between two secular religions, communism and democracy, that know no respect for national boundaries. Ideology, Morgenthau believed, constituted that "dynamic force" prompting the superpowers to intervene at will all over the globe by resorting to tactics ranging from traditional methods of diplomatic pressure to instruments of covert subversion and open force.

America's historic commitment to the moral and legal doctrine of nonintervention, Morgenthau believed, had been of practical significance only in terms of abstention from the political rivalries of Europe during the era of isolationism. The United States, having no concrete interests in the continents beyond the oceans, could afford to judge the affairs of other nations in light of its ideals, oppose oppression, and sympathize with the aspirations of freedom everywhere. In the words of Washington's Farewell Address: "Europe has a set of primary interests, which to us have none, or a very remote relationship. . . . Hence . . . it must be unwise in us to implicate ourselves, by artificial ties, in the ordinary vicissitudes of her politics, or the ordinary combinations and collisions of her friendships or enmities." Popular writers at the time easily equated the uniqueness of America's geographic position with the benevolent workings of Providence, which had prescribed the course of American expansion as well as isolation. Morgenthau cited the example of John Bright's observation to Alfred Love: "On your continent we may hope your growing millions may henceforth know nothing of war. None can assail you; and you are anxious to abstain from mingling with the quarrels of other nations." [34]

Even during the heyday of classical isolationism, however, America's adherence to the principle of nonintervention was qualified by its tendency to intervene at will in the affairs of the Western Hemisphere. The American propensity for self-deception was revealed by treating such examples of intervention as essentially different from the selfish and expansionist ways of traditional European diplomacy. Debating Lloyd Gardner and Arthur Schlesinger, Jr., on the origins of the Cold War, Morgenthau described the Monroe Doctrine as "the most comprehensive, unilateral proclamation of a sphere of influence of modern times."

34. Merle Curti, *Peace and War: The American Struggle 1636–1936* (New York, 1936), 122. See also Morgenthau, *Politics Among Nations*, 37–38; *The Impasse of American Foreign Policy*, 6–7; and *In Defense of the National Interest*, 5–12.

President Wilson, his universal message of democratic self-determination notwithstanding, once referred to the Western Hemisphere as an "implied and partial protectorate." Commenting on the divergence between what Americans *think* their foreign policy is and its actual character, Morgenthau wrote: "The unchallengeable superiority of the United States within the Western Hemisphere, in conjunction with the American ideals at the service of which that superiority was supposed to be employed, made it appear to American eyes as though what was actually intervention was in truth something different, if not the exact opposite."[35]

The distribution of world power following World War II posed additional problems for both the nature and justification of American intervention abroad. The Soviet Union's interpretation of the Yalta agreement, in addition to its declared policy of a competitive, global struggle with the West, threatened American vital interests in both Europe and remote colonial regions. Instead of taking Churchill's lead and reaching a satisfactory spheres-of-influence agreement with the Soviet Union, American officials resorted to that time-honored fallacy of seeking an alternative to "power politics" in the form of a universal, international organization and the universal applicability of democratic institutions as a panacea for political ills. The opposition of key players in the Roosevelt Administration, notably Harry Hopkins and Cordell Hull, to the British-Soviet spheres-of-influence agreement in Eastern Europe was indicative of how the American political mind was at war with both incontestable political realities and its own moral conscience. The United States tried to bridge "the gap between its moral principles and its political practices by juxtaposing its selfless intentions with the evil purposes of other nations— most eloquently propounded . . . by Wilson in justification of the intervention in Mexico."[36]

For Morgenthau, it was obvious "that we are intervening massively and effectively all over the world and what we have foresworn is not intervention *per se*, but only certain kinds of intervention." As much as the Soviet Union intervened in developing countries to promote causes of

---

35. Hans J. Morgenthau, Lloyd C. Gardner, and Arthur Schlesinger, Jr., *The Origins of the Cold War*, eds. J. Joseph Huthmacher and Warren I. Susman (Waltham, Mass., 1970), 86–87; Morgenthau, *The Impasse of American Foreign Policy*, 6.

36. Morgenthau, Gardner, and Schlesinger, *The Origins of the Cold War*, 88–91.

national liberation, the United States championed the political status quo throughout the Third World. When faced with an actual or impending crisis, Morgenthau judged American foreign policy as "incapable of foresight, sureness of touch as regards means and ends, and manipulative skill that are the prerequisites of successful political action." Only by redefining political challenges in military terms have American leaders been able to act "with unambiguous simplicity and without regard for those complexities, uncertainties, and risks inherent in the political act."[37] Evaluating American intervention at various places in the developing and nonaligned world, Morgenthau emphasized the following themes: the error of anticommunist intervention, the self-defeating character of anti-revolutionary intervention, and the failure of American foreign and economic aid.

The interventions of the United States in Cuba, the Dominican Republic, and Vietnam have been largely justified as reactions to communist intervention. Morgenthau never doubted the aggressive and expansionist tenor of Soviet foreign policy; however, he deplored the failure of United States policy-makers to assess objectively the extent to which the infusion of communist revolutionary sentiment in local or regional conflicts threatened American security interests. The intellectual roots of this world view are expressed in the demonological adage "*Ecrasez l'infâme*"—exorcise the witches, hang the Kaiser, execute the leaders of the vanquished as war criminals. This pattern of thought posits a causal nexus between certain individuals or groups and the locus of evil in the world. In the words of William Graham Sumner: "The amount of superstition is not much changed, but it now attaches to politics, not to religion." Morgenthau applied Sumner's observation to the "specter of communism" and how American officials have misunderstood how Stalin and his successors transformed the tenets of communism into instruments of Russia's traditional foreign policy.[38]

From Roosevelt to Reagan, the rationale for projecting American power abroad to contain Soviet expansionist tendencies has depended on one of two answers given to the question concerning the ultimate purpose of Soviet foreign policy. Has the external conduct of the Soviet Union

37. Morgenthau, *Truth and Power*, 329.
38. William Graham Sumner, "Mores of the Present and Future," in *War and Other Essays* (New Haven, 1911), 159; Hans J. Morgenthau, "The Pathology of American Power," *International Security*, I (Winter, 1977), 8.

been limited largely to the security and expansion of the Russian state, or have Stalin's successors merely tried to realize the worldwide Bolshevik aspirations of Lenin and Trotsky? Morgenthau argued that American strategies of intervention and containment have vacillated between two poles of attraction. The corollary to the indiscriminate opposition to communism is the indiscriminate support of governments and movements that profess and practice anticommunism. Although Morgenthau did credit the diplomacy of President Nixon and Secretary of State Kissinger with a more modest statement of American national interest in world affairs, he warned that "the elimination of ideological considerations from our policies is partial, and tenuous where it exists." With reference to the link between ideology and the American policy of intervention in the 1970s, Morgenthau wrote: "Nor does the ideological decontamination of our relations with the Soviet Union signify that our foreign policy has been altogether freed of its ideological ingredients. We still think about foreign policy in demonological terms and allow our actions to be influenced by them. Why are we fighting in Indochina? In order to prevent the communist takeover of South Vietnam is the official answer. Why did we send our troops to the Dominican Republic? Because we cannot have another communist government in the Western Hemisphere, said President Johnson. . . . Only the devil's place of residence has changed."[39]

Morgenthau noted that the propensity for political demonology also finds support in the nature of the Soviet state and the foreign policies it pursues. On the one hand, the Soviet Union, since the time of Stalin, has used ideological factors as means to the end of the Soviet state. For example, the German "fascist beasts" became comrades-in-arms against Western imperialism after the Molotov-Ribbentrop pact of August 1939, and the "neo-fascists" and "revanchists" of West Germany transformed themselves into respectable partners, once they were willing to recognize the territorial status quo. On the other hand, however, the Soviet Union regards itself not only as one nation among others but also as the "Fatherland of Socialism," the leader of all "progressive forces" throughout the world.

Morgenthau acknowledged the need for governments of the great powers to abide by certain rules according to which the game of interven-

39. Hans J. Morgenthau, "Changes and Chances in Soviet-American Relations," *Foreign Affairs*, XLIX (September, 1971), 434.

tion is to be played; yet these rules "must be deduced not from abstract principles which are incapable of controlling the actions of government, but from the interests of the nations concerned and from their practice of foreign policy reflecting those interests." An example of the type of choices and consequences associated with the decision to intervene is particularly well illustrated by Morgenthau's analysis of the ill-fated Bay of Pigs invasion in 1961. President Kennedy had to choose between two incompatible courses of action suggested by his advisers: to stage an invasion of Cuba, with American military support if necessary, or not to intervene. Kennedy attempted to steer a middle course, intervening to uphold American interests but in such a way as not to violate openly the principle of nonintervention. Both objectives, as Morgenthau noted, were in accord with concrete American interests. On the one hand, the United States had a stake in challenging the Soviets' objective of using Cuba as a military and political outpost from which to export instability and threaten American interests within the Western Hemisphere. Yet the United States, on the other hand, also had a diplomatic interest in not alienating those new nations in the developing or nonaligned world. The Kennedy Administration's error was in failing to assign priorities to those two objectives. Administration officials, instead of using prestige as a datum among others in the political equation, "submitted to it as though it were an abstract principle imposing absolute limits upon the actions necessary to achieve success." Not only did the intervention fail, but the United States "lost much prestige as a great nation able to use its power successfully on behalf of its interests."[40]

A more rational approach to the Cuban intervention would have entailed imposing some hierarchy on competing values from which to distill concrete courses of action. American leaders, first of all, should have decided which was more important: to succeed in the intervention or to avoid a loss of prestige among the developing nations. Acceptance of the latter course of action would have dictated against any intervention at all. The former option would have necessitated taking the necessary measures, military and political, to insure the success of the mission regardless of domestic or world public opinion. As the French thinker and sociologist Raymond Aron observed in a 1961 column written for *Le*

40. Morgenthau, *Truth and Power*, 145; *A New Foreign Policy for the United States*, 122–23.

Figaro: "Yet in foreign policy the half measure, the compromise, ordinarily combines the disadvantages of the two possible policies."[41]

With the increasing polycentric nature of international communism, Morgenthau found no simple correlation between the invocation of communist ideology by various revolutionary movements and the qualitative extension of Soviet power. He knew well, and wrote in various essays treating the philosophy and practice of communism, that the history of Marxism-Leninism has from the very beginning been the story of interminable pseudotheological controversies about the true meaning of the doctrine. "Custodians of the doctrinal truth, from Marx to Mao, have argued not so much in terms of what is feasible and . . . ought to be done in view of concrete political circumstances, but of what is required by the truth of communism, correctly interpreted." The monolithic character of the communist camp under Stalin rested upon the moral foundation of the Marxist infallibility of the Soviet Union as incarnated by Stalin. When Khrushchev denounced Stalin's rule in 1956, and thereby stripped him of his Marxist infallibility, he also deprived the Soviet Union of its moral and political claim to lead the communist camp. The subsequent "liberalization" of Soviet society was paralleled by the international phenomenon of polycentrism—a variety of Marxist societies and movements denying in theory and practice the Soviet monopoly of truth, virtue, and power.[42]

Increasingly, the United States confronted a variety of communist regimes and factions pursuing their separate interests throughout Europe and the Third World. The plurality of communisms can be grouped into one of three broad categories according to the degree of subservience to the Soviet Union or China. These include: (1) those nations occupied by Soviet military forces (*e.g.*, the communist nations of Eastern Europe) and other nations economically dependent upon one or the other leading communist power (*e.g.*, Cuba and Albania); (2) those communist nations or institutions that have traditionally taken an independent line from the Soviet Union (*e.g.*, the communist government of Romania or the Italian Communist Party); and (3) those communist nations or groups that might either become independent from, or subservient to, the Soviet

41. Morgenthau, *Truth and Power*, 145–46.

42. Hans J. Morgenthau, "Thoughts on the October Revolution," *New Leader*, November 26, 1967, pp. 13–16.

Union or China according to changing political and military circumstances.[43] What is required of American policy-makers, then, is a dual task: first, a determination of the relations that a communist government or group is likely to have with the Soviet Union or China and how those relations will be influenced by American foreign policy choices; and second, the formulation of policies that seek to minimize the negative effects that communism might have on the interests of the United States.

Although Morgenthau noted that intervention against communism is a dubious proposition with potential for miscalculation, he also realized that policy-makers confront an additional dilemma insofar as revolutionary movements the world over are apt to exhibit some kind of communist component. How can the United States, for example, stabilize a world that is inherently unstable and whose stability is threatened by national and social revolutions that may run the risk of being taken over by communism? Recent examples of American intervention against revolutionary movements have accomplished little more than legitimizing the political status quo and exacerbating deep-seated revolutionary tensions. Regarding American involvement in Southeast Asia throughout the 1960s and 1970s, Morgenthau knew it would be absurd to suggest that the officials responsible for the conduct of American foreign policy were unaware of these distinctions and of the demands they make for discriminating subtlety; yet "they maneuver themselves into a position which is antirevolutionary and which requires military opposition to revolution wherever it is found in Asia, regardless of how it affects the interests and how susceptible it is to the power of the United States." Much as Alexander I and Metternich invoked Christianity against the liberal revolutions, so the foreign-policy doctrine of intervention invokes the abstraction of stability against contemporary revolutionary change. The rational choice open to American foreign policy is not between the status quo and revolution, but between noncommunist and different types of communist revolutions. Morgenthau argued that the United States, far from intervening against revolution, must intervene in competition with the main instigators of revolution—the Soviet Union, China, and Cuba—in behalf of revolution. The purpose of such an intervention would be twofold: to protect the revolution from a communist take-over; and, failing this, to prevent a revolution from turning against American national interests. It

43. Morgenthau, "The Pathology of American Power," 10.

is the task of statesmanship not to oppose what cannot be opposed with a chance of success, but to bend it to one's own interest.[44]

By treating all revolutionary movements as communist dominated and uniformly hostile to the interests of the United States, the American policy of indiscriminate anticommunist intervention would be self-defeating for a number of reasons. First, the United States lacked sufficient resources to deal simultaneously with a number of acute revolutions at any one time. Second, such interventions would fail, because "logic that would make us appear as the anti-revolutionary power . . . would surrender to communism the sponsorship of revolution everywhere." Finally, intervention under the ideological spell of opposition to communism "is bound to corrupt our judgment about the nature and limits of our power." America's self-imposed obligation to establish a new order throughout the world is only fueled by the conviction that the problems of foreign policy will yield to moral conviction and military efficiency. Edmund Burke had the same national hubris in mind when he issued a stern warning to his countrymen: "Among precautions against ambition, it may not be amiss to take one precaution against our *own*. . . . I dread our *own* power and our *own* ambitions; I dread our too much being dreaded. . . . We may say we shall not abuse this astonishing and hitherto unheard-of power. But every other nation will think we shall abuse it. It is impossible but that, sooner or later, this state of things must produce a combination against us which may end in our ruin."[45] Alternatively, Morgenthau emphasized that the principle of selectivity should serve as the criterion for American political and military intervention. The decision to intervene or not to intervene will be defined not by sweeping ideological commitments or the blind reliance on power but by a responsible calculation of the interests involved and the power available.

Morgenthau's widely publicized condemnation of United States participation in the Vietnam War testified to the "anti-revolutionary" stigma attaching to the exercise of American power in the Third World. His incisive criticism, first expressed in 1961, of those personalities and policies shaping America's Indochina policy is worth recalling for several reasons. He was the first prominent American political scientist to rise

44. Hans J. Morgenthau, "We Are Deluding Ourselves in Vietnam," *New York Times Magazine*, April 18, 1965, p. 25.

45. Morgenthau, *A New Foreign Policy for the United States*, 126–27; Burke, "Remarks on the Policy of the Allies with Respect to France," in Burke, *Works*, IV, 457.

above the suffocating air of intellectual conformism within his discipline in order to expose the corruption of power and principle at the highest echelons of the United States government. As a philosopher whose reputation was insulted by a campaign of lies and disinformation perpetrated by political hacks in the Johnson Administration, he never wavered from the Socratic duty of pressing for rational solutions within the existing system of power relations. Of more importance, Morgenthau's objection to American military intervention in Vietnam represents, not a departure from, but a bold affirmation of the ethical core of the American realist tradition. The use and abuse of military force for unattainable political objectives in Southeast Asia is but a natural extension of that crusading moralism by which a nation assumes an exclusive moral worth and duty of a magnitude commensurate with so much power. Similar arguments were advanced by other leading American thinkers such as Walter Lippmann, Reinhold Niebuhr, and George F. Kennan. At a time when the United States is called upon to support "freedom fighters" throughout the world, the loss of lives and a war in Vietnam can now provide meaningful diplomatic lessons for the 1990s.

The various arguments and assumptions shaping Morgenthau's perspective on American military involvement in Vietnam revolved around a single consistently argued theme—the contention that American interests could not be served by fighting a war that was "politically aimless, militarily unpromising, and morally dubious." The rationale underlying the American military engagement in Southeast Asia can be traced back to 1947 and the justification for containing communism that received expression in the Truman Doctrine and Marshall Plan. Yet the problems the United States confronted in Asia were quite different from those that were successfully dealt with in Europe. The threat that faced the nations of Western Europe in the aftermath of World War II was primarily military—the threat of the Red Army marching westward behind the line of military demarcation of 1945. The threat today in much of the Middle East and Asia is not primarily military but political in nature. By the early 1960s, with the fragmentation of the communist bloc into national components, the United States continued the policy of containment as if the political disintegration of South Vietnam were analogous to the North Korean invasion of South Korea. In addition to focusing on the internal origins of instability within Vietnam, Morgenthau examined the American military strategy of counterinsurgency and the various moral problems posed by seeking a military victory over North Vietnam. He singled out the Vietnam crisis as just one conspicuous example of the American preference for "safe routines in support of the status quo" as well as the tendency to "make political problems manageable . . . by redefining [them] in military terms."[46]

The roots of the Vietnamese civil war go all the way back to the very beginning of South Vietnam as a separate state under the leadership of President Ngo Dinh Diem in 1954. In the process of eliminating rival armies and political opponents, he polarized the politics of South Vietnam—on one side, Diem surrounded by his Praetorian guard; on the other, the Vietnamese people, backed by the communists who declared themselves liberators from foreign domination and internal oppression. The possibility of civil war grew inevitable after Diem refused to agree to all-Vietnamese elections, as stipulated by the Geneva accords. The government of South Vietnam—following Diem's death in 1963 and the gradual assumption of power by General Nguyen Van Thieu—relied on the army for its support and represented the interests of an elite group of absentee landowners who would have lost their economic, social, and political privileges had the government really tried to counter the social revolution of the Viet Cong with radical social reforms of its own. As Morgenthau suggested: "A government imposed on an unwilling or . . . indifferent people by a foreign power to defend the status quo against a national and social revolution is by dint of its very nature precluded from doing what Americans expect it to do."[47]

To the end of transforming the hostility or indifference of the South Vietnamese into positive loyalty to the government, American policy relied on such techniques of warfare as counterinsurgency and pacification. The primary characteristic of a counterinsurgency war (*i.e.*, a war fought against a whole people or at least a large segment of it) is that its primary aim is not the conquest of territory but the destruction of the will to fight of the insurgent population by killing insurgents. If that will proves indestructible, then the physical destruction of the insurgent population becomes the primary objective. Pacification programs repeatedly failed over the course of a decade because American officials operated under

46. Morgenthau, *A New Foreign Policy for the United States*, 126.

47. Hans J. Morgenthau, "U.S. Misadventure in Vietnam," *Current History*, LIV (January, 1968), 29–30.

"the misconception that the guerrillas are an alien element within the indigenous population, who therefore can be separated from that population by the appropriate technique." Yet little evidence was forthcoming to disprove what, until 1965, had been official American doctrine: that the main body of the Viet Cong was composed of South Vietnamese and that over 80 percent of their weapons were of American origin. American troops—in Morgenthau's estimation—treated counterinsurgency as a "mechanical contrivance" or as a particular kind of military tactic with which to fight and win an "unorthodox" war. This approach could not account for the difference in motivation between the guerrillas and the army resisting it. The Viet Cong, like the Spanish and Tyrolian guerrillas fighting in the army of Napoleon, were fanatical protagonists of an ideal (*e.g.*, social revolution and national survival) and were prepared to die rather than admit defeat. The South Vietnamese army, by contrast, was viewed by large masses of the people not as the expression of the popular will but as its enemy. The United States government faced the same dilemma here as it encountered in promoting the Alliance for Progress: it was trying to achieve radical social reforms through the instrumentality of governments that have a vital interest in the preservation of the status quo.[48]

These errors in political and military judgment led the United States to embark upon a course of action that was utterly at variance with what the national interest required and was bound to end in failure. America was engaged in a war that it could neither win on the battlefield without risking a direct military confrontation with either the Soviet Union or China, nor terminate without "giving the lie" to the political assumptions upon which policy-makers staked the credibility of the United States government. What Morgenthau found so disquieting is why intelligent and honest men, drawing upon the best expert advice and ample sources of information, were unable to renounce a course of action that should have been recognized as unpromising and potentially disastrous from the outset. Morgenthau, in accounting for the failure of a nation so amply endowed with human and material resources, pointed to defective moral standards that were responsible for prolonging a losing undertaking. What distinguished Morgenthau's commentary from most other observations on the moral liabilities of American military intervention was his

48. Morgenthau, *A New Foreign Policy for the United States*, 133–34.

ability to relate defects in the implementation of policy to the process and style of foreign-policy decision making in government. This line of argument, of course, refutes those critics of Morgenthau's realism who claim that his approach to international politics ignores the linkage between domestic political structures and foreign-policy outcomes.

The methods by which elected officials justified American involvement in Vietnam point to an underlying moral dilemma in the democratic conduct of foreign policy. The moral stamina of democratic policy-makers is put to the test in having to reconcile the need for public accountability while, at the same time, trying to maximize the chances for success. The dilemma of choosing between what is right and what is popular is obliterated if democratic leaders are tempted by short-lived political advantage to sacrifice the permanent interests of the country for the preferences of the people. The "unawareness of this existential dilemma and of the moral choice it requires is worse than yielding to the temptation to make the wrong moral choice." What Morgenthau described as the "moral decay" of democratic society—the sacrifice of universal, objective standards at the core of republican government—points to a vicious circle where government molds public opinion in support of a particular foreign policy and then invokes that opinion with customary zeal to justify that policy. The truth emerges, not from what Justice Holmes described as the "competition of the market," but by fiat of arbitrary rulings when the predominant social and political powers induce the majority and the government to overstep the bounds of the "higher law" covenant. In other words, the issue of the correctness of policy is thus settled before it is really raised. The moral incapacitation of American democracy, "characteristic of our policies in Vietnam, results from the government's destruction of the dynamics of pluralistic debate through which errors can be corrected and the wrong policies set right." If a political elite is convinced it is in the possession of a monopoly of truth, then little room is left for the relativistic ethos of democracy. Dissent is stifled and opponents are punished who speak the truth to power, as Oliver Cromwell pleaded with the representatives of the Church of Scotland: "I beseech you, in the bowels of Christ, think it possible you may be mistaken." [49]

Morgenthau wrote at considerable length about the creeping intel-

49. Morgenthau, *Truth and Power*, 40–44.

lectual conformism within the universities as representing yet another obstacle to the moral accountability of American policies in Vietnam. Despite a few notable exceptions, American educators and professors seldom challenged the government's policies or explanations until the Vietnam War became a political liability in the late 1960s. That many American intellectuals were reluctant to speak forcefully against the escalation of the American troop presence in Vietnam during the Kennedy and Johnson years may be explained, in large part, by the way personal ambition augments the pressure to conform. The military-industrial complex, to which President Eisenhower referred upon leaving office, is paralleled by an academic-political complex in which the interests of the government are inextricably tied to the welfare of large groups of academics. Because of the money, prestige, and awards that flow from government grants and contracts with universities and private foundations, the academic "enters into a subtle and insidious relationship with the government, which imperceptibly transforms his position of independent judge to that of client and partisan." In a revealing passage describing the tragedy of both President Johnson and the intellectuals of America, Morgenthau the political realist wrote:

> These intellectuals must maintain their own regard for the truth in the face of a massive official disregard for it, which goes far beyond the necessities of the political game. The official pronouncements on President Kennedy's assassination and the Vietnam War could perhaps still be justified in terms of reason of state, although they have made civilized public debate with public officials virtually impossible. But it is a different matter to habitually play fast and loose with the truth, regardless of the public ends that might justify such a play and for the sole purpose of enjoying another dimension of power.[50]

The damage that American military involvement in Vietnam inflicted upon the national interest was not limited to Vietnam alone. The United States, Morgenthau believed, lost much of its moral attractiveness, which throughout its history had set it apart from other nations. This was Metternich's war being fought by the nation of Jefferson and Lincoln. On numerous occasions, Morgenthau applied the traditional

50. *Ibid.*, 24–27.

standards of just war—proportionality between the end sought and the means employed—to America's conduct of the war on the ground and in the air. For example, pacification policies were implemented in South Vietnam without discrimination between combatants and civilians. The nation in whose behalf the war was supposedly being fought was "being slowly but surely brought to ruin by the subtlety of the chemical and conventional weapons used and by the complete social, cultural, and spiritual dissolution with which it [was] threatened." In intellectual, moral, and practical terms, nothing is easier and less ambiguous than to deal with a social problem by oppressing and getting rid of the human beings that pose it. Against those who argued that America's credibility and prestige throughout the world would be diminished by an abrupt termination of military hostilities, Morgenthau questioned whether it is a boon to the prestige of the most powerful nation on earth to be bogged down in a war that it is neither able to win nor can afford to lose. Is not the mark of greatness "in circumstances such as these to be able to afford to be indifferent to one's prestige?" [51]

The United States has also attempted to promote its global interests and to counter communist gains through the medium of foreign aid. Throughout the postwar era, Morgenthau remained a vocal critic of both the intellectual rationale and actual operation of American assistance to recipient countries in the developing world. Much as the Truman Doctrine was transformed from an ideology of military containment into a general principle of global policy, the Marshall Plan evolved from a program of economic revitalization limited to Europe into the global principles of foreign aid. The assumption that rich nations have a moral duty to assist poor nations overcome their poverty justified the naïve expectation that the quantitative extension of American aid was actually capable of eliminating poverty on a grand scale. The American philosophy of foreign affairs, Morgenthau alleged, "equated foreign aid with economic development, economic development with social stability, social stability with democracy, and democracy with a peaceful foreign policy." [52]

51. Hans J. Morgenthau, "Johnson's Dilemma: The Alternatives Now in Vietnam," *New Republic*, May 28, 1966, pp. 13–14; "What Price Victory?" *New Republic*, February 20, 1971, pp. 22–23; "The Intellectual, Political, and Moral Roots of U.S. Failure in Vietnam," in William Coplin and Charles Kegley, Jr. (eds.), *Analyzing International Relations* (New York, 1975), 115, 124–26.

52. Morgenthau, *Truth and Power*, 156.

Yet he believed that American foreign-aid efforts have largely failed to promote democratic reforms or significant economic growth in developing societies. By contrast, ambitious strategies of modernization have often led to an uneven distribution of resources and have had little bearing on the redistribution of political power. Morgenthau argued that American policy-makers are just now recognizing the "extent to which the development of other nations depends upon indigenous rational and moral qualities not susceptible to deliberate foreign influence." He believed that the problem of foreign assistance is insoluble if treated as a "self-sufficient technical enterprise" without regard for either the political policies of the donor country or the prevailing political conditions in the receiving country. The conclusion Morgenthau arrived at in his discussion of intervention also applies to the special kind of intervention called foreign aid: it should be selectively oriented toward the political advantage of the donor and, if feasible, the economic benefit of the recipient ought to be the aim of American foreign policy.[53]

Human Rights: The Use and Abuse of Norms in Foreign Policy

Perhaps no moral issue in recent times has divided the American public and their elected officials more than the campaign to promote human rights in foreign policy. Following the political corruption of Watergate and the Vietnam War, the call for a renewal of American values in the conduct of foreign policy was viewed by many as a positive alternative to the private diplomacy of the Nixon-Kissinger team. For one often associated with the iron logic of power politics, it should be noted that few other political thinkers wrote at greater length than did Morgenthau throughout the 1970s about the abuse of power and the crisis of American democracy. Debating human rights with theologians and philosophers before the Council on Religion and International Affairs, he observed: "There has been recently a flood of statements, some of them on the highest authority, that have very little to do with a philosophic or even pragmatic understanding of international morality." Morgenthau's approach raises a fundamental question for human-rights policy: To what degree is a nation obligated to impose its values on others? The

---

53. Morgenthau, *A New Foreign Policy for the United States*, 12, 110.

argument is between those who say let the example speak and those who argue that a nation should express its principles but not necessarily expect to be consistent in following all of them. Morgenthau's writing in this area has the merit of bringing together a concern for diplomatic history with the connections between moral principle and self-interest in concrete examples of a nation's external behavior.[54]

As the previous chapter illustrated, Morgenthau cited numerous examples throughout history to illustrate that statesmen have refrained from certain actions on moral grounds—actions they could have taken physically and that would have been in their interests. Respect for human life, for example, has increased significantly since the fifteenth and sixteenth centuries. The assassination of foreign diplomats and emissaries was as common a practice then as the exchange of notes or summit meetings is today. The Republic of Venice, from 1415 to 1525, employed the services of an "official poisoner" and attempted some two hundred assassinations in order to achieve certain vital foreign-policy objectives. In 1514, John of Ragusa offered to poison anybody selected by the government of Venice for an annual salary of fifteen hundred ducats. The Venetian government hired the man "on trial" and asked him to show what he could do with Emperor Maximilian. In the same period, the cardinals brought their own butlers and wine to a papal coronation dinner for fear that they might otherwise be poisoned; this custom is reported to have been general in Rome, with the host's taking offense at it.

Although such methods to attain political goals are no longer commonplace today, the motives for employing them still exist. "What has changed," Morgenthau once wrote, "is the influence of civilization, which makes some desirable and feasible policies morally reprehensible and . . . impossible of execution." Similarly, since the beginning of history statesmen have decried the ravages of armed confrontation and justified their participation in them in terms of self-defense or religious duty. The avoidance of war, in addition to distinguishing between combatants and civilians, was the legacy of the two Hague Conferences of 1899 and 1907, the League of Nations of 1919, the Kellogg-Briand Pact of 1928 outlawing aggressive war, and the United Nations following World War II.[55]

54. Morgenthau, *Human Rights and Foreign Policy*, 1.
55. Morgenthau, *Politics Among Nations*, 231–35.

Morgenthau also referred to certain objective and psychological factors in the present condition of mankind that point to a definite weakening in those moral restraints that contributed to civilized relations among nations. The moral limitations upon killing are observed to a lesser degree for an age in which mass armies supported by the productive effort of the majority have replaced the smaller armies of the previous centuries. The distinction between combatant and noncombatant is imperiled when military success is defined in terms of eliminating the civilian productive processes and the enemy's will to resist. With the increasing ideological character of international politics, the citizen no longer sacrifices his life for a ruler or the greatness of his nation; rather, he becomes a "crusader" who fights to the death or to "unconditional surrender" against those who adhere to another, a false and evil, "ideal" and "way of life." Finally, the moral limitations on killing have receded at a time when war is "anonymously fought by people who have never seen their enemy alive or dead and will never know whom they killed."[56] New and even more brutal techniques of torture and punishment of "political" criminals—in addition to the use of toxic defoliants and chemical weapons against belligerents in Vietnam, Afghanistan, and Iraq—testify to the dissolution of an ethical system that in the past imposed restraints on the daily operations of foreign policy.

A number of commentators who have opposed the principles and diplomacy of *raison d'état* argue along similar lines that the ethics of American realism subordinates the rights of individuals to the privileges and practices of governments. Critics have seized upon brief quotations from prominent scholars as proof of moral failure in the area of human rights. George F. Kennan, for example, observed that "government, especially democratic government, is an agent and not a principal; and no more than any other agent can it attempt to substitute itself for the conscience of the principal." Kennan could find no absolute standards for defining what human rights ought to be "other than their general utility in assuring the higher moral aims of a given society—in our case the achievement of humane, decent, or orderly social conditions." Reinhold Niebuhr, describing the irony of American history, wrote: "The more we indulge in an uncritical reverence for the supposed wisdom of our Ameri-

56. *Ibid.*, 239–40.

can way of life, the more odious we make it in the eyes of the world, and the more we destroy our moral authority, without which our economic and military power will become impotent. Thus we are undermining the reality of our power by our uncritical pride in it."[57]

Participating in a State Department study group on the role of ethics in foreign policy in 1977, Morgenthau argued that "the purpose of our foreign policy is not to bring enlightenment or happiness to the rest of the world but to take care of the life, liberty, and happiness of the American people."[58] Although these realist scholars have exhibited occasional differences on matters of policy and philosophy, they have refused to consider foreign policy as an enterprise devoid of moral significance. To conclude, therefore, that realism is either amoral or immoral because its spokesmen are willing to qualify the promotion of human rights by other necessities of diplomacy is deficient in two respects. The allegation misrepresents their understanding of the human condition as well as the heritage of moral reasoning in Western civilization.

Foreign policy, like all human activities, "partakes of the judgment made by both the actor and the witnesses to the act when they perceive the act." Realist ethics begins with the premise that there are certain basic moral principles applicable to all human beings. Morgenthau, for example, agreed that "there exists a moral order in the universe which God directs, the contents of which we can guess." He believed "that it is impossible to postulate a plausible moral code without a theological foundation." Morgenthau never wavered from a faith "in a higher power whose designs are inscrutable and who guides the affairs of men toward unknown ends." Fundamental principles concerning the dignity and sacredness of human life are not a product of history, but are "something objective that are to be discovered."[59]

A final verdict on the role of human-rights considerations in foreign

57. George F. Kennan, "Ethics and Foreign Policy: An Approach to the Problem," in Louis J. Halle and Theodore Hesburgh (eds.), *Foreign Policy and Morality: Framework for a Moral Audit* (New York, 1979), 42–43; Kenneth W. Thompson, "Four Perspectives on Ethics and Foreign Policy and Their Implications for Some Central Issues of Current U.S. Policy" (Conference report prepared for the State Department's External Research Program, Charlottesville, Virginia, July 1977), 1.

58. Thompson, "Four Perspectives on Ethics and Foreign Policy," 14.

59. Morgenthau, *Human Rights and Foreign Policy*, 3, 9–10, 25, 36.

policy involves a judgment on ourselves as much as on the actions of others. To neglect the former and its intrinsic bearing on how a democracy conducts its foreign affairs can radically impair the manner in which the national interest is formulated and defended. Morgenthau seriously questioned the idea that the rest of mankind was required to accept the American political and moral tradition. He found that Wilsonian moralism and President Jimmy Carter's campaign for universal human rights exhibited similar defects. First, the universal acceptance of human rights would be impossible to enforce. Second, the United States is a global power with a variety of interests throughout the world. The consistent promotion of human rights in foreign policy could easily jeopardize other valuable military, political, and economic interests. The United States, therefore, is incapable of applying a uniform moral standard to each and every country, because such a policy "must come in conflict with other interests that may be more important than the defense of human rights in a particular instance." Finally, Morgenthau questioned the applicability of the concept of rights to the political transactions of sovereign states in world affairs. "The concept of rights," he argued, "presupposes a society that gives the rights." Although agreeing that there are "certain basic interests which are common to all men," no authoritative sources yet exist above nation-states from which to distill consensual norms and obligations affecting transnational political behavior.[60]

To Morgenthau, the issue of human rights is merely a general example of the connection between morality and foreign policy. Recognition that men and nations proclaim goals transcending national defense or sovereignty is a first step in solving, but is not a solution to, the moral problem in international politics. It is both moral and political wisdom to choose the most moral alternative through which expedience and ethics are served. This experience of insecurity and even powerlessness, although in apparent full control of the implements of power, is an experience common to all statesmen and military leaders. Morgenthau said: "They are called upon to make decisions of the utmost gravity without adequate knowledge of their consequences. In order to withstand the pressures of their responsibility, at odds with their ability to discharge them with confidence, and to be able to act at all, these leaders are in

60. *Ibid.*, 4–6, 15. See also Thompson, *Masters of International Thought*, 89.

need of reassuring themselves that a higher power, however defined, will decide in their favor."[61]

In attempting to formulate a standard for the statesman seeking what is morally and politically right, Morgenthau cited the reply of Abraham Lincoln to a petition by a delegation of Christian ministers who asked him to emancipate all slaves: "In great contests each party claims to act in accordance with the will of God. Both may be and one must be wrong. These are not, however, the days of miracles and I suppose it will be granted that I am not to expect a direct revelation. I must study the plain physical facts of the case, ascertain what is possible and learn what appears to be wise and just."[62]

61. Morgenthau and Hein, *Essays on Lincoln's Faith and Politics*, 9–11; Thompson, *Masters of International Thought*, 90.
62. Morgenthau, *Human Rights and Foreign Policy*, 8.

CHAPTER SIX

The American Realist Tradition in World Affairs

Following World War II, the discipline of international relations represented an *ad hoc* mixture of scholarly pursuits ranging from international law and organization to diplomatic history and descriptive area studies. The scope and methods of the various subfields were influenced, and often overshadowed, by the historic American debate over the significance of power and moral principle in statecraft. It was the lifelong achievement of one scholar-activist, Hans J. Morgenthau, to integrate political realism within the mainstream of American political science and help to establish international politics as an autonomous field of inquiry. The national interest defined in terms of power, the precarious uncertainty of the international balance of power, the weakness of international morality, the decentralized character of international law, the deceptiveness of ideologies, the requirements of diplomacy—these were phenomena his theory of international politics aimed to address in terms of general principles of politics.

Morgenthau's theory of international politics drew upon fundamental philosophical conceptions about man, nature, and politics. Rejecting many of the optimistic and reductionist beliefs of modern liberal thought, he stressed that the political realm is governed by objective laws that have their roots in human nature. One scholar has effectively summarized Morgenthau's intellectual orientation in the following terms: "He was determined both to erect an empirical science opposed to the utopias of the international lawyers and political idealogues, and to affirm the unity of empirical research and philosophical inquiry into the right kind of social order. He wanted to be normative, but to root his norms in the realities of politics, not in the aspirations of politicians or in the constructs of lawyers." Against the wishful thinking and pious hopes of interwar idealism, Morgenthau developed a theoretical approach to international affairs that both described national behavior and provided a framework for policy-makers. "The use of theory, then, is not limited to rational explanation and anticipation," he declared. "A theory of politics also contains a normative element." [1]

More so perhaps than any American student of international relations and foreign policy during the past generation, Hans J. Morgenthau has frequently been judged as the premier spokesman for the *realpolitik*, or "reason of state," approach to international political behavior. Certainly, his formative educational experiences in Germany exhibited a clear appreciation for the statecraft of such standard-bearers of *raison d'état* as Frederick the Great, Richelieu, and Bismarck. Upon embarking on a new career in the United States, he staked out an intellectual position on the tragic side of the social drama and left to others—idealists in the first postwar generation, and peace-centered behavioralists in the second—to side covertly with the angels. [2] Generally neglected, however, has been the philosophy or conception of political ethics underlying Morgenthau's analysis.

Morgenthau's contribution to the American political tradition has been to illuminate the organic connection between political thought and political action. Behind his treatment of particular domestic and foreign-policy problems have been a distinctive conception of the role and importance of political philosophy and a willingness to subject individual manifestations of self-interest and power to the judgment of universal norms and moral principles. Some commentators may criticize Morgenthau's political philosophy for neglecting to provide some indication of future action or a political program to lead mankind to the "brave new world." Yet his understanding of human nature and the limits of all political action was too profound to allow any utopian blueprints or speculative constructs to obscure the unpredictable configurations of the hu-

1. Hoffmann, "An American Social Science: International Relations," 44; Morgenthau, *The Decline of Democratic Politics*, 49.

2. Liska, "Morgenthau vs. Machiavelli," in Thompson and Myers (eds.), *Truth and Tragedy*, 105.

man will as a partisan for the struggle for power in society. Political action itself proceeds in small steps of which the consequences are either not to be foreseen at all or are visible only in the vaguest outlines.

Morgenthau's recognition of why circumstantial ethics are an inescapable by-product of politics and foreign policy—as well as his description of the American purpose as "uniform in procedure and pluralist in substance"—must be judged in the context of his affirmation of the sanctity of the moral law as something objective and binding upon all societies. He quoted Kant, who wrote: "If justice should perish, man's existence on earth would have lost its meaning." To understand the command of ethics, Morgenthau turned to the lessons of the Greek tragedians and biblical prophets for their eloquent testimony to the innate character of man's moral faculty. From his days as a youth, troubled by a strong sense of humiliation and alienation from the anti-Semitism of German society of the 1920s and 1930s, Morgenthau cited the dreadful consequences of those who "flee into the protective cover of the anonymous crowd and judge as it judges and act as it acts."[3] Moral judgments, played out in the soul of man, point to the insufficiency of a self-contained existence and to the individual's need to justify his life and labors by faith in the reality of objects or deities that transcend it.

Morgenthau's political faith was sustained by a vision of a unique American national purpose animated by self-evident truths that speak to common moral and rational aspirations among men in societies that are otherwise culturally and politically diverse. These truths, however formulated in a particular historic epoch, can be subsumed under the general proposition that the individual—his integrity, happiness, and self-development—is the ultimate point of reference for the political order and, as such, owes nothing to any secular or human institution. The American legal system, as Morgenthau acknowledged, "is based upon, and permeated by, moral principles—without . . . which the interpretation of the Constitution by the courts would be impossible." In an essay entitled "The Dilemmas of Freedom," Morgenthau testified to the "philosophic principle" at the heart of "the institution and spirit of liberalism": "It is on this absolute and transcendent foundation that the philosophy of genuine democracy rests, and it is within this immutable

3. Morgenthau, "Notes on Political Theory" (TS in Morgenthau Papers, Box 80), 10–11; *The Decline of Democratic Politics*, 374.

framework that the processes of genuine democracy take place. The pluralism of these processes is subordinated to, and oriented towards, those absolute and transcendent truths."[4]

Realist Philosophy and Principles of International Politics

The varied professional and academic commitments of other prominent American scholars suggest several preliminary considerations relevant for any assessment of realism as a distinctive American tradition of political thought. Along with Morgenthau, the writings of Walter Lippmann, Reinhold Niebuhr, and George F. Kennan accounted for the power of self-interest in the lives of men and nations, as well as the statesman's moral dilemma in seeking to uphold universal norms of conduct in a world of changing and unstable values. At a minimum, the realist world view has seldom been characterized by either its leading proponents or critics as an autonomous or unprecedented agenda of research and political inquiry. In fact, much of the creative energies helping to distinguish the realist approach to international politics emanate from a wide range of intellectual orientations in philosophy, theology, and ethics. Moreover, the divergent paths by which these thinkers arrived at a common body of principles also provide a basis for identifying more specific differences among American realists in matters of conceptualization and policy evaluation.

As discriminating critics of public affairs, they sought to relate specific trends and developments in national policy to the norms and philosophy of American society. Reflecting on the rational requirements of political action in a democracy, Lippmann argued that a large pluralistic nation could not be governed "without recognizing that, transcending its plural interests, there is a rational order superior to canon law." He judged it to be the basic responsibility of the intellectuals to promote "a common conception of law and order which possesses universal validity" and would provide the basis for the American public philosophy.[5]

In terms of America's intellectual history, Niebuhr's special contribution was in formulating and applying a pragmatic Christian ethic to

4. Hans J. Morgenthau, "The Dilemmas of Freedom," *American Political Science Review*, LI (September, 1957), 720–21.
5. Walter Lippmann, *The Public Philosophy* (Boston, 1955), 83.

the struggle for justice in human communities. The Christian view of man as both a sinner and an image of God led him to the conclusion that democracy was a perennially valuable form of polity. As he once wrote: "Man's capacity for justice makes democracy possible; but man's inclination to injustice makes democracy necessary." A system of checks and balances represented the best method of neutralizing special interests and of arriving at the truth by allowing various conceptions of the truth to destroy each other. At the same time, Niebuhr was far from offering one more celebration of American uniqueness. In *The Irony of American History*, he treated the American experience not as a revelation of progress, but as a sign of the indeterminacy of history, of its potential for good and evil.[6] For Niebuhr, the atomic bomb served as the most visible symbol of man's technical fortitude, as well as a sign of the crushing anxiety of modern life.

Although receiving scant attention in academic circles, Morgenthau's *Purpose of American Politics* offered a conclusive rebuttal of the popular misconception that his political thought is concerned exclusively with power to the neglect of purpose and morality. Any great nation, he submitted, must pursue its interests for the sake of a transcendent purpose that gives meaning to the day-by-day operations of its foreign policy. The very uniqueness of the American purpose—the establishment of freedom conceived as equality of opportunity and minimization of political control—brings into being another purpose that "endows the action required by the fundamental purpose with a special . . . responsibility; to maintain equality in freedom . . . as an example for other nations to emulate." In language hardly compatible with the European tradition of "reason of state," Morgenthau wrote: "The American purpose carries within itself a meaning that transcends the natural boundaries of America and addresses itself to all the nations of the world. By pursuing its own purpose and in the measure that it achieves it, America gives meaning to the inspirations of other nations and furthers the awakening and achievement of their purpose."[7]

As one of the principal architects of postwar American diplomacy,

6. Reinhold Niebuhr, *The Children of Light and the Children of Darkness: A Vindication of Democracy and a Critique of Its Traditional Defence* (New York, 1944), xi; Richard W. Fox, *Reinhold Niebuhr: A Biography* (New York, 1985), 146.

7. Morgenthau, *The Purpose of American Politics*, 33–42.

Kennan noted that the diplomatic historian is compelled to take cognizance of the classical problems in the history of political philosophy (*i.e.*, the obligations and restraints in the exercise of governmental power). Like Morgenthau, Kennan conceived of the role of the United States in world affairs as a reflection of the internal purposes and values of American society. Although less willing to assign universal significance to any definition of national purpose, he equated the successful defense of the national interest with America's spiritual and material resolve in coping with the strains and divisions of domestic society. Specifically, Kennan judged America's traditional liberal-rational philosophy as the servant of private interest no longer sufficient to address such negative phenomena as inflation, declining educational standards, pornography, and environmental pollution. Although he called for the reorientation of civic values with a greater sense of collective purpose, Kennan argued that "the ancient conflict of freedom and authority has taken on new forms in this day and age, and ones which assail . . . the very foundations of our political and social philosophy." [8]

The standard of American *realpolitik*, as some critics have alleged, can be demonstrated by the realist preoccupation with: the irrational and egotistic elements in man's nature; the omnipresence of conflict and coercion in all political life resulting from the struggle for power; the nation-state as the most important actor in world politics; the national interest as the objective basis of a state's foreign policy; the importance of classic diplomatic procedures and the balance of power for preserving international stability and reconciling divergent national objectives; and the illusion of moral absolutes in world affairs.

Like their European predecessors, each scholar evaluated in this study affirmed the importance of contrasting perspectives on human nature for generalizing about political behavior at all levels of human existence. Although Lippmann's investigation into the ethical basis of human behavior reflected periodic shifts in viewpoint, he consistently inveighed against the tendency of political scientists to focus exclusively on institutions without an accompanying analysis of "man," who makes and lives under them. Forever trying to strike a balance between the fusion of universal ideals and self-interest in national behavior, Niebuhr's "Christian

8. George F. Kennan, "Lectures on Foreign Policy," *Illinois Law Review*, XLV (January–February, 1951), 729.

realism" drew its inspiration from the dialectical tension between the law of love and the reality of man in an imperfect world.

Similarly, Morgenthau reminded his more empirical-minded colleagues that the commitment to a value-free political science is itself a philosophical predisposition based on certain beliefs about man's nature and the meaning of his political existence. Although generating considerable controversy over America's moral mission in world politics, Kennan certainly shared the conviction of the classical political thinkers that the justification for political action begins with an appreciation of the forces at work in the human soul. In responding to America's radical student left of the 1960s, he suggested that the origin of evil in this world is "not in social or political institutions or the inequities of statesmen, but simply in the weaknesses and imperfections of the human soul itself." [9]

Although often motivated by a broad range of intellectual concerns, these four thinkers testified to the manifold vitalities and contradictory forces at work in human nature. Man is both good and evil, rational and compulsive, part animal and part spirit. The great societies that historically comprise mankind must share the same burdens and strengths. Whereas American realists have, in varying degrees, recognized man's capacity for virtue and moral self-sacrifice in community with others, they have also affirmed one of the key insights of European thinkers—that politics and diplomacy bring out the harshest side of man's nature. Writing in the *Federalist* on the origin of conflict among states, Alexander Hamilton suggested: "To presume a want of motives for such contests would be to forget that men are ambitious, vindictive, and rapacious." [10]

The ineluctable tension between the misery and dignity of human nature had a direct bearing on Lippmann's inquiry into the competing themes of morality and power in modern society. As a dedicated political rationalist seeking to illumine objective standards undergirding all political action, he equated the ethical goal of human development with the triumph of reason over man's passions and natural impulses. Against the chaos and disorder of a large democratic society, the dictates of reason

9. George F. Kennan, *Democracy and the Student Left* (Boston, 1966), 9–11.

10. Alexander Hamilton, James Madison, and John Jay, *The Federalist Papers* (New York, 1961), 54.

filled the "mature man" with an appreciation for universal standards of order and justice superior to the selfish ambitions of private interests backed by power. In an essay prepared for the first issue of the *New Republic*, Lippmann echoed a theme that would be fundamental to all his writing: Man's thoughts and ideas represent the only viable weapons in controlling the irrational resort to violence in both domestic and international politics. Reviewing *The Public Philosophy*, Morgenthau took exception to Lippmann's "rationalistic idealism" and the emphasis he placed on the power of self-sustaining reason to transform the philosophy by which men live. He wrote: "Lippmann believes that men in their political thoughts and actions can be sincerely lucid and rational, and he considers this rationality to be the very foundation of the public philosophy. Herbert Butterfield, Reinhold Niebuhr, myself and others have tried to show how much more ambiguous . . . the relations between reason and politics are than is suggested by this simple rationalistic faith."[11]

Morgenthau's objections to the abstract mechanical formulas of modern rationalist philosophy notwithstanding, his summary review fails to illustrate how Lippmann's thought was influenced by an awareness of both the norms of the American higher-law tradition and the complex interplay of personalities and historical forces in a dark and angry world of unreason. The politics of human reconstruction takes place within a social and political arena in which the vast majority of men are foolish and ever-insurgent against reason, where both groups and individuals seek to realize their desires by force. As a realist, Lippmann realized that there is evil as genuine as goodness; that there are ugliness and violence no less real than joy or love. In a world where conflict and rivalry are a fact, the survival of men and nations cannot be achieved unless power is confronted with power, unless it is checked and balanced.

The ethical realm of man's political existence within society and the more complex international community formed the vital center of Niebuhr's Christian realism. From the perspective of Christian ethics, he alluded to the fundamental existential contradiction of man in history—where there is, on the one hand, man's aspiration to the law of love as the true essence of *humanitas* and, on the other, the tragedy of his

11. Walter Lippmann, *Early Writings* (New York, 1970), 3; Morgenthau, *The Restoration of American Politics*, 66.

consistent betrayal of that law. Niebuhr located the source of this contradiction in man's being situated at an uneasy juncture between necessity and freedom, spirit and nature, the human and the divine. The classical preoccupation with man's unique and rational qualities is often betrayed by man's restless urge to power and brute nature. Alternatively, the more modern perception that man is a product of nature and unable to rise above his immediate circumstances says little of man as "a spirit who stands outside of nature, life, himself, his reason, and the world." As Niebuhr once pointed out: "Christianity . . . recognizes that the dignity of man consists precisely of that freedom which makes it possible for him to sin."[12]

Man's involvement in the paradox of finitude and freedom provided the boundaries within which Niebuhr reflected on the relation between power and moral principle in the political behavior of groups and nations. According to Niebuhr, it is in man's attempt to overcome his own vulnerability to the self-regarding ambitions of others that "all human life is involved in the sin of seeking security at the expense of other life." In both individual and collective life, the human predicament has its roots in the "security-power dilemma"; the margin of power sought is never sufficient to achieve complete security, and the struggle for power continues unabated as both man and nations are caught in a tragic dilemma. The ferocity and intensity of the struggle among groups is so strong that "the only harmonies are those which . . . neutralize this force through the balance of power . . . and through techniques for harnessing its energy for social ends."[13]

More explicitly than some other American realists, Morgenthau suggested that all political relationships are governed by objective rules deeply rooted in human nature. Because these rules are "impervious to our preferences, men will challenge them only at the risk of failure." Viewing man as a self-centered creature whose ego is contaminated by the propensity for sin and evil, Morgenthau acknowledged that forces inherent in human nature prevent the realization of a thoroughly rational or moral political order. Whereas Niebuhr emphasized man's creative

12. Kenneth W. Thompson, "The Political Philosophy of Reinhold Niebuhr," in Charles W. Kegley and Robert W. Bretall (eds.), *Reinhold Niebuhr: His Religious, Moral, and Political Thought* (New York, 1956), 164; Reinhold Niebuhr, *Moral Man and Immoral Society: A Study in Ethics and Politics* (New York, 1932), 51–83.

13. Reinhold Niebuhr, *An Interpretation of Christian Ethics* (New York, 1940), 40.

and destructive tendencies, Morgenthau's doctrine of political man was often couched in extreme, pessimistic terms. "It is impossible," he argued, "to be a successful politician and a good Christian." Calling into question the influence of morality upon social life, he wrote: "There can be no actual denial of lust for power without denying the very conditions of human existence in this world. . . . There is no escape from the evil of power, regardless of what one does. Whenever we act with reference to our fellow men we must sin."[14] Divorced from any transcendent moral authority, man's political life is doomed to produce evil.

Kennan's reference to Niebuhr as "the father of us all" was in large part prompted by the diplomat's recognition of the many human failings that preempt the realization of those moral and civic virtues that form the basis of civilized existence. However, Kennan is perhaps closer to Morgenthau than either Lippmann or Niebuhr in his tendency to stress the demonic more than the divine or rational elements in man. An admitted elitist repulsed by the crass materialism of the Western world that has lost its spiritual stamina, he accepted the reality of coercive power and violence as "the tribute we pay to original sin." Ultimately, Kennan's thought was shaped less by the requirements of human justice (*e.g.*, "There is little that can be done about men's motives") than the need to preserve the tangible order of society by the imposition of restraints on recalcitrant human behavior.[15] Unlike Lippmann, Kennan devoted little consideration to how the self-interest in human nature is moderated by faith in a higher law. Unlike Niebuhr, he provided little insight into why it is necessary to rely upon transcendent moral principles to broaden the conception of self-interest in political life.

Integral to both the continental tradition of *raison d'état* and American realist thought is the assumption that conflicts of power are an inevitable feature of all political relationships—more so perhaps among nation-states than at any other level of political interaction. European theorists viewed the state's struggle for power and security as a fact of nature or a datum of history impervious to human will and control. The best the political philosopher could hope to achieve was to describe the international state of nature and the precarious legal order presumed to

14. Morgenthau, *Politics Among Nations*, 4; Stone, *Reinhold Niebuhr: Prophet to Politicians*, 202. See also Morgenthau, *Scientific Man*, 187–201.

15. George F. Kennan, "Speak Truth to Power—A Reply by George F. Kennan," *Progressive*, XIX (October, 1955), 18; Kennan, *Democracy and the Student Left*, 149–50.

exist among nations. Along with Thucydides and Machiavelli, American realists regarded the lust for power as an intrinsic quality of human nature; however, the political thought of Lippmann, Niebuhr, and Morgenthau more specifically illustrated how the peculiar corruption of political man is magnified by the transference of power impulses from the individual to the state.

Tracing the modern force of nationalism to the loves and prejudices of man's "first" (or irrational) nature, Lippmann noted that the nation absorbs the loyalties that men desire to bestow on an entity more permanent and enduring than themselves. The strength of collective egotism, according to Niebuhr, results from the tendency of groups and nations to express both the virtue and selfishness of their members. One consequence of modern society is that the state delimits and suppresses the individual's desire for power and personal security. Frustrated individuals seek an outlet for their inhibited aspirations by projecting their ego to the level of the national ego. Furthermore, this process of transference is accentuated by the state's appeal to the loyalty and self-sacrifice of individuals. What was egotism and immoral for man in his personal life now becomes patriotic and noble when these impulses are directed by the state itself toward its own ends. Believing that society simply "cumulates the egotism of individuals and transmutes their individual altruism into collective egoism," Niebuhr concluded that no nation "acts from purely unselfish or even mutual intent, and politics is therefore bound to be a contest of power."[16]

Building on Niebuhr's analysis, Morgenthau explained how the diversion of power drives from the individual to the state gives the "lie" to the ethical dualism associated with Machiavellian *raison d'état*. Specifically, those who seek power at all levels of political organization must make it appear that they are aiming at something more worthy of moral approval than power or domination. This objective is usually met by the invocation of political ideologies that conceal and transform the political act into something different from what it actually is. As for the ethical significance of this transference, these ideologies function to blunt man's conscience, in that man becomes oblivious to the corruption of power in the public sphere while still being aware of its private manifestation. With obvious reference to the ethics of *raison d'état*, Morgenthau wrote: "The

16. Thompson, *Masters of International Thought*, 29.

dual morality . . . which justifies what is done for the power of the state but condemns it when it is done for the power of the individual . . . presents but the positive aspect and at the same time the logical consummation of this forgetfulness."[17]

In brief, these American thinkers can be distinguished from their European counterparts in their effort to substantiate more fully the connection between human nature and the power of self-interest in national or group behavior. Whereas continental theorists generally retained a pessimistic view of man, Niebuhr and Morgenthau argued that the international state of nature was a product of *both* the virtuous and selfish aspects of man's nature.

An additional point on which the American school of realism parallels the classical diplomacy of *raison d'état* is the assumption that nation-states are the most significant actors in world politics. Especially following the breakup of medieval Christendom, continental theorists regarded the state as an enduring moral entity whose authority superseded transnational sympathies. The norms of diplomacy and military confrontation observed by Richelieu and Bismarck were efficacious only to the extent that they enhanced the power and security of the French and German states. In fact, the legacy of Bismarckian *realpolitik* was to elevate the state to the level of a "mortal God" for an age that no longer believed in an immortal God.

Although American realists continue to view the governments of territorially organized nation-states as the primary actors on the international stage, they have been no less insistent in refusing to treat the self-centered, parochial national community as a final norm of human existence. Referring to the "anarchism" and "primitiveness" of the modern concept of sovereignty, Kennan asked: "Could anything be more absurd than a world divided into several dozens of large secular societies, each devoted to the cultivation of the myth of its own overriding importance and virtue?"[18] Similarly, Niebuhr suggested that realism must be tempered with morality, that men and states cannot follow their self-interest without claiming to do so in obedience to some general scheme of values. Lippmann's rationalist ethics led him to the conclusion that a

17. Morgenthau, *Scientific Man*, 199.

18. George F. Kennan, "History and Diplomacy as Viewed by a Diplomatist," *Review of Politics*, XVIII (April, 1956), 171.

world-state predicated on the law of reason—or the Law of Nature's God—must be the ultimate norm of all clear-thinking men. Insofar as the dictates of reason are universal and coextensive with mankind, Lippmann could argue that nationalism represented a barbaric retrogression in the criminal rivalry of nations.

Along with Kennan, Morgenthau pointed out that "the contemporary connection between interest and the nation state is a product of history, and is . . . bound to disappear in the course of history." Nowhere is it preordained that nation-states constitute the permanent political units of international life. The paradox of the present age is that the nation-state may have outlived its usefulness, but no wholly viable form of political organization ("more in keeping with the technological potentialities and moral requirements of the contemporary world") has emerged to take its place. In tandem with Lippmann and Niebuhr, Morgenthau considered "the equation between a particular nationalism and the Counsels of Providence as morally indefensible," for it "is liable to engender the distortion in judgment which . . . in the name of moral principles" destroys nations and civilizations.[19] All four American realists are united in the belief that interest is the perennial standard by which political action must be judged and directed; however, they have been much more willing than continental thinkers to recognize the tragic moral dilemma of acting within the political sphere.

Thucydides' statement that "identity of interests is the surest of bonds whether between states or individuals" was echoed by those American realists who appealed to the historic reality of the national interest to account for the goals of postwar United States foreign policy.[20] Although previous chapters briefly noted a number of conceptual and empirical weaknesses of realism as a theory of international politics, the significance of *raison d'état* for the expression of American national interest in world affairs is primarily a problem in political ethics. In other words, the moral dilemma for the statesman inheres in his having to reconcile the requirements of political success with ultimate standards of right and wrong in the behavior of sovereign states. Although our analysis has been restricted to four prominent realist thinkers, each of them

19. Morgenthau, *Politics Among Nations*, 9–11.
20. *Ibid.*, 8.

has acknowledged that the ethical dimension of diplomacy assumes special importance inasmuch as Americans have traditionally viewed the actions of the United States as taking place within a framework of moral restraints and limitations. The projection of American power in war or peace has seldom been justified exclusively by reference to national survival; rather, policies designed to defend and augment national security are viewed in and out of government as standing for moral purposes beyond the state.

To some extent, the charge that these American scholars are little more than modern enthusiasts of hard-headed power politics results from their periodic inclination to draw an overly sharp distinction between moral principle and objective self-interest (backed by power) in foreign policy. Influenced by the geopolitical stratagems of Alfred Thayer Mahan and Nicholas Spykman, Lippmann's classic definition that foreign policy "consists of bringing into balance with a comfortable surplus of power in reserve, the nation's commitments and . . . power" implied that in diplomacy the national interest is a consideration superior to all others. According to some commentators, the Machiavellian tendencies in the thought of Niebuhr may be evidenced by his occasional tendency to portray national self-interest as an inescapable reality from which no state can demur. By viewing group pride as a corruption of individual loyalty, Niebuhr rejected the proposition that a nation can escape the power of self-regard through the proclamations of universal aspirations based on mutual intent. For example, he once noted that during World War II the allied nations were driven by "a stronger desire to come to the aid of stricken peoples [invaded by the fascists] than they had the power to act upon that desire. . . . Every impulse of national pride intervenes to prevent the desired, or at least desirable, action."[21]

In addition, selected passages from the writings of Morgenthau and Kennan appear to stretch the gap between "the moral ideal and the facts of political life" to its breaking point. Specifically, Morgenthau often characterized politics as an autonomous field of inquiry (distinct from ethics) and argued that the statesman's primary obligation is to think and act in terms of interest defined as power. Judging the political act to be

21. Lippmann, *U.S. Foreign Policy*, 9; Niebuhr, *The Children of Light and the Children of Darkness*, 170.

inevitably evil, he called into question the ethical potential of American foreign policy by suggesting that "the invocation of moral principles for the support of national policies is of necessity a pretense."[22]

In equally strident tones, Kennan rejected the proposition "that state behavior is a fit subject for moral judgment"; in most international conflicts, he cautioned, what is morally right or wrong is "simply not discernible to the outsider." Ironically, both of these realists evinced a normative rationale for the pursuit of a national interest unencumbered by the moral abstractions of pretentious idealism. Addressing the Truman Administration, Morgenthau wrote: "Above all, remember that it is not only a political necessity but also a moral duty for a nation to follow in its dealings with other nations but one guiding star . . . one rule for action: the National Interest." Exemplifying the liberal faith that the observance of one's objective self-interest cannot help but serve the common good, Kennan expressed the conviction that "if our purposes at home are decent ones . . . then the pursuit of our national interest can never fail to be conducive to a better world."[23]

Morality and Foreign Policy:
Raison d'État and the Dual Moral Standard

Perhaps more than other American realists, the writings of Niebuhr and Morgenthau explicitly treated the Machiavellian doctrine of *raison d'état* as a distinctive issue in the history of Western political ethics. In fact, the moral realm of man's political existence within both the national community and the more complex international community formed the basis of Niebuhr's realism; he regarded politics as a vital and ever-changing arena where the self-interest of power-seeking men and nations interacts with the demands of conscience. Although Niebuhr claimed to abide by a "frank dualism" in ethical matters, his use of the dialectic denied neither egoism nor altruism, but illustrated how the many facets of man's social life are an inevitable product of both self-seeking and self-giving impulses.

22. Good, "The National Interest And Political Realism: Niebuhr's Debate With Morgenthau and Kennan," 612; Morgenthau, "National Interest and Moral Principles in Foreign Policy," 207, 211.

23. George F. Kennan, *American Diplomacy, 1900–1950* (Chicago, 1951), 88–89, 100; Stone, *Reinhold Niebuhr: Prophet to Politicians*, 203.

Always alert to the errors resulting from an overly consistent realism or idealism, Niebuhr recoiled from the tendency of continental thinkers either to exempt or subordinate morality to the realities of power and self-interest in politics. For example, he considered that the "secular realism" of Machiavelli and Hobbes jeopardized the prospect of achieving standards of discriminate justice in the political order by its cynical preoccupation with the sources of individual and collective egoism. The violent and destructive manifestations of man's fallen nature were recognized by these thinkers only for the amoral purpose of investing the Leviathan or conquering prince with sufficient power to bring order to the conflicting interests in society. As a result, the problem of the larger order between parochial communities disappeared from the moral horizon. Niebuhr concluded that "pulling ethics into the service of justice, however defined, remains one of the paramount problems of an adequate political ethics."[24]

The dual moral standard suggested by *raison d'état* was rejected by Morgenthau for two principal reasons. First, he observed that political philosophers since the time of Plato and Aristotle have routinely embraced the belief that man is not allowed to act as he pleases in the political sphere (*i.e.*, that his behavior ought to conform to a standard higher than success). The test of a morally good action is the degree to which it is capable of treating others not as means to the actor's end but as ends in themselves. In addition, Morgenthau shared the normative sentiment of Niebuhr in recognizing that the struggle for power amid the evil and conflict in political life "must be intelligible as a dialectical movement toward the realization of justice." Doubting whether even the most cynical political act is exempt from ethical significance, he wrote: "The actors on the political scene, however they may be guided by . . . expediency, must pay tribute to these standards by justifying their actions in ethical terms. The actor may subordinate all ethical considerations to his political goal; however, his act cannot be beyond good and evil . . . as long as he makes the apparent harmony of his act with the ethical standards part of the goal to be realized."[25]

Second, Morgenthau took exception to the notion that man acts differently in the political sphere than in the private one because ethics

24. Niebuhr, *The Structure of Nations and Empires*, 144.
25. Morgenthau, *Scientific Man*, 177.

allow him to act differently (*i.e.*, political acts are subject to one ethical standard, whereas private acts are subject to another). This juxtaposition, he believed, was fundamentally mistaken, because it is always the individual who acts either in his own interest or in reference to the goals of others; the action of a society or nation, political or otherwise, has no empirical existence. The opposition between man and society reduces to the opposition between different kinds of actions. There is not one kind of ethical precept applying to political action and another one to the private realm, but one and the same ethical standard applies to both. Morgenthau argued that the difference in moral character between the private and public sphere is at best a relative one: The potential immorality of all human action becomes obviously more present in political behavior, where it is impossible for an action to conform to the rules of politics (*i.e.*, to achieve political success) and to conform to the rules of ethics (*i.e.*, to be good in itself).[26] Niebuhr's admission of a "frank dualism" notwithstanding, both realists viewed the lust for power as ubiquitous empirical fact and its denial as universal ethical norm as the two poles between which the problem of political ethics is perilously suspended.

By implication, the ethical dualism of *raison d'état* poses a central question for the nature of moral choice in a state's external relations: To what extent, and from what perspectives, have American realists maintained a meaningful balance between universal norms and national self-interest? That Lippmann was often described by critics as a proponent of American *realpolitik* was largely the result of his reliance on the methods of classical diplomacy and support for a reinvigorated Atlantic Alliance based on the balance of power and spheres of influence. Yet his faith in the rational dignity of man and his concern for transcendent standards of justice in democratic societies precluded any attempt to decouple power politics from man's inherent capacity for moral judgment.

Although Lippmann considered military and strategic assets the frontline of any nation's power, he also warned that a government would be foolish to disregard the potential impact of ideals in its calculations of foreign policy. During World War II, he defended the national values that shaped the history of American diplomacy with the conviction that "a

26. *Ibid.*, 187–88.

people which does not advance its faith has already begun to abandon it."[27] Even at the height of the Cold War, Lippmann urged American decision-makers to develop and apply their principles of democracy and freedom to counter Soviet ideological fervor in Europe and areas of the Third World. In the final analysis, Lippmann suggested that United States foreign-policy commitments abroad are supported by the fact that they enlist American power as the defender of democracy.

Moreover, Lippmann's geopolitical orientation must be evaluated in the context of his self-admitted internationalism and distinctive cosmopolitan world view. His writings on both American government and American foreign policy reveal a mind-set that is sensitive to the values and interests of many other countries. The prospects for any rational exchange of ideas and beliefs among diverse societies were being jeopardized, he thought, by the imperatives of modern warfare and the globalization of militant ideological confrontation between East and West. To a considerable degree, Lippmann's recourse to diplomatic strategies traditionally associated with *raison d'état* represented the only realistic means by which to salvage his cosmopolitan sympathies. The balance of power and stabilization of alliance systems functioned as self-activating restraints on the irrational resort to imperialism or belligerence by aggressive nations on either side of the Atlantic. Although Lippmann never approached the American national interest as an issue in moral philosophy, his contribution was to illustrate how the ethics of war and peace can never be approached apart from political and territorial questions.

Niebuhr, Morgenthau, and Kennan shared Lippmann's concern that a true realism, grounded on justice and historical standards, was an illusive goal unless "military power has first been organized for security against the threat of great wars."[28] At the same time, these three thinkers took Lippmann's analysis a step further by more precisely focusing upon the consequences and problems of trying to relate self-interest to norms transcending interest in the conduct of foreign policy. By noting both complementary and dissimilar components in the moral perspective of these three thinkers, students of American diplomacy will be able to draw

27. Walter Lippmann, *U.S. War Aims* (Boston, 1945), 40.
28. D. Steven Blum, *Walter Lippmann: Cosmopolitanism in the Century of Total War* (Ithaca, 1984), 132.

on a more informed estimate of how realist ethics can be distinguished from the dual moral standard of *raison d'état*.

American realists begin their analysis of the moral problem in foreign policy by pointing to the inescapable hypocrisy in the nation's claim to being the bearer of transcendent values; however, an important difference occurs at the point of prescribing a remedy to the claims of the pretentious idealist. Kennan recommends that we have the modesty to admit that the national interest provides the only objective standard for American foreign policy. Although Kennan would have policy-makers consult the national interest with restraint and prudent regard for the interests of others, he argued that the error of the legalistic-moralistic approach was to carry over "into the affairs of states the concepts of right and wrong." [29] Even though Morgenthau found it morally indefensible to equate a particular nationalism with the creative work of civilization, he was no less insistent in maintaining that the ends of policy are determined by interest and by available power.

By contrast, Niebuhr consistently urged that the realist understanding of the national interest be broadened and evaluated beyond the aims of the parochial national community. He accepted the reality of national self-interest, although he rejected it as a norm. The recognition of norms beyond the national interest helps to moderate the nation's egoism and assist it in achieving what at least may be regarded as enlightened self-interest. Niebuhr never denied that the nation constitutes a morally defensible entity. What he did question, however, was whether those values that assure the legitimacy of the nation and impart a modicum of dignity to the national interest are ever defined in such a way to accommodate the devotion to principles of justice and established mutualities in a community of sovereign nations. Accordingly, Niebuhr advised that "a narrow national loyalty . . . will obscure our long range interests where they are involved with those of a whole alliance of free nations." [30]

A second important difference among these three thinkers concerns the role of universal norms in the political life of nations. Human existence, Morgenthau stressed, "cannot find its meaning within itself but must receive it from a transcendent source." Against the Hobbesian view

29. Kennan, *American Diplomacy*, 100.
30. Reinhold Niebuhr, *Christian Realism and Political Problems* (New York, 1952), 134–37.

that there is neither morality nor law outside the state, he claimed that there are absolute moral principles that "do not permit certain policies to be considered at all from the point of view of expediency."[31] Paradoxically, Morgenthau's rather vaguely defined transcendent ethic is so ethereal in distancing sinful man from a "wholly other Divine Being" that it can play only a judgmental role in saving man from hypocrisy (*i.e.*, by demonstrating that man is not God and that every political act is therefore inconsistent with the moral law). By contrast, he is far less instructive on how and in what ways moral absolutes may serve as the directive force and constant goal of political life. This line of inquiry is preempted by Morgenthau's more pronounced tendency to conceive of politics as an autonomous realm with its own operational rules. Although these rules may derive from universal norms, they are ultimately distorted (and relativized) by individual selfishness and the tragic presence of evil in all political action.

Perhaps more than any other prominent American realist, the ethical precepts shaping the international thought of Kennan defy precise categorization. Although "moral principles have their place in the heart of the individual," he warned that the "unavoidable necessities" of the national interest (*i.e.*, maintaining the military security and political integrity of the state) are "not subject to classification as either good or bad." If Kennan has looked to "the traditional devices of political expediency" as a remedy for idealistic and utopian abstractions, he has also sought to distance himself from the national cynicism of *raison d'état* by occupying the less dangerous middle ground of moral relativism.[32]

Throughout the postwar decades, Kennan exhorted Americans to rely upon principles "of a moral and ethical nature which we like to consider as being characteristic of the spirit of our civilization," without presuming that those principles are valid for others.[33] Elaborating on the connection between power and responsibility, he suggested that American moral conduct in world affairs must be founded on, and limited to, the nation's traditional principles of justice and propriety. In contrast to Morgenthau's "sense of transcendence," Kennan's formal ethic is imma-

31. Morgenthau, *The Purpose of American Politics*, 358; *Politics Among Nations*, 231.

32. George F. Kennan, *Realities of American Foreign Policy* (Princeton, 1954), 48; "Morality and Foreign Policy," *Foreign Affairs*, LXIV (Winter, 1985–86), 206.

33. Kennan, *Realities of American Foreign Policy*, 213–14.

nental; morality in foreign policy is a function of the values and normative order of American society. Unfortunately, his "humane relativism"
often failed to designate the source or type of American principles necessary for the pursuit of a just and ordered world community.

The realism of Niebuhr was distinguished by his lifelong concern to
reconcile the transcendent articles of Christian faith with the inevitable
tendency of men and nations to pursue their own selfish interests. In Niebuhr's estimate, Morgenthau's concept of transcendence could hardly
provide a viable political ethic insofar as his overly pessimistic outlook
on human nature functioned to obscure the search for moral principles
beyond the operative political reality of any one particular group or nation. In opposition to Morgenthau's contention that man's political life is
doomed to produce evil, Niebuhr insisted on the mixture of good and
evil; he found politics, like man, morally ambiguous rather than the
"prototype of all possible corruption." The responsibility for defining
standards of order and justice in the human community can only be acted
on "if the individual is known in terms of both his capacity for love and
self-love." [34]

In addition, Morgenthau's somewhat fatalistic preoccupation with
man's sinful nature neglects the always-precarious balance between the
destructive and creative vitalities of the human will. Niebuhr argued that
the "radical freedom" of the individual personality forces us to acknowledge that to will evil implies the freedom to will the good. Although the
community of perfect justice cannot be achieved, a narrow but real margin of moral choice may be preserved if the "higher loyalty" to norms
beyond self-interest saves the "lower loyalty" (*i.e.*, self-regard) from cynicism and self-defeat. At the very least, these universal principles can serve
political man by pointing to those areas in which self-interest intertwines
with the interest of others. Whereas Morgenthau spoke of the impossibility of reconciling the moral requirements of Christianity and politics,
Niebuhr's reliance on the importance of Christian social teaching regarding the responsibility for order and justice reduced the impossibility to a
tension-filled possibility. [35]

Certainly, Niebuhr was aware that when applied to the behavior of
nations the dialectical balance between power and principle is subject to

34. Reinhold Niebuhr, *The Self and the Dramas of History* (New York, 1955), 234.
35. Stone, *Reinhold Niebuhr: Prophet to Politicians,* 201.

enormous strains. He joined with other American realists in maintaining that "there can be no complete self-sacrifice or even generosity in political or collective relations." Although an enlightened self-interest is often considered the most attainable virtue of states, Niebuhr stipulated that "nations are . . . subject, as are individuals, to an internal tension between the claims of the self and the larger claims of love." At a deeper level, and in vivid contrast to the relativism of Kennan, he wrote: "It is possible for . . . individuals and groups to relate concern for the other with interest and concern for the self. . . . A valid moral outlook for both individuals and for groups . . . sets no limits to the creative possibility of concern for others and makes no claim that such creativity ever annuls the power of self-concern . . . if the force of residual egotism is not acknowledged." Specifically, Niebuhr drew upon his profound faith "to remind the nation of a majesty greater than its own, of obligations beyond its own interest, and of a divine judgment . . . against the complacent and proud."[36]

The Responsibility and Limits of American Power

The allegation by some commentators that the realist perspective simply recapitulates the logic of *raison d'état* often takes the form of a loosely worded indictment against those writers who define the primary interest of the United States according to the calculus of military and diplomatic gains in the enduring rivalry among hostile states. Often obscured by this line of reasoning, however, is the extent to which American scholars repeatedly emphasized the necessity for *restraints and limits upon the actions of the United States,* as the leader of the Western alliance and the champion of democracy around the globe.

For almost four decades, peace has been maintained in the world through the maintenance of an effective nuclear deterrent by the two major superpowers. Not one of the American thinkers examined in this study has ever argued against the need for a deterrent capacity sufficient to prevent a debilitating "first strike" by the Soviet Union. What they have objected to is, first, the conviction of some strategic thinkers and government officials that the management and control of nuclear war is

36. Niebuhr, *The Structure of Nations and Empires,* 30–31; Reinhold Niebuhr, "The Perils of American Power," *Messenger,* May 22, 1951, p. 6.

no different from the fine tuning of military strategy throughout the ages; and, second, the naïve belief that deterrence can be stabilized and American security enhanced by adding increasing numbers of new and more sophisticated weapons with which to threaten a potential aggressor.

At the height of the Cold War, and with the concept of massive retaliation in mind, Lippmann warned of the militarization of American diplomacy that would substitute a temporary monopolization of nuclear power for a more constructive diplomatic approach to resolving the territorial and political questions that lie at the center of Soviet-American strategic differences. Along with Kennan, he objected to basing the defense of Western Europe on offensive missiles and called for the withdrawal of Soviet and American forces from Central Europe. Referring to the moral predicament of the statesman in the nuclear age, Niebuhr pointed out that "we are caught in the dilemma of doing the evil we do not want." Moreover, Niebuhr questioned whether American policymakers could ever find a moral vantage point from which to justify a retaliation-in-kind in the event of a preemptive Soviet strike. Although his Christian faith revealed that there are no solutions to the ultimate ethical problems of man's political existence, Niebuhr believed that peace might be enhanced if "both sides were . . . more conscious of the common danger which transcends their enmities." [37]

In addition to the escalating costs and unparalleled risks that continue to multiply in the military competition between the United States and the Soviet Union, all four American thinkers acknowledged several important limitations upon American diplomatic influence throughout the Third World. Viewing the Truman Doctrine and containment strategy in relation to the developing world, Lippmann argued that the implicit suggestion of globalized military confrontation with the Soviet Union would commit the United States to an "ideological crusade" and a dangerous policy of indiscriminate intervention in the affairs of weaker and disorderly states. Niebuhr cautioned the West against overestimating its moral authority among the new nations; by the mid-1960s, he judged that the claims of capitalism and communism were largely irrelevant to the many diverse liberating movements of nationalism and modernization in Africa and Asia.

37. Harry R. Davis and Robert C. Good, (eds.), *Reinhold Niebuhr on Politics* (New York, 1960), 326; Niebuhr, *The Structure of Nations and Empires*, 273.

Focusing on the major strongholds of military-industrial strength that have a direct bearing on American national security, Kennan maintained that the smaller states of the non-European world are poorly constituted to make a useful contribution to the global strategic balance. Furthermore, Morgenthau concluded that American foreign-aid efforts have been ineffective in promoting democratic reforms and economic growth insofar as policy-makers have failed to recognize the extent to which the development of other nations depends on indigenous rational and moral solutions. Specifically, he believed that the problem of foreign aid is insoluble if treated as a "self-sufficient technical enterprise" without regard for either the political problems of the donor country or the prevailing political conditions in the receiving country.[38]

Another integral concept associated with the diplomatic execution of *raison d'état*, and repeatedly emphasized by leading American realists as a standard for United States foreign policy, is the balance of power. Although the precise origins of the balance of power have been the subject of considerable debate among diplomatic historians, the principle generally served continental thinkers and statesmen as an indication of the methods by which foreign policy is conducted and a prescription shaping the successful defense of state objectives. As Inis Claude observes, "the trouble with the balance of power is not that it has no meaning, but that it has too many meanings."[39] In the writings of our four American scholars, the balance concept has been variously construed to mean an existing distribution of power, an equilibrium or certain amount of stability that under favorable conditions is produced by an alliance or other devices, a particular manifestation of a general social principle, an approximately equal distribution of power, a search for superiority, and a law of universal application whenever a number of armed sovereign states coexist and compete for power.

Although American realists have drawn on a wide variety of definitions to characterize the workings of the balance of power, their interpretation of this perennial concept has frequently drawn on a number of common assumptions. First, the fact that decisions can be taken in one or more independent states that may drastically affect the national well-being and vital interests of other nations means that foreign policy must

38. Morgenthau, *The Restoration of American Politics*, 255.
39. Inis Claude, *Power and International Relations* (New York, 1962), 13.

be shaped with the end-in-view of neutralizing the power threat implicit in such a state system. One solution—indeed, the most frequently adopted solution—is for each nation to seek alliances that will counterbalance the power of its principal rivals and its allies. In this way, an alliance system is established that may enhance national security by balancing rival nations and rival power blocs. In the words of Lippmann: "Where coercive force exists, it must either be neutralized by force or employed in the interests of what we regard as civilization." [40]

Second, the interests and objectives of the American Republic going back to the Founding Fathers were restricted to maintaining a preponderance of power in the Western Hemisphere and a balance of power elsewhere in the world. For well over a century, the only serious threat to the security of the United States could come from a major outside power—and this meant a *European* power—given the preponderance of great powers within Europe and the proximity of Europe to the bulge of Brazil in the Southern Hemisphere. [41] As Morgenthau and Kennan pointed out, American entry into the world wars of the twentieth century was justified by the traditional conviction that the subjugation of European powers by any one predominant nation would put the very safety of the United States in the Western Hemisphere in jeopardy.

Third, the traditional balance-of-power framework composed of a multiplicity of states with roughly equal strength and sharing a common political culture was radically altered in the postwar years by the emergence of a bipolar system of world power. Concerning the requirements and consequences of the new international distribution of power, American realists have often displayed significant differences and pointed to a number of unresolved puzzles for calculating the relevance of balance strategies in the nuclear age. For example, Lippmann's optimism that "third states" might serve to moderate conflicting interests between the major powers was rejected by Morgenthau and Kennan.

Against Morgenthau's belief that the balance of power is "an essential stabilizing factor in a society of nations," Niebuhr suggested that the balance of power may degenerate into domination and tyranny by creating a coerced unity of society in which the freedom and vitality of its members are impaired. [42] Kennan's use of the balance of power, restricted

---

40. Walter Lippman, *The Stakes of Diplomacy* (New York, 1915), 221–22.
41. Thompson, *Moralism and Morality in Politics and Diplomacy*, 50.
42. Morgenthau, *Politics Among Nations*, 167.

to initiatives designed to support an equilibrium among the geopolitical strongholds of the world, provided few clues about how such policies can possibly be responsive to his more recent concern for the common environmental and military dangers transcending all nations. Furthermore, political realists in general have devoted little attention to how balance techniques can be usefully applied to the nuclear "balance of terror." Aside from seeking some numerical parity in the weapons of mass destruction, what viable options does a statesman possess in seeking to preserve his nation's security in a world where the rational relationship between force as a means and end of foreign policy no longer applies?

Conclusion

From the venue of either political philosophy or international ethics, to single out these four thinkers as either vigorous or unwitting advocates of cynical *raison d'état* is intellectually indefensible. The American realist tradition affirms that political actors come under moral judgment and are witness to the values of their society. Its leading spokesmen since the time of Washington and Hamilton maintained a consistent regard for the underlying purposes and ideals of American society. "From the time of the Declaration of our Independence," according to Henry Kissinger, "Americans have believed that this country has a moral significance for the world."[43] The United States was created in a conscious act by a people dedicated to a set of political and ethical principles they held to be of universal meaning. Whereas continental theorists of *raison d'état* propounded an autonomous ethics of state behavior, American thinkers have been unwilling to admit of any separate ethics for state behavior. Insofar as a state is a legal abstraction, or fictitious personality, it is not the state that decides and acts but always individuals, though they are sometimes called "statesmen."

Furthermore, the ethical perspective of American realists may, in part, be distinguished by their implicit affirmation of the classical and Christian principles that characterize the higher-law background of American constitutional law. The Founding Fathers were practical philosophers whose views on democratic government and foreign policy

43. Henry A. Kissinger, "Morality and Power," in Ernest W. Lefever (ed.), *Morality and Foreign Policy* (Washington, D.C., 1977), 59.

were based on a clear-cut conception of the nature of man, the state, and the world. Edward S. Corwin, one of America's leading constitutional historians, argued that the early American statesmen succeeded in translating principles of transcendental justice into terms of personal and private rights. These principles of natural law, he wrote, "were made by no human hands; indeed, if they did not antedate deity itself, they still . . . express its nature as to bind and control it. . . . They are eternal and immutable. In relation to such principles, human laws are, when entitled to obedience . . . merely a record or transcript, and their enactment an act not of will or power but one of discovery and declaration." Similarly, Lippmann wrote that the American founders were the adherents of a public philosophy—"of the doctrine of natural law, which held there was law above the ruler and the sovereign people . . . above the whole community of mortals."[44]

That transcendent purpose, which Morgenthau deemed essential for the successful workings of a democratic government, encompassed a common conception of law and order based on the natural rights of man. Because imperfect man aspires to the good but is frequently betrayed by a propensity for sin, the best system of government is one that harnesses his virtues to serve good purposes and limits his vices through legal and institutional restraints. Niebuhr's perception of the manifold forces at work in human nature and his belief that the balance of power stands at the forefront of whatever justice is achieved in human relations were reflected earlier in the political thought of James Madison. In the pages of the *Federalist*, Madison opined: "Ambition must be made to counteract ambition. The interest of the man must be connected with the constitutional rights of the place. It may be a reflection on human nature that such devices should be necessary to control the abuses of government. But what is government itself but the greatest of all reflections on human nature? If men were angels, no government would be necessary. If angels were to govern men, neither external nor internal controls on government would be necessary."[45]

The central moral problem of government, since the early days of

44. Edward S. Corwin, *The "Higher Law" Background of American Constitutional Law* (Ithaca, 1979), 4–5. See also Ellis Sandoz, "Power and Spirit in the Founding," *This World*, No. 9 (Fall, 1984), 66–77; Lippmann, *The Public Philosophy*, 76.

45. Hamilton, Madison, and Jay, *The Federalist Papers*, 322.

the Republic, has been to strike a just and effective balance between free-dom and authority. In short, what Blackstone saluted as "the eternal, immutable laws of good and evil" were institutionalized within a consti-tutional system of checks and balances designed to achieve the best that is possible among mortal and finite, diverse and conflicting men.

Evaluating the potential significance of American ideals for the re-alities of international politics, realist thinkers acknowledged that the principles of morality and the necessities of power are not mutually ex-clusive categories by which to define the scope and objectives of the na-tional interest. Clearly, a responsible foreign policy must begin with the practical necessities of survival and the maintenance of a balance of power—a scope for action, a capacity to shape events and conditions. At the same time, the higher-law tradition and transcendent values of the American people ensure that a policy directed solely at manipulating force would lack all conviction, consistency, and public support.

Any number of historical examples can be cited to illustrate how the confluence of self-interest and the ethics of national purpose have distinguished America's relations with the world for over two centuries. For example, the Founding Fathers were driven to manipulate the rival-ries of European powers in order to secure the independence of a nation committed to the rule of law and to reap the blessings of ordered liberty. After World War II, the Marshall Plan, as well as several other recent foreign-policy initiatives (attempts to promote human freedom behind the Iron Curtain; efforts to promote democratic governments in Latin America, Africa, and Asia; programs designed to eliminate or reduce poverty and hunger throughout the Third World; campaigns to promote the international observance of human rights; and initiatives to achieve strategic arms control and disarmament) have served both moral and practical ends, and can be sustained only with idealistic conviction and practical wisdom.

At a time in our history when both liberals and conservatives fre-quently judge the nation's interest and foreign-policy commitments ac-cording to universal principles of justice and human rights, the legacy of realism for American diplomacy in the 1990s can be stated briefly. Al-though sensitive to the force of self-interest in the political conduct of men and nations, realist scholars have exhorted America to maintain the courage of its moral convictions, to seek the enhancement of freedom and basic human liberties together with other national objectives. As Kennan suggested, the implementation of these convictions requires a renewed sense of the basic decency of this country so that the American public and policy-makers may continue to have the pride and self-confidence to remain actively involved in the world. Furthermore, American realists are well aware that underlying the traditional historic and geopolitical conflict between the two leading superpowers is a pervasive ideological and spiritual "struggle for the minds of men." The conflict between freedom and totalitarianism is not transient or incidental; it is a moral conflict, of fundamental historical proportions, that gives the modern age a special meaning.

The error of moral perfectionists, as Morgenthau and Kennan submit, is to make an unjustifiable leap from the omnipresence of the moral element in foreign policy to the conclusion that the United States has a mission to apply its own moral principles to the rest of humanity. Abstract principles of human rights and individual liberty not only come into conflict with other diplomatic and strategic interests that America may possess in a given instance; in addition, the actual impossibility of consistently pursuing the global defense of self-evident truths enshrined in the American polity may be evidenced by the lack of effective enforcement mechanisms and the predominance of universal ideological claims in the foreign policy of nondemocratic states. Secretary of State John Quincy Adams, in an early expression of the American realist tradition, maintained that it was not for the United States to impose its own principles of government upon the rest of mankind, but, rather, to attract the rest of mankind through the example of the United States. Speaking before the citizens of Washington on July 4, 1821, Adams offered an eloquent testimony to the normative foundations of American diplomacy.

> Wherever the standard of freedom and independence has been or shall be unfurled, there will be America's heart, her benedictions, and her prayers. But she goes not abroad in search of monsters to destroy. She is the well-wisher to the freedom and independence of all. She is the champion and vindicator only of her own. She will recommend the general cause by the countenance of her voice, and by the benignant sympathy of her example. She well knows that by . . . enlisting under other banners than her own, were they even the banners of foreign independence, she would involve herself be-

yond the power of extrication, in all the wars of interest and in-
trigue, of individual avarice, envy, and ambition, which assume the
colors and usurp the standards of freedom. . . . She might become
the dictatress of the world. She would no longer be the ruler of her
own spirit.[46]

Regarding the relation between moral principles and foreign policy,
American realists have exemplified a distinctively pragmatic approach to
the universal application of American standards of action to others. To
their minds, moral principles are not realized in the real world of conflicting interests by moral fervor alone, but instead by a pragmatic calculation of the means to an end or by a rational anticipation of the actual
consequences of a given action. Summarizing what is distinctive in the
American approach to foreign policy, Secretary of State Kissinger has
written: "Since Tocqueville, it has been observed that we are a pragmatic
people, commonsensical, undogmatic, undoctrinaire—a nation with a
permanent bent to the practical and an instinct for what works. We have
defined our basic goals—justice, freedom, equality, and progress—in
open and libertarian terms, seeking to enlarge opportunity and the human spirit rather than to coerce a uniform standard of behavior or a
common code of doctrine and belief."[47] Because international society is
morally and institutionally imperfect, it is also inevitable that the effective
means for achievement of even the loftiest goals will fall short of ideal
standards.

In other words, universal norms must be filtered through the intermediary of historic and social circumstances, which will lead to different
results in different times and under different circumstances. As Morgenthau pointed out, "There exists of necessity a relativism in the relation
between moral principles and foreign policy that one cannot overlook if
one wants to do justice to the principles of morality in international politics." The ancient virtue and art of prudence provided American realists
with a standard to acknowledge the persistence of self-interest without
sacrificing the practical moral requirement of adjusting interest to norms
above the national community. In language that could not fail to com-

46. Walter LaFeber (ed.), *John Quincy Adams and American Continental Empire*
(Chicago, 1965), 42–46.
47. Kissinger, "Morality and Power," in Lefever (ed.), *Morality and Foreign
Policy*, 59.

mand the acquiescence of his colleagues, Niebuhr wrote: "Prudence is a civic virtue because it is necessary not only to strive for justice, but to take cognizance of all contingencies in preserving the stability . . . of a community. Prudence is the wise application of principles of justice to the contingencies of interest and power in political life. . . . Political tasks require a shrewd admixture of principle and expediency, of loyalty to general standards of justice and adjustment to actual power."[48]

48. Morgenthau, *Human Rights and Foreign Policy*, 4; Louis J. Halle and Theodore Hesburgh (eds.), *Foreign Policy and Morality: Framework for a Moral Audit*, 58.

BIBLIOGRAPHY

Works by Hans J. Morgenthau

MANUSCRIPTS

Hans J. Morgenthau Papers. Alderman Library, University of Virginia, Charlottesville.

BOOKS

In Defense of the National Interest. New York, 1951.
Dilemmas of Politics. Chicago, 1958.
Essays on Lincoln's Faith and Politics. With David Hein. Lanham, Md., 1983.
Human Rights and Foreign Policy. New York, 1979.
A New Foreign Policy for the United States. New York, 1969.
The Origins of the Cold War. With Lloyd C. Gardner and Arthur Schlesinger, Jr. Edited by J. Joseph Huthmacher and Warren I. Susman. Waltham, Mass., 1970.
Politics Among Nations. 5th ed. New York, 1973.
Politics in the Twentieth Century. 3 vols. Chicago, 1962.
Principles and Problems of International Politics. With Kenneth W. Thompson. New York, 1951.
The Purpose of American Politics. New York, 1960.
Science: Servant or Master? New York, 1972.
Scientific Man vs. Power Politics. Chicago, 1946.
Truth and Power: Essays of a Decade, 1960–1970. New York, 1970.

243

ARTICLES AND ESSAYS

"An Atomic Philosophy." *Saturday Review*, February 10, 1961, pp. 18–19.

"Changes and Chances in Soviet-American Relations." *Foreign Affairs*, XLIX (September, 1971), 429–41.

"Daniel Berrigan and Hans Morgenthau Discuss the Moral Dilemma in the Middle East." *Progressive*, XXVIII (March, 1974), 31–34.

"Decline of Democratic Government." *New Republic*, November 9, 1974, pp. 13–18.

"Dilemma of the Summit." *New York Times Magazine*, November 11, 1962, pp. 25, 117–18, 120, 122.

"The Dilemmas of Freedom." *American Political Science Review*, LI (September, 1957), 714–33.

"The Evil of Politics and the Ethics of Evil." *Ethics*, LVI (October, 1945), 1–18.

"Fighting the Last War." *New Republic*, October 20, 1979, pp. 15–17.

"The Four Paradoxes of Nuclear Strategy." *American Political Science Review*, LVIII (March, 1964), 23–35.

"Globalism: Johnson's Moral Crusade." *New Republic*, July 3, 1965, pp. 19–22.

"Hannah Arendt on Totalitarianism and Democracy." *Social Research*, XLIV (Spring, 1977), 127–31.

"The Influence of Reinhold Niebuhr in American Political Life and Thought." In *Reinhold Niebuhr: A Prophetic Voice in Our Time*, edited by Harold R. Landon. Greenwich, Conn., 1962.

"An Intellectual Autobiography." *Society*, XV (January–February, 1978), 63–68.

"The Intellectual, Political, and Moral Roots of U.S. Failure in Vietnam." In *Analyzing International Relations*, edited by William Coplin and Charles Kegley, Jr. New York, 1975.

"International Relations: Common Sense and Theories." *Journal of International Affairs*, XXI (1967), 207–14.

"To Intervene or Not to Intervene." *Foreign Affairs*, XLV (April, 1967), 425–36.

"Johnson's Dilemma: The Alternatives Now in Vietnam." *New Republic*, May 28, 1966, pp. 12–16.

"The Limitations of Science and the Problem of Social Planning." *Ethics*, LIV (October, 1943), 174–85.

"The Machiavellian Utopia." *Ethics*, LV (January, 1945), 145–47.

"The Moral Dilemma in Foreign Policy." In *The Yearbook of World Affairs, 1951*. London, 1951.

"National Interest and Moral Principles in Foreign Policy." *American Scholar*, XVIII (Spring, 1949), 207–12.

"Our Thwarted Republic." *Commentary*, XXX (June, 1960), 473–82.

"The Pathology of American Power." *International Security*, I (Winter, 1977), 3–20.

"The Political Conditions for an International Police Force." *International Organization*, XVII (January, 1963), 393–403.

"A Positive Approach to a Democratic Ideology." *Proceedings of the Academy of Political Science*, XXIV (January, 1951), 79–90.

"Science of Peace: A Rationalist Utopia." *Social Research*, XLII (Spring, 1975), 20–34.

"Thought and Action in Politics." *Social Research*, XXXVIII (Winter, 1971), 611–32.

"Thoughts on the October Revolution." *New Leader*, November 26, 1967, pp. 13–16.

"The Twilight of International Morality." *Ethics*, LVIII (January, 1948), 79–99.

"The U.N. of Dag Hammarskjöld Is Dead." *New York Times Magazine*, March 14, 1965, pp. 32–39.

"US and UN." *Foreign Policy Bulletin*, XXXIII (September, 1954), 5–6.

"U.S. Misadventure in Vietnam." *Current History*, LIV (January, 1968), 29–34.

"Views of Nuremberg: Further Analysis of the Trial and Its Importance." *America*, December 7, 1946, pp. 266–67.

"We Are Deluding Ourselves in Vietnam." *New York Times Magazine*, April 18, 1965, pp. 25, 85–87.

"What Ails America?" *New Republic*, October 28, 1967, pp. 17–21.

"What Price Victory?" *New Republic*, February 20, 1971, pp. 21–23.

Raison d'État: Statesmanship and Political Thought

Aristotle. *Nicomachean Ethics*. Translated by M. Ostwald. New York, 1962.

Aubrey, John. *Brief Lives*. Edited by Oliver L. Dick. Ann Arbor, 1957.

Bentham, Jeremy. *Emancipate Your Colonies*. London, 1830.

Bloom, Allan. *"The Republic" of Plato*. New York, 1968.

Bluhm, William T. *Theories of the Political System: Classics of Political Thought and Modern Political Analysis*. Englewood Cliffs, N.J., 1965.

Bull, Hedley. "Hobbes and the International Anarchy." *Social Research*, XLVIII (Winter, 1981), 717–38.

———. "Martin Wight and the Theory of International Relations." *British Journal of International Studies*, II (Spring, 1976), 101–16.

Burke, Edmund, *The Works of the Rt. Honourable Edmund Burke*. 12 vols. Boston, 1889.

Burnham, James. *The Machiavellians*. New York, 1943.

Butterfield, Herbert. *The Statecraft of Machiavelli*. New York, 1956.

Butterfield, Herbert, and Martin Wight, eds. *Diplomatic Investigations: Essays in the Theory of International Politics.* London, 1966.

Church, William F. *Richelieu and Reason of State.* Princeton, 1972.

Donelan, Michael, ed. *The Reason of States.* London, 1978.

Dorpalen, Andreas. "The German Historians and Bismarck." *Review of Politics,* XV (January, 1953), 53–67.

Dunne, John C. "*Realpolitik* in the Decline of the West." *Review of Politics,* XXI (January, 1959), 131–50.

Finley, John H. *Thucydides.* Cambridge, Mass., 1942.

Fleiss, Peter J. *Thucydides and the Politics of Bipolarity.* Baton Rouge, 1966.

Friedrich, Carl J. *The Age of Baroque, 1619–1660.* New York, 1952.

Germino, Dante. *From Machiavelli to Marx: Modern Western Political Thought.* Chicago, 1972.

Gibbon, Edward. *The Decline and Fall of the Roman Empire.* 3 vols. New York, 1932.

Gilbert, Allan H., ed. *Machiavelli: The Chief Works and Others.* 3 vols. Durham, N.C., 1965.

Gomme, A. W., ed. *A Historical Commentary on Thucydides.* 3 vols. Oxford, 1945–56.

Gooch, G. P. "Bismarck's Legacy." *Foreign Affairs,* XXX (July, 1952), 518–30.

Hallowell, John. *Main Currents in Modern Political Thought.* New York, 1950.

Hamerow, Theodore, ed. *Otto von Bismarck: A Historical Assessment.* Lexington, Mass., 1972.

Hegel, Georg Wilhelm Friedrich. *Philosophy of Right.* Translated by T. M. Knox. New York, 1976.

Hobbes, Thomas. *Behemoth; or, The Long Parliament.* Edited by F. Tonnies. New York, 1969.

⸻. *Leviathan.* Edited by Michael Oakeshott. Oxford, 1947.

Hume, David. *Essays Moral, Political, and Literary.* 2 vols. London, 1875.

Kennan, George F. *The Decline of Bismarck's European Order: Franco-Russian Relations, 1875–1890.* Princeton, 1979.

Medlicott, W. N. *Bismarck, Gladstone, and the Concert of Europe.* London, 1956.

Meinecke, Friedrich. *The German Catastrophe: Reflections and Recollections.* Translated by Sidney B. Fay. Cambridge, Mass., 1960.

⸻. *Machiavellianism: The Doctrine of "Raison d'État" and Its Place in Modern History.* Translated by D. Scott. London, 1957.

Molesworth, Sir William, ed. *The English Works of Thomas Hobbes of Malmesbury.* 11 vols. London, 1836–45.

O'Connell, D. P. *Richelieu.* New York, 1968.

Plato. *Republic.* Translated by Benjamin Jowett. New York, 1941.

Proudhon, Pierre Joseph. *Oeuvres Completes.* 13 vols. Paris, 1868.

Reddaway, W. F. *A History of Europe, 1610–1715.* London, 1952.

Ridolfi, Roberto. *The Life of Niccolo Machiavelli.* Chicago, 1963.

Russell, Frank M. *Theories of International Relations.* New York, 1936.

Savigear, Peter. "European Political Philosophy and the Theory of International Relations." In *Approaches and Theory in International Relations,* edited by Trevor Taylor. London, 1978.

Schnabel, Franz. "The Bismarck Problem." In *German History: Some New Views,* edited by Hans Kohn. Boston, 1954.

Snyder, Louis. *The Blood and Iron Chancellor.* Princeton, 1967.

Sorel, Georges. *Reflections on Violence.* Translated by T. E. Hulme and N. Rolfe. New York, 1950.

Sterling, Richard. *Ethics in a World of Power.* Princeton, 1958.

Strauss, Leo. *Thoughts on Machiavelli.* Glencoe, Ill., 1958.

Thucydides. *The Peloponnesian War.* Translated by R. Crawley. New York, 1910.

Tolstoy, Leo. *War and Peace.* Translated by Constance Garnett. New York, 1966.

Voegelin, Eric. "Machiavelli's *Prince:* Background and Formation." *Review of Politics,* XIII (April, 1951), 142–68.

———. *The New Science of Politics.* Chicago, 1952.

Wallbank, T. Walter, Alastair M. Taylor, George B. Carson, and Mark Mancall. *Civilization Past and Present.* 2 vols. Glenview, Ill., 1969.

Warmington, Eric H., and Philip G. Rouse. *Great Dialogues of Plato.* Translated by W. H. D. Rouse. New York, 1956.

Wight, Martin. "The Balance of Power and International Order." In *The Bases of International Order,* edited by Alan James. London, 1973.

Wiser, James L. *Political Philosophy: A History of the Search for Order.* Englewood Cliffs, N.J., 1983.

Zeitlin, Jacob, ed. *The Essays of Michel de Montaigne.* 3 vols. New York, 1936.

Realism, Science, and the Philosophy of International Politics

Bailey, Thomas A. *A Diplomatic History of the American People.* New York, 1946.

Basler, Roy P. *The Collected Works of Abraham Lincoln.* 9 vols. New Brunswick, N.J., 1953.

Blum, D. Steven. *Walter Lippmann: Cosmopolitanism in the Century of Total War.* Ithaca, 1984.

Cahn, Edmond. *The Sense of Injustice.* Bloomington, 1949.

Churchill, Winston S. *The Second World War.* 6 vols. Boston, 1951.

Claude, Inis. *Power and International Relations.* New York, 1962.

Clinton, W. David. "The National Interest: Normative Foundations." *Review of Politics,* XLVIII (Fall, 1986), 495–519.

Corwin, Edward S. *The "Higher Law" Background of American Constitutional Law.* Ithaca, 1979.

Crabb, Cecil V. *American Foreign Policy in the Nuclear Age.* 4th ed. New York, 1983.

Crabb, Cecil V., and June Savoy. "Hans J. Morgenthau's Version of *Realpolitik.*" *Political Science Reviewer,* V (Fall, 1975), 189–228.

Curti, Merle. *Peace and War: The American Struggle 1636–1936.* New York, 1936.

Davis, Harry R., and Robert C. Good, eds. *Reinhold Niebuhr on Politics.* New York, 1960.

Farrand, Max, ed. *The Records of the Federal Convention of 1787.* 4 vols. New Haven, 1911.

Feller, A. H. "In Defense of International Law and Morality." *Annals of the American Academy of Political and Social Science,* No. 282 (July, 1952), 77–83.

Fish, Max H., ed. *Selected Papers of Robert C. Binkley.* Cambridge, Mass., 1948.

Ford, Paul, ed. *The Works of Thomas Jefferson.* 12 vols. New York, 1905.

Fox, Richard W. *Reinhold Niebuhr: A Biography.* New York, 1985.

Good, Robert C. "The National Interest and Political Realism: Niebuhr's Debate with Morgenthau and Kennan," *Journal of Politics,* XXII (1960), 597–619.

Graebner, Norman A. *Ideas and Diplomacy.* New York, 1946.

Haas, Ernst B. "The Balance of Power: Prescription, Concept, or Propaganda." *World Politics,* V (July, 1953), 361–80.

Halle, Louis J. *Civilization and Foreign Policy.* New York, 1955.

Halle, Louis J., and Theodore Hesburgh, eds. *Foreign Policy and Morality: Framework for a Moral Audit.* New York, 1979.

Hamilton, Alexander, James Madison, and John Jay. *The Federalist Papers.* New York, 1961.

Hare, J. E., and Carey B. Joynt. *Ethics and International Affairs.* New York, 1982.

Harrison, H. V. *The Role of Theory in International Relations.* Princeton, 1964.

Hoffmann, Stanley. *Primacy or World Order: American Foreign Policy Since the Cold War.* New York, 1980.

———. "An American Social Science: International Relations." *Daedalus,* CVI (Summer, 1977), 41–60.

Hoopes, Townsend. *The Devil and John Foster Dulles.* Boston, 1973.

Jaspers, Karl. *The Future of Mankind.* Chicago, 1958.

Jeans, Sir James. *The New Background of Science.* New York, 1933.

Joad, C. E. M. "Pacifism: Its Personal and Social Implications." In *In Pursuit of Peace*, edited by G. P. Gooch. London, 1933.

Kahn, Herman. *On Thermonuclear War.* Princeton, 1960.

Kennan, George F. *Democracy and the Student Left.* Boston, 1968.

———. "Ethics and Foreign Policy: An Approach to the Problem." In *Foreign Policy and Morality: Framework for a Moral Audit*, edited by Louis J. Halle and Theodore Hesburgh. New York, 1979.

———. "History and Diplomacy as Viewed by a Diplomatist." *Review of Politics*, XVIII (April, 1956), 170–77.

———. "Lectures on Foreign Policy." *Illinois Law Review*, XLV (January–February, 1951), 718–42.

———. "Morality and Foreign Policy." *Foreign Affairs*, LXIV (Winter, 1985–86), 205–18.

———. *Realities of American Foreign Policy.* Princeton, 1954.

———. "Speak Truth to Power—A Reply by George F. Kennan." *Progressive*, XIX (October, 1955), 18.

Kissinger, Henry. "Hans Morgenthau." *New Republic*, August 2–9, 1980, pp. 12–14.

———. "Morality and Power." In *Morality and Foreign Policy*, edited by Ernest W. Lefever. Washington, D.C., 1977.

Knorr, Klaus, and Sidney Verba, eds. *The International System: Theoretical Essays.* Princeton, 1961.

Kuhn, Thomas S. "Reflections on My Critics." In *Criticism and the Growth of Knowledge*, edited by I. Lakatos and A. Musgrave. Cambridge, Mass., 1970.

———. *The Structure of Scientific Revolutions.* Chicago, 1970.

LaFeber, Walter, ed. *John Quincy Adams and American Continental Empire.* Chicago, 1965.

Lang, Daniel G. *Foreign Policy in the Early Republic: The Law of Nations and the Balance of Power.* Baton Rouge, 1985.

Lijphart, Arend. "The Structure of Theoretical Revolutions in International Relations." *International Studies Quarterly*, XVIII (March, 1974), 42–59.

Lippmann, Walter. *Early Writings.* New York, 1970.

———. *The Public Philosophy.* Boston, 1955.

———. *The Stakes of Diplomacy.* New York, 1915.

———. *U.S. Foreign Policy: Shield of the Republic.* Boston, 1943.

———. *U.S. War Aims.* Boston, 1945.

Niebuhr, Reinhold. *The Children of Light and the Children of Darkness: A Vindication of Democracy and a Critique of Its Traditional Defence*. New York, 1944.

――――. "Christianity and Communism: Social Justice." *Spectator*, November 6, 1936, pp. 802–803.

――――. *Christian Realism and Political Problems*. New York, 1952.

――――. *An Interpretation of Christian Ethics*. New York, 1940.

――――. *Moral Man and Immoral Society: A Study in Ethics and Politics*. New York, 1932.

――――. "The Perils of American Power." *Messenger*, May 22, 1951, pp. 5–6.

――――. *The Self and the Dramas of History*. New York, 1955.

――――. *The Structure of Nations and Empires*. New York, 1959.

Niemeyer, Gerhart. "Foreign Policy and Morality: A Contemporary Perspective." *Intercollegiate Review*, XV (Spring, 1980), 77–84.

Osgood, Robert. *Ideals and Self-Interest in America's Foreign Relations*. Chicago, 1953.

Parkinson, F. *The Philosophy of International Relations*. Beverly Hills, 1977.

Planck, Max. *The Philosophy of Physics*. New York, 1936.

Polanyi, Michael. "Commentary on T. S. Kuhn's 'The Function of Dogma in Scientific Research.'" In *Scientific Change*, edited by A. C. Gombie. London, 1963.

Russell, Greg. "Balance of Power in Perspective." *International Review of History and Political Science*, XXI (November, 1984), 1–16.

――――. "The Ethics of American Statecraft." *Journal of Politics*, L (May, 1988), 503–17.

Sandoz, Ellis. "Power and Spirit in the Founding." *This World*, No. 9 (Fall, 1984), 66–77.

――――. *The Voegelinian Revolution*. Baton Rouge, 1981.

Schuman, Frederick L. *International Politics*. 6th ed. New York, 1958.

Stone, R. *Reinhold Niebuhr: Prophet to Politicians*. Lanham, Md., 1981.

Sumner, William Graham. *Earth Hunger and Other Essays*. New Haven, 1913.

――――. "Mores of the Present and Future." In *War and Other Essays*. New Haven, 1911.

Teller, Edward, and Allen Brown. *The Legacy of Hiroshima*. Garden City, N.J., 1962.

Thompson, Kenneth W. "Four Perspectives on Ethics and Foreign Policy and Their Implications for Some Central Issues of Current U.S. Policy." Conference report prepared for the State Department's External Research Program. Charlottesville, Virginia, July, 1977.

――――. "The Limits of Principle in International Politics: Necessity and the New Balance of Power." *Journal of Politics*, XX (August, 1958), 437–67.

————. *Masters of International Thought.* Baton Rouge, 1980.

————. *Moralism and Morality in Politics and Diplomacy.* Lanham, Md., 1985.

————. *Morality and Foreign Policy.* Baton Rouge, 1980.

————. "Moral Reasoning in American Thought on War and Peace." *Review of Politics,* XLIX (July, 1977), 386–99.

————. "The Political Philosophy of Reinhold Niebuhr." In *Reinhold Niebuhr: His Religious, Moral, and Political Thought,* edited by Charles W. Kegley and Robert W. Bretall. New York, 1956.

Thompson, Kenneth W., and Robert J. Myers, eds. *Truth and Tragedy: A Tribute to Hans J. Morgenthau.* New Brunswick, 1984.

Tocqueville, Alexis de. *Democracy in America.* 2 vols. New York, 1945.

Vasquez, John A., ed. *Classics of International Relations.* Englewood Cliffs, N.J., 1986.

Voegelin, Eric. *Anamnesis.* Translated by Gerhart Niemeyer. Notre Dame, 1978.

————. *Science, Politics, and Gnosticism.* Chicago, 1968.

Waltz, Kenneth. *Man, the State and War.* New York, 1959.

————. *Theory of International Politics.* Menlo Park, Calif., 1979.

Wight, Martin. "Why Is There No International Theory?" In *Diplomatic Investigations: Essays in the Theory of International Politics,* edited by Herbert Butterfield and Martin Wight. London, 1966.

Wolfers, Arnold. *Discord and Collaboration.* Baltimore, 1962.

————. "Statesmanship and Moral Choice." *World Politics,* I (January, 1949), 175–95.

INDEX

136–37, 140–41, 151, 162–63, 167, 211; on national purpose, 86–92, 216; criticism of social science, 92–96; on power, 94, 97–98, 113–14, 119–21, 147; on ethics in politics and diplomacy, 96, 100–102, 113, 120, 141–50 *passim,* 155–58, 209, 222–23, 227–28; on political idealism, 97–108 *passim,* 159, 166, 186; defense of national interest, 99–100, 103–119 *passim,* 161, 166, 195, 226; on Hobbes, 101–102, 150, 160–61, 230–31; on balance of power, 112, 113, 118, 122–28; on nationalistic universalism, 116–17, 130, 169; on Cold War, 118–19, 130–31, 152, 176, 191–92; criticism of Vietnam War, 119, 195–206; on diplomacy, 121, 128–36, 165–66, 176; on Lincoln, 138, 211; on international law and organization, 172–79; on intervention, 188–206 *passim;* approach to human rights, 206–211; criticism of Lippmann, 219
Moscow Conference, 113

Napoleon I, 202
Napoleon III, 134
Napoleonic Wars, 110
Narcissism, 75–76
National interest: 2, 74, 99, 103–104, 161, 195, 224, 226; moral dignity of, 58, 86–87, 107–108, 153–54, 166–67; permanent and variable elements of, 104–107, 117–18; rational character of, 105–106; and three phases of American diplomatic history, 108–111; following World War II, 113–14; relation to nationalistic universalism, 116–17
Nation-state, 12–13, 50, 60, 99–100, 210, 223
Natural law, 91–92, 238–39
Neumeyer, Karl, 64
Ngo Dinh Diem, 201
Nguyen Van Thieu, 201
Nicolson, Harold, 136
Niebuhr, Reinhold: 150, 219, 222, 226;

on human rights, 209; and Christian political ethic, 215–16; on realism, 219–20; on national interest, 225, 230; ethical dualism of, 226; criticism of Machiavelli and Hobbes, 227; and transcendent principles, 232–33; on nuclear war, 234; on balance of power, 236; on prudence as civic virtue, 241–42
Niemeyer, Gerhart, 13
Nietzsche, Friedrich, 150, 181
Nixon, Richard, 134, 206
Nuclear age, 70, 132
Nuclear war, 85, 179–88, 234

Oncken, Herman, 63–64
Osgood, Robert, 57–58

Paradigm: and international political theory, 13–14, 55
Penn, William, 11
Philosophy of history: cyclical and transcendental conceptions, 143–45; and international affairs, 146–48
Pinckney, Charles, 87
Pindar, 71
Planck, Max, 95
Plato, 69, 71, 78–79, 82, 145, 148, 227
Polanyi, Michael, 14
Political ethics: in foreign policy, 51–52, 109, 166–67, 213–15, 224–25; and human existence, 69–70, 82–83, 89–91, 96, 145, 157–58
Political philosophy, 56, 78–86 *passim,* 137–38, 156
Political science: intellectual and moral confusion of, 1, 69
Political theory: and international relations, 10–17 *passim,* 73–74, 97–99, 149
Pollock, Frederick, 83
Polybius, 29
Positivism: in political science, 69, 173; and international law, 173–74
Power, 2, 7, 15, 16, 51, 69, 72, 94, 113–14, 119–21
Pragmatism, 67, 99, 115, 163, 170, 177, 206, 241